VERONICA'S ROOM

AND OTHER DRAMAS

WORKS BY IRA LEVIN

NOVELS

Son of Rosemary

Sliver

The Boys from Brazil

The Stepford Wives

This Perfect Day

Rosemary's Baby

A Kiss Before Dying

PLAYS

Footsteps

Cantorial

Break A Leg

Deathtrap

Veronica's Room

Dr. Cook's Garden

General Seeger

Critic's Choice

Interlock

No Time For Sergeants

(from the novel by Mac Hyman)

MUSICALS

Drat! The Cat!

(music by Milton Schafer)

VERONICA'S ROOM

AND OTHER DRAMAS BY IRA LEVIN

INTERLOCK, DR. COOK'S GARDEN, AND VERONICA'S ROOM

BLACK STONE PUBLISHING

Published in 2025 by Blackstone Publishing
Cover and book design by James Egan of Bookfly Design

Printed in the United States of America

ISBN 979-8-212-64274-3
Drama / American / General

Version 1

Blackstone Publishing
31 Mistletoe Rd.
Ashland, OR 97520

www.BlackstonePublishing.com

CONTENTS

STAGE DIRECTION REFERENCE

"One word of advice to those not accustomed to reading plays: Don't worry too much about the chairs and tables. It rarely matters whether they're at stage right or stage left, or whether the doors are upstage or down. What does matter is the dialogue. Try to hear it, and try to hear the pauses too, that's where the shivers are."

—Ira Levin, Introduction to
"The Mousetrap" and Other Plays

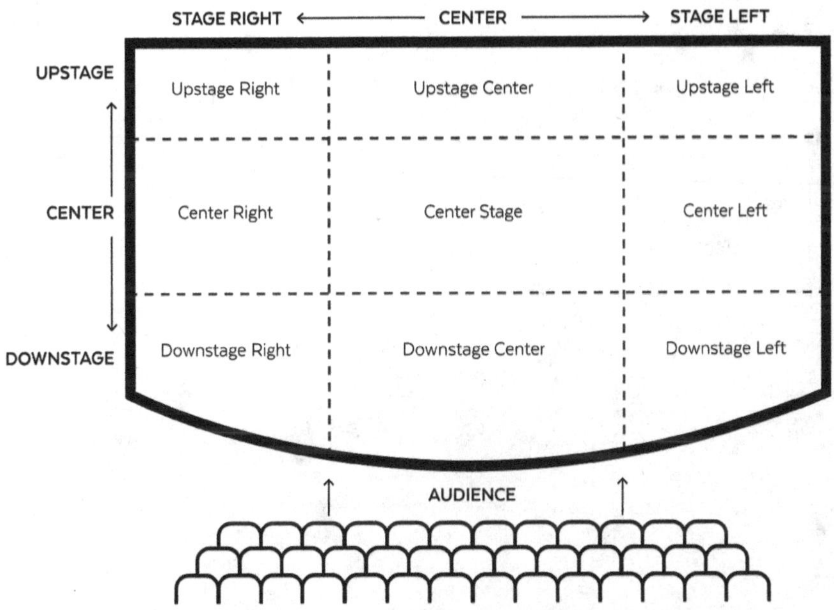

INTRODUCTION TO THE COLLECTION

It's ironic that the main point I'm led to make in presenting this first compilation of the plays of my father Ira Levin ends up being the same one he made when writing the introduction to a 1978 collection of Agatha Christie's plays: that they're their novels' undeservedly lesser-known cousins. (Both he and Christie wrote about a dozen stage works alongside their well-known books.)

My father's love of the theater ran deep; he viewed himself as a playwright who wrote novels, and not the reverse. He'd saved the *Playbill* from every show he'd ever attended, and referred to that pregnant moment when the house lights dim in advance of the curtain's rise as "*magic time.*"

Though Levin's novels often featured "high-concept" conceits (think of the plots of *Rosemary's Baby*, *The Boys from Brazil*, or *The Stepford Wives* for example), his plays were far more intimate *chamber* affairs. And just as Christie's own plays (surprisingly) did not feature her best-known characters (*Hercule Poirot*, *Miss Marple* . . .), Levin's stage works are almost entirely absent the grand themes associated with his novels—occultism, globe-spanning conspiracies, techno-oppression, etc. His plays' primary focus is *human relations*; the conflicts that arise between and within individuals. The human animal. (That said, you'll still stumble on the occasional antecedent of some of those more fantastic designs in these pages.)

An element that *is* common to both Levin's books and plays is their lack of morality lessons and tidy resolutions. He resented works of art that preach, believing that people were "*good enough that they deserved to be entertained*" and not lectured to. Here, just as in real life, the bad guys sometimes win. And you're occasionally left to determine for yourself who the bad guys *are*, and what exactly constitutes *winning*.

Even in his dramas though, Levin's wit peeks through—they're not without their laugh-out-loud moments. What's perhaps most surprising in reading these weightier offerings is the fact that he also wrote out-and-out *comedies*—the riotous *Break A Leg*, the *bon mot*-laden *Critic's Choice*, and the Andy Griffith juggernaut *No Time For Sergeants* among them. (A companion volume showcases Levin's stage comedies, while a second one spotlights his *triad* of plays set in the military.)

Something those who are only familiar with Levin's novels often mistakenly believe is that all his female characters are *victims*; you'll find that a high percentage of the works herein prove otherwise.

Another common misconception: since Levin's stage plays enjoyed less commercial success than his novels, taken on the whole, that must mean they're lesser works. Not at all. The theater's a fundamentally different business than book publishing—for starters, its collaborative nature requires welcoming other cooks into the kitchen. Then, unlike a book, a play requires continued financing beyond its initial release—and producers can sometimes prove skittish, pulling up stakes before a show has had a chance to "find its audience." (An impactful consideration for an envelope-pushing author like Levin.) Despite all that, nearly as many of Levin's plays have been adapted for film and TV as were his books.

But the house lights are starting to dim; it's *magic time.* Here then are three masterfully-crafted plays, written by as ardent a lover of the medium as you'll find.

Nicholas Levin
January 2025
New York City

You can read more about Levin's work at IraLevin.org

INTERLOCK

(1958)

INTRODUCTION

(*INTERLOCK*)

Ira Levin changed genres like typewriter ribbons—from suspense to horror to science fiction and back . . . even a Broadway musical. (*Drat! The Cat!*) In its review of *Interlock,* the *Washington Evening Star* commented: *"[Levin] burst upon the theater three seasons ago as adapter of* No Time For Sergeants, *an exercise in hilarity that could not make his change of mood more astonishing."*

Helmed by the deceptively capable Mrs. Price (one of Levin's most masterful female characters), *Interlock* showcases his handling of pure drama; the play's single set and lack of intruding external events and persons keeps the focus solely on the intense interplay between the three individuals who make up the work's central "triangle." (An abstracted triangle design featured prominently in the show's original poster.)

In Mrs. Price's dealings with her young companion Hilde, and Hilde's talented but conflicted classical-pianist fiancé Paul, Mrs. Price provides the prototype for a character common to some of Levin's most recognized later works—an outwardly solicitous benefactor who traffics in sly manipulation and gaslighting to achieve their own concealed agenda—resulting in a game of cat and (unwitting) mouse—or mice, as the case may be.

The manipulation's not only coming from Mrs. Price, however; the revered critic Walter Kerr observed of *Interlock*: *"Mr. Levin is also good at anticipating an audience's protests, having his character make the same protest [. . .] Just as we are about to ask—aloud, even—why [Paul] doesn't get up and get out [. . .] he does get up and say, 'I'm getting out of here.'"* Jordan Peele cited that very element of Levin's technique as key to the plotting of 2017's Stepfordian *Get Out.*

We're also subjected to the same power imbalance that Paul is, by virtue of knowing only Mrs. Price's surname (which is surely a tipoff though that her favor comes at a *cost.*) Paul has the capacity to give as good as he gets, however—and when he's ultimately taken into his patron's full confidence, it's as if the two are truly meeting for the first time, as equals. (Once having read the play, I recommend translating its last few lines—they speak volumes.)

Mrs. Price serves as something of a maternal stand-in for Paul. The first several pages of Act Two (in which Paul describes his mother, as Mrs. Price sketches his likeness) provide an excellent example of the type of hidden parallels Levin often wove into his works. Paul describes his mother as nearly *frozen*—a "*Snow Queen . . . a cool statue of a woman, with ice-blue eyes, and a smile that never rose above her lips.*") Mrs. Price is herself constitutionally *frozen* (as it were) in her wheelchair. And Paul himself, in those same pages, sits *frozen*, as Mrs. Price sketches him. (You may also hear in Paul's reminiscences a future echo of Levin's *The Boys from Brazil.)*

But this is not a funeral! Levin's trademark wit is still present—Mrs. Price and Paul's initial meeting has nearly enough laughs to do double-duty as a *Borscht Belt* routine.

Though *Interlock*'s two remaining characters—the married *Lucille* and *Everett*—are largely the utilitarian "domestic" characters common to works of the time, Levin still characteristically imbues them with views and agency beyond that role—Lucille speaks to Mrs. Price as more of an equal than

Hilde can—and Everett shows Hilde the empathy his wife is unwilling to summon. You'll find that "the domestics" (as I'll call them) resurface in both of the later plays in this volume—in some *interesting* permutations.

Not uncommonly for Levin, there's an autobiographical component to *Interlock*. While majoring in English and philosophy at New York University, he'd lived in an apartment situated in the play's NYU-adjacent *Gramercy Park* neighborhood. (It might even be a self-directed dig when Mrs. Price brands Paul a "*personal philosopher.*")

At the time of its opening, some critics faulted the subtle, cerebral nature of *Interlock's* dealings. The *New Yorker* wrote that the play was concerned only with "*an intellectual triumph of evil.*" *Rosemary's Baby* would receive similar criticism on its release—too *cerebral*; not enough *horror*. (Now that sort of subtlety's a feature, not a bug.)

Levin was aiming at something beyond the status quo. The *Washington Evening Star* understood this: "*Audiences may feel, and the New York critics may say, that* Interlock *ought to be less like life and more like Agatha Christie, with more ingeniously mechanical twists and turns, with comfortably black-and-white characters, and with some astonishing trick of violence at the finale. I found* Interlock *a continuously entertaining study in corruption by logic, with something of the acid view of the sex-and-power struggle that marks a number of the better plays from Europe.*" The review further praised *Interlock*'s "*theatrical–literary quality.*" (Levin, it must be noted, was a devout Christie fan and acolyte!)

On Broadway, Mrs. Price's cunning charms were doubtless enhanced by Celeste Holm's portrayal of her. The part of Paul was played by Maximillian Schell (in his first American role). A talented pianist, Schell played all of Paul's piano music live at each performance. (For the curious, that included Brahms'

G Minor Rhapsody, Chopin's fiery "*Revolutionary*" etude, and a piece written for the production by composer George Kent, titled (appropriately) "*Nocturne.*")

Levin structured *Interlock* in the then-prevailing *three-act* classical format. (Movies are often still structured in three acts, though plays seldom are anymore. For those interested, Levin regarded playwright Patrick Shanley's 1945 "*The Hasty Heart*" as a prime example of the three-act form.)

A 2015 review of a Baltimore production of *Interlock* summed up: "*This sharp drama is a reminder of a lost genre; a throwback to a time nearly forgotten in the midst of poppy new musicals and edgy political works* [. . .] *a true classical treat.*"

We hope you enjoy your visit to Mrs. Price's townhouse.

Nicholas Levin
January 2025
New York City

INTERLOCK

INTERLOCK was presented by Richard Myers, Julius Fleichmann and Walter N. Trenerry at the ANTA Theatre on February 6, 1958. It was directed by Philip Burton and the set was designed by Howard Bay. The cast was as follows:

HILDE . . . . Rosemary Harris
LUCILLE . . . . Georgia Burke
EVERETT . . . . John Marriott
MRS. PRICE . . . . Celeste Holm

The action takes place in Mrs. Price's home in the Gramercy Park section of Manhattan, several years after the Second World War. There are two scenes in each act.

ACT ONE: OCTOBER
ACT TWO: NOVEMBER
ACT THREE: DECEMBER

SETTING

The play's single setting represents a room in a Gramercy Park town house built in the 1870's. A sombre elegance characterizes the room: its woodwork is dark and elaborately carved, its walls are covered with dark green brocade, its architectural details are subtly Gothic.

There is a staircase UPSTAGE CENTER, ascending in a curve toward stage RIGHT and leading to a second floor balcony which runs parallel to stage front. The balcony extends off RIGHT, but its continuation is blanked from view by the set's RIGHT wall, which is angled inward and reaches the full two-story height of the room. There is a large pair of sliding doors in RIGHT wall, leading to the main downstairs hallway (off). A bell in wall UPSTAGE of doors. A second door, in UPSTAGE wall of balcony leads to a bedroom (off). (Hilde's room.) The outer curve of the staircase is walled by a curving mullioned window of great size. Drapes can be drawn over the entire window; when opened they hang LEFT of foot of staircase. Through the window can be seen the stone exterior wall of the bedroom wing, the top of a bare-branched tree, neighboring buildings and gray sky. In UPSTAGE wall, LEFT of foot of staircase, are built-in cabinets and bookcases, some of which contain phonograph records. Liquor and glasses are in one of the cabinets. Over them hangs a full-length bridal portrait of Mrs. Price, who was 28 at the time and smiling. The light over the portrait works independently of the room's main lighting, and is controlled by a hanging switch directly beneath the portrait. Main lighting is controlled by two switches in RIGHT wall; one DOWNSTAGE of sliding doors, the other at balcony height. Wall LEFT contains more cabinets and bookcases, and built-in phonograph equipment. Principal furniture consists of table with telephone, DOWNSTAGE of sliding doors; side chair, UPSTAGE of sliding doors; couch, DOWNSTAGE RIGHT, angled toward LEFT; end table, LEFT of couch; large hassock, LEFT of end table; concert grand piano, UPSTAGE CENTER in curving area formed by staircase, keyboard toward RIGHT; wing chair, between end of piano and foot of staircase. The only furniture in the room's shallower section, LEFT of foot of staircase, is a single small table, standing well into the room, curiously isolated. Ashtrays on the various tables.

ACT ONE: OCTOBER

SCENE ONE

The curtain rises in darkness. Lights dim up, accenting HILDE *standing at* CENTER STAGE *facing* RIGHT, *motionless in the act of removing her coat, and* PAUL, *standing in doorway* RIGHT, *his coat over his shoulders European-style. There is darkness outside the window. When lights are up full,* HILDE *finishes taking off her coat.* SHE *is 30, stockily-built, healthy looking, neatly and simply dressed.* PAUL *is 30, gaunt, shabbily dressed.*

HILDE

(*A trace of a German accent.*)

Come in, Paul. Please do. Come in! Please . . .

(PAUL *steps hesitantly into the room.*)

Nobody is here. The maid sits in the basement with her ear against a radio; if a bomb were to explode she would not hear it.

(PAUL *advances farther into the room, holding himself stiffly, looking about with reserve.* HILDE *puts her coat on wing chair, goes to window and pulls cord, drawing drapes across it.*)

That is my room up there. In the entire house it is one of the very best! Mrs. Price *insisted* I take it.

PAUL

(Motionless, his eye caught by the staircase. A German accent more marked than HILDE*'s.)*

It is like home . . . the staircase . . .

HILDE

No, it is English, not German. The wood is from England, the wall-coverings from Belgium, the marble of the front stairway from Italy. Her grandfather imported everything when he built the house. In the living room is a chandelier from a palace in France, but a sheet is pinned over it now and the room is closed. Eighteen rooms and only seven in use!

(She presses switch beneath portrait UPSTAGE LEFT, *and its overhead light goes on.* PAUL *makes a fractional movement toward it.)*

PAUL

She is an attracting woman . . .

(His coat slips from his shoulders, he catches it automatically.)

HILDE

Attractive.

PAUL

Attractive . . .

(Puts coat mechanically over back of couch.)

HILDE

Yes. And still so today, poor thing. This was fifteen years ago, her wedding portrait.

(Turns from portrait, crosses and removes decorative scarf from piano, folds it.)

PAUL

(*Still looking at portrait.*)

Hilde . . . I have seen the house . . .

(*Faces* HILDE, *with a forced assurance.*)

I have seen the house and find it quite the mansion you described. Now I should leave.

HILDE

Leave? Without even touching the piano?

PAUL

I feel . . .

(*The assurance dropping.*)

small and uncomfortable, sneaking in here like a schoolboy . . . I should not have let you bring me.

HILDE

(*Coming down.*)

We are not sneaking, Paul. She *asked* me to bring you last year, when you first arrived. You will not come when she is in, so we come when she is out.

PAUL

(*Firmly again.*)

It is wrong for me to be here.

HILDE

(*Putting folded scarf on end table.*)

You're being silly, darling. What is wrong is that you refuse to meet her; this fine woman with such an interest in art and music and—

PAUL

(*Interrupting gently.*)

Hilde, please. Twice we have discussed it. Not again. Please . . .

HILDE

All right, but do not say we sneak. In this house I am not a servant, Paul; I am her companion. That means "friend." I may have visitors any time I choose. Besides . . .

(*Going up to piano.*)

it is bad for a piano not to be played occasionally. You told me that yourself, didn't you? The night before last?

PAUL

(*Pause.*)

I suppose that I did.

HILDE

(*Lifts piano top, props it open.*)

It was tuned only two weeks ago. I said to her, "Even if no one plays it, a fine instrument such as this should be tuned, taken care of."

PAUL

You knew two weeks ago that I would come here tonight?

HILDE

I did not *know* . . .

(*Smiling at him.*)

but I hoped . . .

PAUL

(*Wryly shaking his head.*)

You astound me, Hilde. When you left Germany you were forthright and simple.

HILDE

At fifteen all girls are forthright and simple.

PAUL

(*Ruefully.*)

And it seems that by thirty they have all become schemers . . .

HILDE

(*Injured.*)

I'm not a schemer!

(*Comes down.*)

I'm *not.* Scheming is when one does something for oneself.

(*Takes his hand.*)

I do this for *you*, because I love you, because I want you to be happy.

(*Drawing him* UPSTAGE *toward piano.*)

I am not a schemer . . .

PAUL

(*Touches piano longingly with* LEFT *hand.*)

All right. . . .

(*Puts* RIGHT *hand on* HILDE'*s cheek.*)

You are a most *un*scheming lamb and I love you.

(*He kisses her softly on the lips. Her guilt melts into happiness.* PAUL *slides in behind keyboard of piano,* HILDE *opens it.* PAUL *strikes a few paired notes.*)

HILDE

A good piano, isn't it?

PAUL

God, yes . . .

(*Strikes several one-handed chords.*)

HILDE

Sit! Play! It will be a concert and I will have a first-row seat!

(Enthusiastically she draws wing chair around from end of piano, while PAUL *lowers himself slowly to piano bench. He rubs his hands nervously.* HILDE *kneels on seat of chair, arms folded over one wing.)*

Play! It won't bite you!

*(*PAUL *begins to play, with restraint at first, then with growing confidence. He plays very well.* HILDE *listens raptly, her cheek on her folded arms. After a few moments,* PAUL *stops, as though the joy of playing were too much to bear.* HILDE *applauds.)*

Bravo! Bravo, Maestro Paul!

PAUL

(Looking at piano adoringly.)

God! Do you know when it was that I last played such a piano?

HILDE

Not since Stuttgart!

PAUL

(Nods.)

Almost half my life ago . . . ! The day I was arrested . . .

(Touches a few light, trilling notes.)

I knew they would be coming for me, but I did not run. Instead I went into the music room and played every piece I knew. At sixteen it is so easy to be heroic!

(A few more airy notes.)

When they finally came, they split open the top of the piano with a steel bar. For no reason, of course.

(Another light phrase.)

HILDE

Oh, that beautiful piano . . . And those beautiful poses you used to strike!

PAUL

Only because I knew you were watching from the garden!

HILDE

I watched for *years* before you saw me!

PAUL

(*A contradicting laugh.*)

Every day, behind this bush or that bush, there was your little rump sticking out!

HILDE

Beast!

PAUL

(*Resumes playing.*)

God, I will steal this piano!

HILDE

Paul . . . Stop for a moment.

PAUL

(*Stops playing.*)

What is it?

HILDE

Paul, listen. Anything I do, like bringing you here or . . . anything else . . . it is only because I love you.

PAUL

"Anything else"?

HILDE

. . . If I were to do anything else . . . because I want you to be happy . . .

PAUL

(*A suggestion of nervousness.*)

You have . . . done something else?

HILDE

She will be here at any moment. Mrs. Price.

PAUL

(*Pause.*)

You told me she would not be back until very late.

HILDE

I lied to you.

(*Pause.*)

She is leaving as soon as they have finished the dinner. She said she would be back by ten-thirty, and it is past that now.

PAUL

(*Rises.*)

Then I must leave.

(*Moves* DOWNSTAGE *toward coat.*)

HILDE

(*Following.*)

Why won't you meet her, Paul? You don't know this woman! Her mind is a—a hungry bird, hopping here—here—here.

(*Takes his arm.*)

It is because of her misfortune! Always she is searching for new interests. And she *loves* music! And such a generous woman!

PAUL

(*Pause, then quickly draws his arm free.*)

My situation is not so desperate that I must bow and light cigarettes for rich widows.

(*Picks up his coat.*)

HILDE

She would not *want* you to bow and light her cigarettes!

(PAUL *faces her for a moment, then turns and goes toward door.*)

For foolish pride you are making us lose more of our lives! We are passing thirty!

PAUL

(*Stops, turns.*)

To have a little pride . . . is foolish?

HILDE

When it makes us wait extra years to get married; yes, it is.

(*Pleadingly.*)

This is today, Paul! Your . . . your father is gone, the money is gone, the factory . . .

PAUL

I know that, Hilde.

HILDE

Then . . . why do you still keep your old pride?

PAUL

(*Shakes his head.*)

Old? The pride is not old, Hilde; it is the newest thing I own. Do you know why it took me so long to approach you when we were children? Because my dear mother told me that the servants' daughter was beneath me, and I believed her for a long time. That was vanity, not pride.

(*Returning slowly toward* HILDE.)

For nine years in the camps I did my job and no one heard me whimper or complain. Vanity, not pride. If I had had pride, I would have tried to escape. The pride is new, Hilde. Here, now, in this past year I have found it.

HILDE

(*Entreatingly.*)

Where would be the harm if she took an interest in your welfare?

PAUL

I am going to get out of the bakery in my own way, Hilde. In a few months there will be enough money for a good piano; a year of study and we will have everything we want. *Then* I will meet your Mrs. Price and be charming and gracious to her.

(*Smiling.*)

We will invite her to *our* home and let her see a genuine mansion!

(*SOUND: Three blasts of auto horn, off* RIGHT. *Paul turns, listens, turns slowly to Hilde again.*)

HILDE

(*Guiltily, yet hopefully.*)

The car. She is here. Meet her, Paul . . .

(PAUL *takes up his coat.*)

If you go out through the front door, you will only have to explain to her . . .

(PAUL *stays motionless.* HILDE *moves hesitantly* UPSTAGE RIGHT *and presses wall button* UPSTAGE *of door. She calls through the doorway.*)

Lucille!

(*Presses button again, then allows her eyes to meet* PAUL*'s.*)

Mrs. Price has treated me not as an employee but as a sister. Her condition makes her lonely; she doesn't go out for months at a time. And she has pride; she will respect yours.

PAUL

(*Pause.*)

Since I am here, I will meet her. I will say "good evening," and I will go.

(*He puts his coat on the couch.* HILDE *comes down, takes it, carries it to wing chair.*)

HILDE

Be civil to her. That is a very small thing to ask.

(*She puts wing chair, with their coats on it, back into its original place.* LUCILLE *enters* RIGHT*; a heavy-set black woman in her mid-fifties, wearing a maid's uniform. Her attitude to* HILDE *is sullen.*)

LUCILLE

Yes?

HILDE

Everett sounded the horn, Lucille. Where is the chair?

LUCILLE

(*Looking curiously at* PAUL.)

Up front, by the elevator.

HILDE

Bring it in here, please.

LUCILLE

She's been out like this, she'll want to go right upstairs.

HILDE

In here, please, Lucille.

(LUCILLE *exits* RIGHT. *Pause.* HILDE*: uncomfortably.*)

Don't be angry with me, Paul.

PAUL

(*Bitterly.*)

I am not angry.

HILDE

(*Pause.*)

There *is* a back door, if you . . .

PAUL

(*A pause, then an irritated shrug.*)

Aah, where would be the sense in running away? Back doors . . .

(*Pause.* LUCILLE *enters* RIGHT. *pushing a wheel chair of gray mohair and chrome.* HILDE *goes to her, takes chair.*)

HILDE

Go help Everett. Quickly.

(LUCILLE *exits.* HILDE *crosses with chair, places it* CENTER LEFT, *facing* DOWNSTAGE, *next to small table. She takes a book and a handkerchief from seat, puts them in compartments in sides of chair, brushes seat with her hand.*)

PAUL

(*Moving* UPSTAGE *near wing chair.*)

But if she offers any kind of assistance, I must refuse, do you understand? I will not fuss over her and flatter her and dance attendance on her.

(*SOUND: Front door closing, off* RIGHT.)

HILDE

(*Standing behind wheel chair.*)

I told you before; she would not *want* you to bow and light her cigarettes. She is not that sort of woman at all.

(EVERETT *enters* RIGHT; *a burly black man of 55 in a chauffeur's uniform. He carries* MRS. PRICE *in his arms. She is in her early forties, a beautiful woman with pale skin foreign to sunlight. She is wearing a white dinner gown, a fur stole, a diamond necklace and large diamond earrings. In her hands are a sequined evening bag and a single red rose. She smiles radiantly at* HILDE *as* EVERETT *carries her across the room, with* LUCILLE *following.* EVERETT *lowers* MRS. PRICE *carefully into the wheel chair,* HILDE *assisting.*)

MRS. PRICE

(*To* HILDE.)

I promised you I would escape early!

HILDE

(*Removing the stole, smiling.*)

Was it as "horrible" as you expected?

MRS. PRICE

No, no, no! Not at all! It turned out to be deliciously amusing!

(HILDE *passes stole to* LUCILLE.)

LUCILLE

I sewed the fancy buttons onto your blue robe, Mrs. Price. It's up in your room. I'm going to get some more and do the green one too.

(EVERETT *crosses to door* RIGHT., *waits.*)

MRS. PRICE

Bless you, Lucy. Pleasant dreams.

LUCILLE

Yes, ma'am. Have an easy night now.

MRS. PRICE

Thank you. Good night, Everett. You drove as though you'd invented the car yourself!

(LUCILLE *exits* RIGHT.)

EVERETT

(*Unsmilingly.*)

Thank you, ma'am. Good night. Miss Hahn . . .

(*Glances curiously at* PAUL.)

HILDE

Good night, Everett.

(EVERETT *exits* RIGHT.)

MRS. PRICE

I made him race through two red lights; he's riddled with guilt!

(HILDE, *smiling, moves to* LEFT *of wheel chair.* PAUL *remains* UPSTAGE, *watching.*)

HILDE

Mrs. Price, I hope you don't mind the chair not being by the elevator. I was afraid you would go—

MRS. PRICE

(*Cutting in.*)

I don't mind *anything*, dear! Four glasses of champagne, *and* a brandy! Have you ever seen me so light-headed?

HILDE

(*Smiling.*)

No, I haven't. And who gave you the lovely rose?

MRS. PRICE

Gave me? I'll have you know I stole it! At a moment when no one was watching me—and I must admit there *was* a moment when no one was watching me—I plucked it from the centerpiece and hid it beneath my napkin.

(*Giving the rose to* HILDE.)

Pour toi, sweetie. A piece of the party.

HILDE

Oh, thank you . . . Mmmmm . . .

(*Inhales the scent of the flower.*)

MRS. PRICE

Doctors, Hilde; all of Dr. MacLeod's friends are doctors! One was sitting on either side of me and I wish you could have seen them! It must be a doctor's dream come true—a woman in a wheel chair, with *diamonds!*

(HILDE *laughs.* MRS. PRICE *takes off her earrings.*)

By the end of the meal I expected the two of them to be treating each other for indigestion! And poor Dr. MacLeod, leaving tomorrow for the Auld Sod and seeing them courting his prize patient . . . *He* won't get a good night's sleep the whole trip!

(*Puts earrings in evening bag.*)

That's a very sweet dress, Hilde. I was right about that collar, wasn't I?

HILDE

Yes, you were. Mrs. Price . . .

MRS. PRICE

What is it, dear?

HILDE

There is a reason I did not have the chair by the elevator.

MRS. PRICE

A reason?

HILDE

There is someone I want you to meet.

MRS. PRICE

(*Pause.*)

Someone—to meet?

HILDE

Paul. My fiancé.

MRS. PRICE

(*Pause. A note of alarm.*)

He's here? Now?

(*Nodding.* HILDE *gives chair a partial turn toward* RIGHT *as* PAUL *comes* DOWNSTAGE.)

PAUL

How do you do, Mrs. Price?

MRS. PRICE

I didn't know anyone was—I didn't—

(*Glances distractedly at* HILDE.)

HILDE

Mrs. Price, this is Paul Schildger. Paul, Mrs. Price.

PAUL

How do you do.

MRS. PRICE

How do you do, Mr.—

HILDE

Schildger.

MRS. PRICE

Schildger . . .

(*Fumbles earrings from bag, attempts to put them on again.*)

I wasn't expecting anyone. I've been at a dinner party. My doctor thinks I remain in the house too much . . .

PAUL

(*Standing before her, watching intently.*)

I came only to visit Hilde. She insisted that I stay to meet you.

MRS. PRICE

Of course. She was right.

(*Giving up with the earrings, fisting them before her.*)

Oh, damn these earrings!

(*Aware that her strain is visible.*)

The champagne. Makes my fingers . . . hard to control.

HILDE

(*Puts rose on table, takes earrings.*)

Here, let me . . .

PAUL

Really, there is no need to trouble yourself, Mrs. Price. I am soon to leave.

(HILDE *begins putting earrings on* MRS. PRICE.)

MRS. PRICE

No, no . . .

(*A deep breath, bringing a degree of composure.*)

It's a matter of principle now. They go on if we have to nail them on.

HILDE

There's one . . .

MRS. PRICE

Sit down, Mr. Schildger. Do sit down. You look like a policeman.

PAUL

(*Hesitates, then lowers himself slowly to the couch.*)

I must go soon . . .

MRS. PRICE

You've been in America since last autumn, haven't you? Do you like it?

PAUL

Yes . . .

HILDE

He *loves* it. He says it is the only country in the world where the cars grow old in a year and the women never grow old at all!

(MRS. PRICE *laughs,* PAUL *flushes and smiles self-consciously.* HILDE, *finished with the earrings, stands behind* MRS. PRICE.)

MRS. PRICE

That's charming! It should be carved on the skirt of the Statue of Liberty.

(*Pause.*)

Hilde tells me that you work in an enormous commercial bakery.

PAUL

(*Pause.*)

That is correct . . .

MRS. PRICE

Don't tell me you're the man who breaks up all the cookies before they put them in the boxes.

PAUL

(*A slight smile.*)

Oh, no, that is the work of a specialist.

MRS. PRICE

(*Smiling.*)

And what is your job?

PAUL

(*Pause. Flatly.*)

I remove a tray of loaves from the oven, wheel it into the cooling room, and return to the oven for another tray.

MRS. PRICE

Surely you could have found more—more suitable work. You've had an education . . .

PAUL

It was interrupted in my sixteenth year.

MRS. PRICE

But the knowledge of two languages; wasn't that a help?

PAUL

My English last year was much poorer than it is now, and German is not the most popular language. So I went back to the bakery.

MRS. PRICE

Went back?

PAUL

It is the same work that I did in prison camps.

MRS. PRICE

(*Pause. Compassionately.*)

Oh, no . . . I should think you would have taken *any* job rather than that.

PAUL

It was a job I knew. Also it is a means now rather than an end, which makes quite a difference. Then too, the work has an attraction—or compensation, perhaps I should say. I mean that it leaves the mind free.

HILDE

He can think of his music.

MRS. PRICE

Yes, I understand you're a pianist of great promise.

PAUL

You flatter me . . .

HILDE

No! Three professors said so, last winter!

PAUL

(*Reproachfully.*)

Hilde . . .

MRS. PRICE

Oh, Hilde's already told me about that. It's a pity you weren't eligible for the fellowship. When will you become a citizen?

PAUL

(*With a dry smile.*)

Not for four more years. And then I will be too *old* for the fellowship.

MRS. PRICE

(*Shaking her head.*)

What a world we live in . . . !

HILDE

(*Pause. Leaning toward* MRS. PRICE.)

Paul was playing Chopin just before you arrived . . .

PAUL

Brahms. It was Brahms.

MRS. PRICE

How I wish I had heard! It must have been lovely! Will you play for me now?

PAUL

I would like to . . . but it is close to eleven o'clock.

MRS. PRICE

No matter; the walls of this house are solid stone.

PAUL

(*Evasively.*)

I mean that I am tired, and would not play my best.

MRS. PRICE

Well, then, you must come back another evening. I would enjoy very much being—"serenaded."

PAUL

Some evening, perhaps . . .

MRS. PRICE

It's criminal, really, for that fine instrument to stand untouched. Hilde tells me that your piano is a secondhand upright. Perhaps you could do your practicing here . . .

HILDE

Oh, that is so kind of you, Mrs. Price! It would—

PAUL

(*Rising, cutting in firmly.*)

Bitte, Hilde, lass das. Du Treibst mich da in etwas hinein—

HILDE

Aber warum denn? Wenn du hier die Moglichkeit hast—

PAUL

Ich will aber nicht und damit basta!

MRS. PRICE

(*Pause.*)

I do hope there are going to be English sub-titles.

PAUL

I apologize, Mrs. Price. I apologize for our rudeness, and for being here without invitation. I will leave now.

MRS. PRICE

I offered you the use of the piano.

PAUL

Thank you. I cannot accept.

MRS. PRICE

(*A hint of her earlier tension.*)

Why not? Do I offend you in some way?

PAUL

No, it is only that I do not wish to make myself . . . the object of charity.

MRS. PRICE

Charity?

(*Pause, then smiling.*)

I said you might practice on the piano; I didn't say I was going to give it to you.

PAUL

(*A strained smile.*)

I fear there is very little difference between the two. A gift from a stranger is charity, even if it is only the use of a thing which is given.

MRS. PRICE

And has charity become a sin? I was under the impression that it was a virtue.

PAUL

For the one who gives it, yes; but for the one who accepts it, I am not sure.

MRS. PRICE

Well, I see I will have to brush up a bit on my German philosophy.

PAUL

It is not a question of my nationality, Mrs. Price; it is a matter of . . . a *personal* philosophy.

HILDE

Please try to understand, Mrs. Price; the Schildgers were a fine family and it is difficult for Paul to—

PAUL

(*Silencing* HILDE.)

Bitte, lass das . . .

MRS. PRICE

A "personal philosophy," you said?

PAUL

Ja. My present situation will not last forever and I think some benefit may come of enduring it. You must see, this is the first time in my life when there is no one directing me; neither parents, nor guards, nor workers of the Red Cross and such. I am—what is the phrase?—*on my own*. It is not easy, but it is a benefit, I think. And I ought to continue on my own until it *becomes* easy.

MRS. PRICE

(*Radiantly.*)

It's because I'm a woman, isn't it!

PAUL

(*A bit taken aback.*)

Not at all.

(MRS. PRICE *propels her chair a bit closer to him.* HILDE *follows behind her.*)

MRS. PRICE

Of course it is! If not for my being a woman you wouldn't have the slightest compunctions about accepting so small a favor!

PAUL

I assure you it is not a question of your sex.

MRS. PRICE

(*A tense pause.*)

I think you are . . .

(*Forcing a tone of archness.*)

something of a fake, Mr. Schildger!

HILDE

Oh, no, Mrs. Price!

MRS. PRICE

Forgive me, but if you really were the thwarted artist of whom I've heard so much from Hilde, my being a woman would count for nothing, your "personal philosophy" would count for nothing; all that would matter to you at this moment would be that piano. I have read biographies of more than a dozen artists, and the common characteristic of these men was a deep and very unphilosophical selfishness, which would let nothing come between them and their work; nothing, not even their own pride.

(*Charming now, femininely reproving.*)

I would have expected to find the same attitude in you . . . Instead, though, I find—well, it's an interesting pose that you strike; very male and very satisfying to your ego, I imagine. But an artist would not have the time for it.

PAUL

(*Lets coat slip to couch. Slowly, bluntly.*)

You must not call me a fake, Mrs. Price.

MRS. PRICE

I'm sorry . . . But, Mr. Schildger, what *is* your prime ambition?

PAUL

(*Firmly, but with an underlying defensiveness.*)

To be a . . . great pianist.

MRS. PRICE

And in order to become that, you must study, mustn't you?

PAUL

(*Pause.*)

I must study.

MRS. PRICE

Is the piano you study on as good as this one?

PAUL

No, it is not.

MRS. PRICE

Wouldn't your studying bring better results if you were working with a better instrument?

PAUL

Yes . . .

MRS. PRICE

But because of a "personal philosophy" you refuse a better instrument when it is offered you.

PAUL

(*Pause.*)

Yes.

MRS. PRICE

Then to be a great pianist is only your second ambition, Mr. Schildger. Your prime ambition is to be—a personal philosopher.

(*Pause.*)

I don't mean to poke fun at you. I only wish to point out your inconsistency.

(*Pause.*)

This piano of yours; you rent it, I understand.

PAUL

(*Pause.*)

That is correct . . .

MRS. PRICE

Very well then, why not rent *my* piano?—If that will satisfy your moral principles.

PAUL

I could not afford a reasonable rental.

MRS. PRICE

What would *be* a reasonable rental? May I ask what you pay now?

PAUL

Eight dollars a month.

MRS. PRICE

For a piano that is in your room, available twenty-four hours a day, whereas this one is here, and would be available only three or four hours every evening. Don't you think its quality is countered by its inaccessibility? Eight dollars a month would be more than reasonable.

PAUL

No, you are making it easy . . .

MRS. PRICE

We must bargain backwards, I see. All right, would ten dollars a month be enough of a burden for you?

HILDE

Please, Paul—

(*She starts to move toward him, but* MRS. PRICE *restrains her with a hand on her wrist.*)

MRS. PRICE

Your firmness is admirable, Mr. Schildger. I only wish you had it working *for* your ambition instead of *against* it.

PAUL

(*Pause.*)

You turn things upside-down, Mrs. Price. It is difficult to resist . . . your logic . . .

HILDE

Oh, Paul!

(*Goes to him, takes his arm happily.*)

MRS. PRICE

Finito. At the risk of offending you, I'll give the payments to charity!

(PAUL'*s stance relaxes, his gaze is inward, uncertain of what he has done.* HILDE *kisses him on the cheek.*)

For myself I will keep only the pleasure of hearing you play.

PAUL

(*Still within himself.*)

You are too kind . . .

HILDE

Mrs. Price, I—

(*Rushes to her.*)

Oh, God will bless you!

(*Takes her hand, kisses her cheek.*)

MRS. PRICE

(*Defending herself.*)

Hilde, please . . . You'll smother me . . .

HILDE

(*Standing ecstatically between the two.*)

Oh . . . Play for her now, Paul! Please do! Please!

MRS. PRICE

Yes, do. Anything at all. If you're terribly tired I could even suffer "Claire de Lune."

PAUL

(*A thin smile.*)

I play "Claire de Lune" unusually well.

(MRS. PRICE *wheels her chair back toward table* LEFT.)

HILDE

Play the nocturne!

(*To* MRS. PRICE.)

When he was fourteen he wrote a nocturne and won a magnificent medal for it! You've seen the medal! My luck charm!

(*Flashing a gold disc that she wears on a thin chain about her left wrist.*)

PAUL

(*Going to piano.*)

Hardly magnificent, Hilde. A plain little disc . . .

HILDE

(*Going quickly to* MRS. PRICE.)

No, don't listen to him! Look! You see the head of Wagner, and here, the inscription—"The Wagner Medal," it is called!

MRS. PRICE

Mmmmm . . . "Paul August Schildger . . ."

HILDE

Good luck it brings me . . .

PAUL

The school gave out medals and my father had money so they gave one to me.

(*Sits at piano.*)

HILDE

No! No one played half as well as he did! Oh, there was such a party that night!

(*Crosses enthusiastically toward* PAUL.)

Remember? Your mother presented you to the guests as though you were Paderewski himself! And then the dancing—and the dishes we prepared!

(*Turning toward* MRS. PRICE.)

The Schildgers' kitchen was as big as a restaurant's. Extra cooks had been brought in, and everywhere one turned there was platter after platter; ducks the size of geese, geese the size of turkeys . . . You have lost something?

MRS. PRICE

(*Emptying her evening bag, a cigarette in one hand.*)

A cigarette holder the size of a cigarette holder.

(*Smiles at* HILDE.)

My gold one. I left it at Dr. MacLeod's, and he's off to Europe in the morning.

HILDE

(*Pause.*)

If you'd like me to, I'll get it.

MRS. PRICE

No, no, no. See if the light is still on in Everett and Lucille's room. Everett would love to drive without me in the car!

HILDE

I will get it.

(*Goes to wing chair.*)

It won't take long. And Paul can play for you.

(*Picks up coat.*)

MRS. PRICE

All right. Take a cab, though.

(*Holds out folded bills.*)

Do you know the address?

(PAUL *strikes a few desultory notes on piano.*)

HILDE

(*Taking bills.*)

It's on Eighty-ninth and Park, isn't it?

MRS. PRICE

The northwest corner.

HILDE

(*While putting on coat, to* PAUL.)

I'll only be half an hour. Play the nocturne and the piece you played before—the Brahms—and—

(*Charading it with crossed hands.*)

you know, the—the impossible one!

(*Exits* RIGHT.)

MRS. PRICE

(*Replacing things in bag.*)

When Hilde is happy, she swims in it.

PAUL

She was often so when we were children . . .

(PAUL*'s eyes meet* MRS. PRICE*'s. For an instant we feel the tension of this first moment alone for the two.* MRS. PRICE *puts her evening bag on the small table.*)

MRS. PRICE

I was beginning to think you didn't exist. When Hilde started to work for me two years ago, it was nothing but "Paul," "Paul," "Paul." "Paul is like this," "Paul is like that" . . . And then she finally arranged your immigration, and—I saw no Paul.

PAUL

The bakery and the studying . . . leave little free time.

MRS. PRICE

Of course. I understand . . .

PAUL

I too have learned much about you.

MRS. PRICE

Nothing incriminating, I hope.

PAUL

No. Only good things. I am grateful to you, Mrs. Price, for being so kind to Hilde. She has been alone in this country for many years. Both her parents died soon after they left Germany.

MRS. PRICE

Yes, I know . . . Well then, let us hear the famous nocturne!

(*Propels chair to* CENTER STAGE.)

PAUL

Really, it is not exceptional. I was only fourteen.

MRS. PRICE

(*Smiling.*)

When *I* was fourteen, no one gave *me* medals. No medals at all . . .

(PAUL *begins to play.* MRS. PRICE *brings her chair a bit closer to the piano. When* PAUL *has played for a few moments,* MRS. PRICE *strikes a cigarette lighter and, with her eyes intent on* PAUL, *touches the flame to a cigarette in a gold holder.* PAUL *continues playing for a few moments, then stops in mid-phrase.*)

PAUL

Is that the cigarette holder for which you sent Hilde?

MRS. PRICE

(*Off guard. Trying to cover.*)

Why, yes, it is. It must have been in my purse all along. I suppose I took it out automatically, I was so intent on your nocturne. It's quite lovely.

PAUL

(*An accusation:*)

Your purse is on the table. The holder was in your hand.

MRS. PRICE

(*Pause.*)

I will try to make my explanation without being maudlin, Mr. Schildger.

PAUL

(*Rises. Curtly:*)

I do not know the meaning of that word.

(*Moves* DOWNSTAGE.)

MRS. PRICE

It means "overly sentimental." I will try to avoid that. Eight years ago, in a particularly unpleasant accident, I lost the use of both my legs. The muscles in them are completely dead; the nerves are very much alive. I am in almost constant pain. The enjoyable moments in my life are few and far between, and when I see one coming I try to insure it. Hilde is like a sister to me; she is good, she is charming, she is honest, she is sweet. But—she is also a chatterbox. To insure my enjoyment of your playing, I invented a harmless errand for her. It was selfish of me, I admit, but I think I am entitled to a bit of selfishness on occasion.

PAUL

(*Facing her. A deeply-felt reprimand.*)

She wanted very much to stay!

MRS. PRICE

(*Her gaze drops. Painfully.*)

I know she did . . .

(*Looking up at him again, forcefully.*)

What can I do? The lie has been told. I'll make it up to her tomorrow! The beautician is coming; a new hair-do for Hilde, a facial or a manicure; she likes that!

(*Pause. Forthrightly.*)

I'll pay for the lie. Let me have the good of it.

(PAUL *hesitates, then returns to the piano.*)

Play it from the beginning. It's a lovely composition! Such longing and sorrow . . . And only fourteen . . . !

(PAUL *sits.*)

To whom did you dedicate it? Hilde? No, no—of course; your mother.

PAUL

(*Pause.*)

To . . . to no one . . .

(*He begins to play.* MRS. PRICE *watches him. The lights dim to darkness.*)

THE CURTAIN FALLS

ACT ONE

SCENE TWO

The curtain rises on the fully lighted set. Drapes opened, darkness outside. Portrait light on. Sheets of music are stacked neatly on DOWNSTAGE *corner of piano, and a new, functional-looking lamp (unlighted)*
is appropriately placed nearby. Hassock has been moved a few feet toward LEFT, *so that there is a space between it and end table.*

HILDE, *dressed differently than in previous scene, stands at telephone* RIGHT. *There is an ornamental silver pin on the bosom of her dress.*

HILDE

(*Into telephone.*)

I understand he is not there now; I would like to know whether he has been in at all this evening.

(*Pause.*)

Would you let me speak to your mother, please?

(*Pause.*)

Hello, Mrs. Gross? This is Hilde Hahn, Mr. Schildger's fiancée. Has he been to his room this evening?

(LUCILLE *enters on balcony* RIGHT, *crosses and descends stairs.*)

If he does come in, would you please tell him that I am expecting him? Thank you. Good-bye.

(*She hangs up,* LUCILLE *begins drawing drapes across window.*)

Mrs. Price is ready to come down?

LUCILLE

She's in the elevator now. All dressed up pretty. You can make another phone call.

HILDE

(*Pause.*)

I am grateful to you for helping out, Lucille, but you know that the doctor said we must not spoil her by having too many people attend her.

LUCILLE

She was ready, and I was there. You were busy on the telephone.

(*Crosses* RIGHT)

HILDE

Please, if that happens again, call me.

LUCILLE

(*Not looking at* HILDE, *straightening something on end table.*)

I tended to her long before you ever come here. I can do it all right.

HILDE

I know you can, Lucille. It is only that the doctor makes a suggestion and we must follow it, mustn't we?

LUCILLE

(*Sotto, moving toward door* RIGHT.)

Doctor ain't running this household . . .

(EVERETT *wheels* MRS. PRICE *in through door* RIGHT. *She wears a beige garment on the order of a hostess gown, with a diamond brooch at the bosom.*)

MRS. PRICE

How happy I am that the program's not started! I'm sorry I'm late, but this concert hall is such a long, long drive from . . .

(*Her exuberance trailing away.*)

way down on Gramercy Park . . .

(LUCILLE *takes chair, pushes it* CENTER LEFT. EVERETT *exits* RIGHT.)

HILDE

Paul isn't here yet, Mrs. Price.

MRS. PRICE

(*Pause.*)

It's past nine. He's never been later than eight-thirty. Maybe a week of our company was enough for him.

HILDE

Oh, no. He'll be along soon. I'm sure of it.

LUCILLE

You want anything, Mrs. Price?

MRS. PRICE

No. No, thanks . . .

LUCILLE

If you do, you just buzz for me.

(LUCILLE *exits* RIGHT. MRS. PRICE *settles herself* CENTER LEFT.)

MRS. PRICE

Why should he be late tonight of all nights?

(*Looking at* HILDE.)

You didn't tell him what I have in mind, did you?

HILDE

You only told *me* this afternoon.

(*Pause. Smiling.*)

I called his rooming house. He hasn't been there. Probably he has worked overtime.

MRS. PRICE

He gives them eight hours a day. It's cruel of them to demand more!

HILDE

There is extra pay for overtime. Paul jumps at the chance.

MRS. PRICE

It's wrong . . .

HILDE

(*Sits on hassock. Pause.*)

Mrs. Price . . . don't you think it might be . . . too soon to make the offer you are thinking of?

MRS. PRICE

Too soon?

HILDE

I am afraid he will refuse it, refuse everything, even to continue using the piano. If you would wait another week or so, maybe it would be easier.

MRS. PRICE

He shouldn't waste one more day in that wretched bakery.

HILDE

I agree. I am only afraid you will undo the good you have already done. For him to rent the piano is one thing, but to accept money, clothing . . .

MRS. PRICE

You've heard my arguments; logic is on my side, isn't it?

HILDE

You do not know Paul as well as I do, Mrs. Price. Things have been done to him in the past, terrible things, which now make him . . . hold people away from him. It surprises me even that he came to dinner last night.

MRS. PRICE

(*An edge of asperity.*)

But he came, didn't he?—and said he enjoyed it more than any dinner since before the war?

(*Pause. Covering tension with a smile.*)

Let me tell you something, Hilde. You say you know Paul better than I do, but I say I know men in general better than you do. There were four of them in this house, my three brothers and my father. I've watched men all my life. First them, and then my husband. Paul may be more clever and sensitive than most men, but at heart he is not so very different from the rest.

HILDE

(*A diffident smile.*)

I think he may also be more stubborn than most other men.

MRS. PRICE

I'll make my offer, he'll protest, but in the end he'll accept. I'll bet on it.

HILDE

(*Resignedly.*)

I hope you are right.

MRS. PRICE

But you think I am wrong.

HILDE

Yes, I do.

MRS. PRICE

(*Pause.*)

Would you care to bet on it?

HILDE

No.

MRS. PRICE

(*Pause. With a longing envy.*)

So self-assured, so sure of *him* . . .

(*An edge of resentment.*)

Is it—woman's intuition?

HILDE

I am not *sure* of anything, Mrs. Price, but I have known Paul for many—

MRS. PRICE

I am sure! He'll accept!

(*Pause. Bringing herself down to a conversational level, not without effort.*)

You think I don't know men! Oh, Hilde, just what do you think was my major field of study through four years of college? I used my notebooks for date books and did my homework where homework shouldn't be done! Lost my roommate on that account. A sweet little thing with eyes like skies and a mind like a dungeon—invented all sorts of slanders, but that was the *real* cause of discord between us; envy of my greater popularity—with those men about whom *you're so sure I know nothing.*

HILDE

(*Pause.*)

Mrs. Price, I said only that you do not know Paul as well as I do.

MRS. PRICE

You implied, my dear; you implied most clearly and distinctly!

HILDE

(*Pause.*)

I am sorry, then. Believe me, it was not intentional.

(*Rises. With a placating smile.*)

We are both of us on edge because Paul is late. We must box his ears when he arrives.

(MRS. PRICE *sits rigidly, tensely.*)

Friends?

(HILDE *reaches toward* MRS. PRICE*'s hand.* MRS. PRICE *snatches it away as though from fire.* HILDE *stares at her, baffled, offended.*)

Mrs. Price . . . !

MRS. PRICE

(*Suddenly naked.*)

I—I'm sorry—

(*Turns her chair, moves swiftly away, straining for breath and composure.)*

(SOUND: Door chime, off RIGHT.)

HILDE

There is Paul!

(HILDE *heads quickly toward door* RIGHT. MRS. PRICE *turns sharply, with a suggestion of panic.*)

MRS. PRICE

Let Everett take it!

(HILDE *looks back at* MRS. PRICE.)

Come here.

(HILDE *returns to* MRS. PRICE.)

I want to make that bet!—He'll protest against my offer, but in the end he'll accept!

HILDE

Mrs. Price . . .

MRS. PRICE

That clip you're wearing, against this clip of mine!

HILDE

There is no *reason* for us to bet.

MRS. PRICE

(*Forcing a smile.*)

Come on, Hilde; your woman's intuition against mine!

HILDE

But . . . this clip is only silver, and yours has a dozen diamonds!

MRS. PRICE

That's my concern; I'll risk the high odds!

(*SOUND: Door chime repeat.*)

Do we have a bet?

HILDE

Not unless you insist, Mrs. Price.

MRS. PRICE

I insist.

(*She draws chair back a bit and turns it more toward door.* PAUL *and* EVERETT *can be heard off* RIGHT.)

EVERETT

They're waiting for you inside.

PAUL

Thank you, Everett.

HILDE

I'm sorry that I have offended you.

MRS. PRICE

You haven't, Hilde. You've made the evening! Betting always excites me! Ah, here he is!

(PAUL *enters* RIGHT. *He wears the same suit, but his appearance is neater than in previous scene. His hands are behind his back.*)

PAUL

Observe my creation!

(*Brings forth his left hand, with a miniature loaf of bread upon it.*)

Hand-baked bread of whole wheat, and inside—raisins!

(*Going to* MRS. PRICE, *offering it to her.*)

Thank you for the lovely dinner.

(MRS. PRICE *takes the bread.* HILDE *comes to* PAUL*'s left side, takes his arm and kisses his cheek.*)

HILDE

You are late, darling.

PAUL

(*Kisses her lightly.*)

Overtime.

MRS. PRICE

Thank you, Paul. Thank you more than I can say. I shall treasure it always.

PAUL

That would be a great deal wiser than eating it.

(MRS. PRICE *puts bread on small table. She extends her hand.* PAUL *does not take it.*)

MRS. PRICE

May I have a handclasp, too?

(PAUL *hesitates, then takes her hand. There is a bandage on the back of his right hand.*)

Oh, my God . . .

HILDE

What happened to you? What is it?

MRS. PRICE

(*Over* HILDE*'s second line.*)

What happened?

PAUL

It is nothing! Nothing! A minor burn! The nurse put salve upon it; in two days it will be healed.

MRS. PRICE

(*Bitterly.*)

Nothing . . .

HILDE

(*Distressed.*)

Oh . . . How did this happen?

PAUL

I brushed against one of the trays. It was my own fault!

MRS. PRICE

Can you move your fingers?

PAUL

Of course.

(*Withdraws his hand from hers, flexes his fingers demonstratively.*)

It will not interfere with my playing in the least.

(MRS. PRICE *and* HILDE *make little sounds of distress.* PAUL *moves back toward piano. To* MRS. PRICE*:*)

My Lord, I expected a bit of sympathy from you, but if I had known there would be *such* commotion I would not have come at all.

MRS. PRICE

You should not be working in that bakery!

PAUL

When the foreman saw me taking that little bread from the oven, he said the very same thing!

HILDE

You were dismissed?

PAUL

Oh, no. Men with my experience are not so readily come by.

(*He turns his attention to the pile of music on the piano, pulls out one sheet, looks for another.* HILDE, *meanwhile, sits on couch.*)

MRS. PRICE

Paul.

(PAUL *turns to her.*)

May I have a few minutes of your time before you start to play? I'd like to speak to you.

PAUL

Yes, of course.

(*Puts down music, comes* DOWNSTAGE. MRS. PRICE, *with a gesture, invites him to sit. He sits at end of couch,* HILDE *on his* RIGHT. MRS. PRICE *brings her chair into space between end table and hassock, turning herself toward* PAUL. *She takes a folded sheet of letter-size paper from a compartment of her chair.*)

MRS. PRICE

I have something I want you to look at.

(*She unfolds paper, glances at it, passes it to* PAUL, *who takes it curiously.* HILDE *looks questioningly at* MRS. PRICE, *who nods, indicating that* HILDE *may also look.* HILDE *does so.* MRS. PRICE *gives them a moment to scan the paper's contents.*)

I receive such statements quarterly from the lawyers who administer my affairs. The figures vary, in that they grow a bit larger with each accounting. The first figure represents the value of holdings which I own jointly with my three brothers. The second figure, underlined, is twenty-five per cent of that, which is my share. The other underlined figures represent properties under my sole ownership, in which my brothers have no part. The total, down below, represents—the total. It does not include savings accounts, U. S. bonds, and a large block of Irish Free State Bonds which my father gave me on my twenty-first birthday.

PAUL

You are an extremely . . . fortunate woman, Mrs. Price.

(*Looks at paper for another moment, then extends it toward her. Warily.*)

Why do you show me this?

MRS. PRICE

(*Takes paper, folds it.*)

Doesn't this paper strike you as being just a little bit—ludicrous?

PAUL

(*Not knowing the word.*)

Ludicrous?

HILDE

Komisch.

PAUL

No, I find nothing ludi-crous in wealth.

MRS. PRICE

(*Holding paper before her.*)

My grandfather made a fortune in silver, my father compounded it in railroads and shipping, my husband became a tributary—more railroads, more shipping. This widening river, fed by three generations, reaches its end—

(*Lets paper drop into her lap.*)

in a cripple's lap. That strikes me as more than a little "ludi-crous."

(*She replaces paper in compartment of chair.* PAUL *watches her silently.*)

I have more money than I can conceivably spend, just as I have a piano that I cannot play. There are more rooms in this house than I can conceivably live in. There is more food at each meal than I, and Hilde, and Lucille and Everett can conceivably eat.

PAUL

What are you saying to me, Mrs. Price?

MRS. PRICE

I am saying that common sense, if nothing else, should tell you to give up that job of yours and move into this house, where you can study in earnest, making use of your God-given talent as God intended.

PAUL

(*Looks at her for a moment, turns to* HILDE.)

Did you—

(HILDE *shakes her head slowly.*)

MRS. PRICE

This is my idea, not Hilde's!

PAUL

(*Turning back to her.*)

You know I cannot do it . . .

MRS. PRICE

Can not or *will* not?

PAUL

Both!

MRS. PRICE

You said that charity was a gift from a stranger! Am I still a stranger to you?

PAUL

No, you are a friend, a good friend, but you offer a gift I can never repay. That is how friendships are ended!

MRS. PRICE

You could repay it! Not now, perhaps, but in the future. There will be concerts and recordings . . .

PAUL

(*Smiling.*)

Oh, Mrs. Price, those lawyers would tremble at such a doubtful investment.

MRS. PRICE

Other women have invested in talent! And other men have accepted their help!

PAUL

(*Pause. Leans close to her. Gently.*)

Mrs. Price, you have much money and you have even more generosity. All I have is a little pride. If I let that go from me, all I will have is your money and your generosity, and nothing of my own.

(*Pause.*)

For a year Hilde has been telling me of you. I wanted to meet you and yet I was afraid; afraid that something like this would happen, that I would say yes when it did. My childhood was spent in a house like this one; to live so again is a great temptation. But by thirty, one should be building one's own house.

(*Smiling.*)

The "personal philosopher" has not quite vanished.

(*Pause.* MRS. PRICE *sits stonily.*)

Because we are friends, I thank you sincerely for the help you would give me. And because I wish us to remain friends, I ask you never to mention the subject again.

(*He backs a few steps* UPSTAGE, *watching her.* MRS. PRICE*'s gaze turns to* HILDE, *who shifts uncomfortably, embarrassed by her vindication.* MRS. PRICE *removes her diamond clip, holds it out toward* HILDE.)

HILDE

Mrs. Price, I don't want it . . .

MRS. PRICE

You've just cost me forty-three hundred dollars, Paul.

PAUL

What do you mean?

HILDE

Please, Mrs. Price . . .

MRS. PRICE

(*Her voice is stretched tight over the beginnings of hysteria.*)

We made a bet, Hilde and I. I was peeved and I forced her to bet with me. She thought you would act foolishly and I thought you would act intelligently. I have lost.

(PAUL *turns away angrily, thrusts his hands into his pockets and moves* UPSTAGE. HILDE *rises, goes to* MRS. PRICE, *who still holds out the clip.*)

HILDE

(*Gently.*)

I don't want your clip, Mrs. Price.

MRS. PRICE

You won.

HILDE

I only bet because I did not want to annoy you further. It would be ridiculous for me to take such an expensive clip. When would I wear it?

MRS. PRICE

We made a bet and you are the winner!

HILDE

You know I did not *want* to bet!

MRS. PRICE

(*Refastens clip awkwardly to her robe. Her tone is humorous, but betrays the growing hysteria:*)

All right . . . *you* don't want my clip . . . *he* doesn't want my money . . . nobody wants *anything* from me . . .

(*Begins sobbing, her hands to her face.*)

HILDE

Oh, Mrs. Price . . .

MRS. PRICE

(*Through the sobs.*)

I'm sorry . . . I'm sorry . . . I don't want to . . .

HILDE

(*Kneeling, soothing her.*)

Ah, hush now, shhhh . . . shhhh . . . please don't . . .

(PAUL *comes* DOWNSTAGE *and looks on, frightened.* HILDE *tucks a handkerchief in* MRS. PRICE*'s hands.*)

Shhhh, here . . . ahh . . . See, there is Paul, looking as though he watches a ghost . . . We don't want to frighten him to death, do we?

MRS. PRICE

(*Into the handkerchief.*)

Oh, no, mustn't frighten Paul . . .

(*Raises her face toward him.*)

We mustn't let Paul see us crying! Because—

(*Sends chair swiftly backward toward* LEFT, *cries out.*)

Paul has pride! And pride forbids crying, doesn't it, Paul?

(*She wipes at her eyes and moves chair* UPSTAGE *and toward* RIGHT, *circling* PAUL. HILDE *rises slowly from her kneeling position.*)

Paul has Pride and Principles! I've got money and generosity, but Paul owns the pride monopoly!

PAUL

Mrs. Price, I—

MRS. PRICE

(*Pointing to hassock.*)

You sit down there. I'll show you how little pride you've left me!

PAUL

Please, Mrs. Price—

MRS. PRICE

Sit down! Or doesn't that philosophy of yours include common courtesy?

(PAUL *sits on hassock.* MRS. PRICE *brings chair down into space between it and end table.*)

HILDE

Mrs. Price, you should not let yourself get so excited!

MRS. PRICE

(*Over the above, with a sharp gesture toward couch, her attention still on* PAUL.)

Sit! Sit.

(*Reluctantly,* HILDE *sits on edge of couch.*)

You come here spouting of pride and principles, suffering nobly in your bakery and your prisons . . . I'm going to tell you something about—

(*Indicates wheel chair.*)

my prison!

(*Pause.*)

HILDE

You should not discuss this.

MRS. PRICE

(*Points at her knees.*)

Do you know how this happened, Mr. Schildger?

PAUL

You said there was an accident . . .

MRS. PRICE

I lied. Last week I still had pride enough for that.

(*Pause.*)

This chair was a present, Paul, a dying present, bequeathed by my husband along with the ships and the railroads.

(*Pause. She is in command of herself again, choosing words carefully, but the hysteria lingers in her eyes.*)

The Fourth of July, eight years ago. A lake with a long Indian name in the state of New Hampshire. The clan had gathered for the holidays; the three brothers, the three happy sisters-in-law—and he and I. He took me for a speed-boat ride on Sunday afternoon, and in the middle of the lake he turned the boat around and headed back for shore. I didn't see what was happening, not until a patrol boat signaled us to cut our speed. Then I saw . . . purpose in his eyes, and the whiteness of his knuckles on the wheel; heard the rising scream of the engine, felt the boat tilting upward, straining for flight—straight at the shore ahead. I wrestled with his arms; they were steel. The shore loomed up; umbrellas, beach chairs. I tried to jump—

(*Pause.*)

He died instantly, crushed behind the wheel, his neck broken over the edge of the windshield. I was thrown from the boat and landed feet-first, on flagstones. If I had been an animal, they would have shot me then and there.

(*Pause.*)

A human being, though, is delivered to the hospitals. If you're poor, they operate once and either kill you or cure you, but if you're rich, God help you, they operate a thousand times. Thirty-seven, to be exact—then send you home in a wheel chair, saying, "You're fine, you'll live to be eighty"—as though that were something devoutly to be wished.

PAUL

Why did he do such a thing?

MRS. PRICE

Why? We had been married for seven years, without children; perhaps he imagined that comments were being made. He was many years older than I, a bitterly sensitive man. Maybe he feared I would leave him; separation had been spoken of. Well, he separated us, despite himself. My brothers reported an accident. Every control on the boat had failed simultaneously; an accident. The police were gullible. Or bribable.

(*Pause.*)

That is how I got into my prison camp, Paul. Unlike the ones you knew, it allows no hope of eventual freedom. And I can do nothing to justify my existence, not even bake bread. I tried to put an end to it last April—didn't I, Hilde?—but I choked on the pills and dropped the bottle, and Hilde came running with my friends, the doctors. So here I am, without function, without purpose, without reason; with no talent, no skill, and no future until eighty. But lots of money. How rich I am!

(*A new urgency begins growing.*)

Last week you came here, and for five evenings I have had the illusion of purpose. Hearing your music, I have told myself, "*This* is what I am doing, helping this man to achieve greatness." I would like to hold the illusion during the day too, but your pride prevents it. I would like to say, "Without me he'd be struggling, trapped in that bakery. Without me he'd be wasted; this is my purpose!" But your pride prevents it.

(PAUL *rises.*)

I would like to say, "Without me he'd be useless; therefore I'm useful! Without me he'd be needy, therefore I'm needed!" *But your pride prevents it!*

PAUL

Mrs. Price—

MRS. PRICE

Offering charity? Is that how you see me? I'm *begging* for charity! Must I fall on my knees?

(*With both hands she attempts to push herself out of the chair.* HILDE *leaps up and restrains her.*)

HILDE

Mrs. Price!

(PAUL *rushes to chair, helps* HILDE. MRS. PRICE *struggles against them.*)

MRS. PRICE

Say yes! "Yes, Mrs. Price, we'll help each other! Yes, Mrs. Price! Yes! Yes!"

PAUL

Yes! Yes, Mrs. Price! Yes . . .

MRS. PRICE

(*To* HILDE, *incredulously.*)

Yes . . . Yes . . . Thank you . . . thank you . . . thank you . . .

(*Crying, she turns her chair swiftly around and propels herself a few feet* UPSTAGE. HILDE *makes a movement toward her, then stops, turns toward* PAUL. *He is still overwhelmed by* MRS. PRICE'*s emotion.* HILDE *goes to him, takes his hands in hers, kisses them. She then returns* RIGHT, *standing in front of couch.* MRS. PRICE *has by now recovered herself, she reverses chair and comes down to her former position, between end table and hassock. A final wipe with the handkerchief leaves her eyes glistening happily. She extends her left hand to* PAUL.)

Listen, can you quit that place tomorrow?

PAUL

Yes . . .

(*Going to her, taking her hand, smiling.*)

Yes!

MRS. PRICE

Good! Everett will bring the car to your rooming house tomorrow afternoon and we'll have you moved over here in time for dinner!

(*Holds out her right hand to* HILDE.)

Hilde . . .

(HILDE *takes her hand.*)

Tomorrow morning, first thing, you and Lucille will go up to the third floor and open one of the rooms, whichever one you choose. See that she does a good job cleaning it.

HILDE

Oh, yes! I will help her!

MRS. PRICE

(*Looks at their two hands in hers, squeezes them, then releases them and clasps her hands together.*)

Dinner tomorrow must be a banquet!

(*To* HILDE.)

We'll plan it together, you and I.

PAUL

Mrs. Price, it is I who should say "thank you" to you, and I—

MRS. PRICE

Shhh! Silence on that subject, forevermore! Is anybody else as desperate for a drink as I am?

PAUL

Most desperate!

HILDE

(*Starting toward bookcases.*)

I'll get—

MRS. PRICE

(*Catching* HILDE*'s hand.*)

No, this is an occasion for brandy, and a man should do the honors!

PAUL

(*Going to bookcase.*)

Of course!

MRS. PRICE

We'll drink to the future!

(PAUL *opens built-in liquor cabinet.* HILDE *and* MRS. PRICE *smile at each other.* MRS. PRICE *tucks away handkerchief.*)

PAUL

I am very good at pouring brandy!

MRS. PRICE

There are glasses on the bottom shelf.

(PAUL *crouches down to get glasses.* MRS. PRICE *extends her hand palm upward toward* HILDE. HILDE *looks at it for a moment, not understanding gesture.*)

PAUL

Bisquit Dubouche! I thought I would never smell this again! My father used to take it with his coffee.

(*Pours.*)

MRS. PRICE

He must have had excellent taste!

(MRS. PRICE *points with gay impatience, still holding out her hand to* HILDE. *Now* HILDE *understands the gesture. Slowly she removes the clip from her dress and puts it in* MRS. PRICE*'s hand.* MRS. PRICE *examines it, happily possessive.*)

PAUL

My father? Not at all. He was unable to distinguish one brandy from the next. It was my mother who chose it.

MRS. PRICE

I think I've some more of it down in the cellar. You'll have to go exploring among the cobwebs.

(MRS. PRICE *puts* HILDE*'s clip into a compartment of her chair and shuts it closed.* PAUL *turns, holding two brandy glasses.*)

PAUL

For the ladies . . .

(*He gives the glasses to* MRS. PRICE *and turns* UPSTAGE *for the third glass.* MRS. PRICE *offers a glass to* HILDE. HILDE *makes no move to accept it. She studies* MRS. PRICE *as though seeing a stranger. The offered glass wavers in* MRS. PRICE*'s hand.* PAUL, *with his own glass in hand, sees the attitude of the two women.* PAUL*: a surprised laugh.*)

You are not going to drink with us, Hilde? Come, come, come. Don't spoil the party!

(*Slowly, swallowing her reluctance,* HILDE *takes the glass. To* MRS. PRICE.)

She does not drink very often.

(*Throws his arm about* HILDE*'s shoulders.*)

Brandy is good for you!

(*He kisses* HILDE *fondly on the cheek, the kiss one gives a dear, foolish child.* MRS. PRICE *watches blankly, then quickly turns and takes up her glass.*)

MRS. PRICE

(*Forcing the return of her earlier joy.*)

A toast seems absolutely inevitable!

(*Thinks for an instant.*)

To the months ahead; may they bring happiness and achievement!

(*Raises her glass.*)

PAUL

And growing friendship!

(*He touches his glass to* MRS. PRICE'*s.* HILDE, *slowly and still expressionlessly, extends her glass and brings it against their two. All three glasses touch.*)

THE CURTAIN FALLS

END OF ACT ONE

ACT TWO: NOVEMBER

SCENE ONE

The curtain rises in darkness. Lights dim up slowly.

PAUL *is seated on the hassock, facing directly* DOWNSTAGE, *holding a rolled-up sheet of music in his hands.* HE *is perfectly motionless, staring into space.* HE *is in his shirt-sleeves, with tie clip and cufflinks of gold. The jacket of his new suit is neatly folded on the couch.* MRS. PRICE *is seated at* LEFT. *facing* PAUL*'s side. A caster table with panelled sides—a companion piece to the wheel chair—spans her lap, upon it, a writing board and a sheet of sketching paper, on which* SHE *works with the careful concentration of the amateur, referring frequently to* PAUL, *her subject. The small table is at her* LEFT. *side* (DOWNSTAGE), *bearing drawing equipment and a china jar with a dozen pencils in it.* MRS. PRICE *wears a russet gown and harlequin-framed glasses. It is night. The drapes are closed. Portrait light and piano work lamp are on, the latter casting a pool of empty light on the keyboard and the music rack, where a sheet of music stands open. A moment after the lights come up,* PAUL *speaks. His pose prohibits any motion.*

PAUL

I call myself German, but in truth I am something of a half-breed. My father was German, and his father, and his . . . But my mother was Swedish; a cool statue of a woman, with ice-blue eyes, and a smile that never rose above her lips. They had met at a ski-resort; "The Snow Queen," he called her. They married within a week. He was growing old and wanted a son. She supplied one for him. What *she* wanted was never known. My father was invisible to her; she seemed always to be waiting for someone else to enter the room. I was invisible, too, except when I would smash a piece of her precious porcelain. Or win a prize that her friends might envy. At parties . . . she *sparkled!* until the guests were gone away.

(*Pause.*)

When the Nazis began parading through Stuttgart my father helped some Jewish friends escape. The taste of adventure made him feel young again; he helped others. Our house became like a secret hotel. Through it all . . . my mother walks in some restless, private daydream. My piano used to please her; now even that can't reach her ears.

(*Pause.*)

One day this silent woman dressed herself in her finest clothes and walked away from the house. That night my father was arrested, along with a professor of law whom he had been hiding in our wine-cellar. They were dragged off; I never learned where. And my mother, who had been the informer, became a heroine; the foreign-born woman who was a better German than her native-born husband. Her picture appeared on the front pages of the Nazi newspapers. She made a speech on the radio. I heard it. A week later she returned. Her cheeks were glowing. The Snow Queen had melted. I was her son, she said, and there was a place for me in the glory she had finally found. All I must do was denounce my father's activities. She described the honors, the dinners, the life we would share . . . Her eyes were . . . bright blue lights . . .

(*The rolled-up sheet of music crumples in his hands.*)

There was a fireplace in her bedroom. I took up the poker and made myself strike her. Once. Twice. Three times. She ran from the house, crying of "arrest" and "punishment." Two hours later the Brownshirts came for me.

MRS. PRICE

(*Exchanging pencil for another one from the china jar.*)

Is she still alive?

PAUL

God knows.

(*Pause.*)

I hope not.

(PAUL's *hands uncrumple the sheet of music.*)

MRS. PRICE

Would you like to rest for a minute?

PAUL

No, no. I am not uncomfortable.

MRS. PRICE

Fine.

PAUL

(*A smile.*)

I think you are purposely working slowly, so there will be no time left for Double Solitaire.

MRS. PRICE

Don't gloat. You only win because I taught you so well.

PAUL

(*Pause.*)

The last time my portrait was drawn, I was holding a toy sailboat.

MRS. PRICE

(*Erasing.*)

That may *remain* the last time. I'm trying to be Gainsborough and your eye keeps coming out Picasso.

PAUL

(*Pause.*)

Perhaps you are a great impressionist and don't know it.

(HILDE *emerges from her room, carrying a pile of LP records topped with a stack of file cards. With her free hand she pulls the door closed behind her.* PAUL *and* MRS. PRICE *freeze for a split-second.* PAUL, *not turning.*)

Hello! I am being captured for posterity!

MRS. PRICE

So soon, Hilde? You haven't finished, have you?

HILDE

(*Descending stairs, watching* PAUL *and* MRS. PRICE *impassively.*)

Two index cards for each record; one for the composer, one for the performer. The shift key on the typewriter is broken again. You are lucky, Paul.

(*Putting records on cabinet* UPSTAGE LEFT.)

When Mrs. Price was to draw *my* picture, she changed her mind at the very last moment. And there I was, all dressed up in one of her most beautiful gowns, with my hair—

MRS. PRICE

Hilde—

(*A quick smile.*)

Visitors in the studio may watch, but they mustn't talk.

(HILDE, *silenced, withdraws. She takes a file box from the bookshelf. During the following she files the cards in the box and puts the records in their proper places on the shelves.*)

PAUL

Are those new records you have there?

MRS. PRICE

You said my collection was weak on piano, so I rubbed the magic lamp, and lo!—the lack has been remedied. The Beethoven Sonatas—

PAUL

All of them?

MRS. PRICE

One through umpty-nine! *And* the Chopin Preludes. *And* the Mozart Concertos.

PAUL

Marvelous!

MRS. PRICE

File them carefully, Hilde. We'll have a "musicale" tomorrow evening.

HILDE

(*Filing records.*)

There's to be no more evening practicing?

(*A silent moment, and the faintest reaction of stiffening from* PAUL *and* MRS. PRICE.)

PAUL

(*Trying for naturalness.*)

No one said there's to be . . . no more evening practicing.

HILDE

(*Turning.*)

But—

PAUL

(*Defensively.*)

This evening I am—taking a little rest . . . I worked very well this afternoon.

MRS. PRICE

(*A beat.*)

Don't talk now, Paul. I'm doing your mouth.

(*A moment passes.* HILDE *files records,* MRS. PRICE *draws,* PAUL *sits as before, but the comfort is fading from his face.*)

PAUL

Hilde is right . . . There *is* no more evening practicing. Sitting here, talking about the past . . .

MRS. PRICE

(*Soothingly.*)

Shhhh . . .

PAUL

This is the second—the third night in a row. Last night, the Double Solitaire; the night before, reading aloud . . .

MRS. PRICE

Now honestly, you've been playing those complicated scales six hours a day, every day for three weeks. I think if you were to slap the side of the piano it would play them by itself!

PAUL

Not six hours a day. Five hours, four . . .

MRS. PRICE

Hilde demands too much of you. He's not a robot, you know.

HILDE

I meant no criticism; I was only asking—

PAUL

(*Out of the pose, turning toward* MRS. PRICE.)

She's right; two hours each evening was part of my schedule—

MRS. PRICE

(*Cutting in, a desperate calming motion with both hands.*)

Now please! Please! Just let me have five minutes more. This is coming so beautifully now! Please. Five minutes. You'll make up for it tomorrow.

PAUL

Tomorrow . . . That is the best way never to do something; leave it for tomorrow.

MRS. PRICE

Please. Just five minutes more. This evening has been so *pleasant*, Paul!

PAUL

(*Pause, grudgingly.*)

All right . . .

(*He assumes the pose once again.* MRS. PRICE *resumes drawing with a quick intensity.*)

Five minutes . . .

MRS. PRICE

Thank you, thank you . . .

(HILDE, *watching, sighs with an edge of disappointment.*)

Paul, listen, tomorrow morning I'm going to have Lucille take all those old party gowns out of the big closet in your room! Whichever are worth keeping will go into the smaller closet and you can transfer your clothes into the big one!

PAUL

It's kind of you. Thank you.

MRS. PRICE

(*Intent on her work.*)

You should have told me sooner! Why didn't you?

PAUL

"Told you sooner"?

MRS. PRICE

That you haven't been given enough room for your clothing.

PAUL

(*A long, uncomfortable pause.*)

I did not say that . . .

MRS. PRICE

You most certainly did. Before dinner. I was admiring your suit and said something about what a good job Huberman is doing in fitting you, and you said that the suit would look even better if it had not been crushed in the closet.

(HILDE *turns, looks at* PAUL. *He seems to feel her gaze, he stirs discomfitedly.*)

PAUL

I did not intend that to be a complaint . . .

MRS. PRICE

And the next thing you said was that good clothing is an investment and should be cared for as such. That's right, you know. Before you put *anything* into the big closet, I'll have Everett spray it with whatever one—

PAUL

(*Interrupting, rising and turning toward her.*)

Mrs. Price, I cannot sit here like a statue all night!

(*Crushing sheet of music.*)

I am not a professional mannikin!

MRS. PRICE

(*Laying down pencil and writing board.*)

All right, we'll rest a while. This has been coming along so beautifully that I didn't realize—

PAUL

(*Cutting in.*)

I do not wish to rest; I wish to practice!

HILDE

(*Placatingly.*)

Paul . . .

MRS. PRICE

I'm just at the end of it; a few more lines . . .

PAUL

(*Pause.*)

I'm sorry, Mrs. Price, but I cannot pose any more this evening.

MRS. PRICE

(*Pause. Managing a smile.*)

Posterity will think you had no chin.

PAUL

It is better, I think, that they should know I had fingers.

MRS. PRICE

Very nicely put . . . but really, Paul, you just promised me five more minutes . . .

(*Another difficult smile.*)

I so rarely finish a sketch . . .

PAUL

(*Gently, but firmly.*)

Can't you see this from my view-point, Mrs. Price? You are so kind to me, you offer so much . . . When I find myself taking everything and *not studying*, I feel ashamed of myself and of . . . my position in this house.

MRS. PRICE

And five minutes would be too much to endure?

PAUL

It would be *more* than five minutes. You know it would. Whenever we talk or play cards or—sit like this, time runs away . . .

(*Pause.*)

I'm sorry, but I *must work.*

(*Turns away.*)

MRS. PRICE

(*Pause. Puts pencil and drawing on table.*)

All right, we will hear the beautiful scales.

(*Pushes table away from her lap and rolls it around to* UPSTAGE *side of chair.*)

PAUL

(*Stops, turns. Pause. Tensely.*)

I like the scales as little as you do, but they are essential for build my technique!

(*Turns toward piano.*)

MRS. PRICE

(*Removing eyeglasses, airily.*)

Essential for *building* your technique . . .

PAUL

(*Turning furiously.*)

What would you have me play for you, pretty little love songs? I did not come into this house to be an entertainer!

HILDE

Paul!

MRS. PRICE

Nor were you brought here to shout like a policeman!

(*A moment of deadlocked tension between* PAUL *and* MRS. PRICE.)

HILDE

Paul, Mrs. Price, please . . . Listen to yourselves . . .

MRS. PRICE

All I wanted was five more minutes!

PAUL

(*Pause. Trying to contain himself.*)

Mrs. Price, we must have an understanding right now.

MRS. PRICE

Can posterity spare the time for it?

PAUL

(*Going to her.*)

I came here to study and I set myself a schedule; two hours in the morning, two hours in the afternoon, two hours in the evening. It is not easy for me to keep myself to such a schedule; when you work against the better part of me, it becomes impossible!

MRS. PRICE

(*Angrily.*)
Work against the better part of you?

HILDE

(*Coming down to* MRS. PRICE*'s side.*)
That is not so, Paul. Mrs. Price hasn't *meant* to hinder you in your studies.

PAUL

I do not say there was intention to do so; I only say that it has been done!

MRS. PRICE

Work against—Whose idea was it that I draw you this evening?
(*Taking up drawing, pointing at it.*)
Your idea! You *wanted* to sit for me! *Your* idea!

PAUL

(*A moment of blocked fury, then explosively.*)
No more, then! No card games! No reading! No portraits! No—

(*On the word "portraits" he has snatched at the sheet of paper in* MRS. PRICE*'s hands—and ripped away the upper half.* MRS. PRICE *utters a little cry.*)

HILDE

Paul!

PAUL

(*Pause.*)
I'm sorry—I did not mean to—

(*Pause.*)

I'm sorry.

(*Awkwardly* PAUL *offers his half of the drawing to* MRS. PRICE. *She turns away, crumpling her half. A beat.* PAUL *crumples his half, hurls it to the floor, turns and goes to the piano. Angrily he starts a series of complex scales.* HILDE *goes to pick up the paper.*)

MRS. PRICE

Leave it!

HILDE

But—

MRS. PRICE

Leave it!

(*Confused,* HILDE *goes to* MRS. PRICE*'s chair.*)

HILDE

Let's go into the library and—

MRS. PRICE

No!

(*She waves* HILDE *sharply back toward the record cabinets.* HILDE *retreats uncertainly.* PAUL *goes on playing.* MRS. PRICES *smooths out her half of the drawing.*)

Paul.

(PAUL *continues playing.*)

Paul!

(PAUL *stops.*)

May I have the other piece of my drawing, please?

(*A beat.*)

HILDE

(*A movement forward.*)

I'll pick it up for—

MRS. PRICE

(*Overlapping.*)

File the records, Hilde!

HILDE

But you want—

MRS. PRICE

File the records!

(HILDE *freezes, confused.*)

May I have it, please, Paul? I think the drawing might be mended.

(*A moment of silence.* PAUL *rises, turns, and goes to press the button beside the door.*)

Do not touch that buzzer! I will not have Lucille brought in here unnecessarily.

PAUL

I am not your servant!

MRS. PRICE

(*Tautly.*)

I don't care what you are. You threw a piece of paper on the floor, and I can't get it. I want it.

(*Pause.*)

May I have it?

(PAUL *stands adamantly.* MRS. PRICE *waits, watching him. By degrees, almost as if a drug were taking hold of him,* PAUL*'s* *rigidity flakes away. Reluctantly he begins moving forward toward* MRS. PRICE *and the paper on the floor. Lowering himself to a semi-crouching position, he picks up the paper, averting his eyes from* MRS. PRICE. MRS. PRICE *extends her hand.* PAUL *gives her the paper.*)

PAUL

(*Softly, hatefully.*)

Weibsbild . . .

HILDE

(*Mingled surprise and reproach.*)

Paul . . .

MRS. PRICE

(*Her voice urgent with fear.*)

What did you call me?

(PAUL *turns, goes toward piano.*)

HILDE

Nothing, he said nothing.

MRS. PRICE

(*Puts paper blindly on table.*)

He called me something and I want to know what it means!

HILDE

He was angry; it means nothing.

MRS. PRICE

Nothing? Words without meaning? What did that word mean?

(*She propels her chair toward* CENTER STAGE. PAUL *turns to face her.*)

What did you call me?

HILDE

Paul . . .

PAUL

I called you—"Weibsbild."

HILDE

For pity's sake!

MRS. PRICE

(*The urgency compressed now to an ice-hard tension.*)

What does it mean?

HILDE

Paul!

PAUL

It means—bitch.

HILDE

(*A beat.*)

Forgive him, Mrs. Price! Please! He's angry and he doesn't mean to—

PAUL

Stop apologizing for me!

(*Pause.* MRS. PRICE*'s body relaxes, and in the relaxation there is a suggestion of relief and something bordering on satisfaction.* HILDE *watches her reaction anxiously,* PAUL *coldly. When her breathing has steadied itself, she speaks.*)

MRS. PRICE

I'm going to my room, Hilde. Come upstairs when you're finished with the records. And leave the clearing-up for Lucille.

HILDE

Yes, Mrs. Price. I'll be with you in two minutes. I'm nearly done.

(MRS. PRICE *propels her chair toward the door, stops, turns toward* PAUL.)

MRS. PRICE

(*With difficulty.*)

I—want an apology in the morning, Paul.

(*She exits.* HILDE *crosses to* PAUL, *takes his arm.*)

HILDE

Paul, did you have to—

PAUL

(*Moving away to small table.*)

You saw what she made me do!

(*Takes up the papers.*)

She would not want me to bow and light her cigarettes, you said. Oh, no! I must only get on my knees before her!

HILDE

(*Going to him.*)

She behaved terribly, I admit. It was you who threw the paper down though, and tore it in the first place.

PAUL

(*Angrily mocking.*)

"Five more minutes." "Five more minutes."

HILDE

Both of you behaved terribly. I think apology should go in both directions.

PAUL

(*Contemptuously.*)

Apology . . .

HILDE

(*Takes his arm. Gently.*)

Yes, apology. And from you first, because you are sound and she is crippled.

PAUL

It is *she* who is the sound one! She glides about in that chair like—an empress enthroned. "May I have the paper, please?"

(*Slaps the papers onto the table.*)

What made me obey her?

HILDE

(*Soothingly.*)

Paul, she has been unkind to me, too; more than one time in

the past month. I try to forget. I ask myself, how kind would I be if I had her misfortune? Do the same. Please . . .

(*She kisses him on the cheek, waits a moment, then goes up to the cabinet and resumes filing the records.* PAUL *prods the papers dourly.*)

PAUL

Apology . . . I suppose to apologize I will also have to . . . get down on my knees . . .

(*His hand fists and strikes his thigh.*)

I hate that woman!

HILDE

(*A bit impatient with such dramatizing.*)

Oh, now, Paul, you're very fond of Mrs. Price, and you know you are.

PAUL

(*Turns slowly toward* HILDE.)

What makes you say a—foolish thing like that?

HILDE

Foolish? The attention you've been paying her? If she were ten years younger I would be as jealous as a—what's jealous: a tigress? That's how I would be: jealous as a tigress.

PAUL

(*Pause. Flatly.*)

She is spoiled and selfish and inconsiderate. I am not fond of her.

HILDE

(*Takes his hands. Pause. Firmly.*)

Paul, this whole ugliness will be patched up in two minutes in the morning. You have a great opportunity here; you mustn't let go of it!

(*Pause.*)

You will apologize to each other and everything will be fine again. You'll see . . . Now I must go to her.

(*Starts toward door* RIGHT.)

PAUL

Hilde!

HILDE

(*Stops, returns to him.*)

What is it?

PAUL

We have not been together since I came into this house. . . .

HILDE

I know . . .

PAUL

(*Taking her in his arms.*)

You and I, and no one else in the world . . .

(*Kisses her.*)

HILDE

Paul, darling . . .

PAUL

(*Vehemently.*)

Even if she *were* ten years younger, I swear you would have no reason for jealousy!

HILDE

I know that . . .

(PAUL *kisses her again, then takes her hands and draws her* UPSTAGE.)

PAUL

Sweet Hilde . . . I have been in your room only once or twice, and then for the shortest moment . . .

HILDE

(*Withdrawing her hands, smiling.*)

Not now, Paul . . . She is waiting for me.

PAUL

(*Backing toward staircase, trying to match her smile.*)

And here am I, also waiting for you.

HILDE

(*Amused protestation.*)

She—needs me! I should be there now!

PAUL

And here am I, also . . . needing you . . .

HILDE

Now I *know* you are not serious. Never before have you said you *needed* me.

PAUL

(*Backing up the first few stairs.*)

I *am* serious, Hilde . . . I am . . .

HILDE

(*With concern.*)

Paul, what's wrong?

(PAUL *turns and goes quickly up the stairs and into* HILDE*'s room, leaving the door partially open. There is a light within.*)

Paul . . . !

(HILDE *mounts the stairs with increasing concern. On the balcony she hesitates, looking off* RIGHT, *then at the door, then off* RIGHT. *again.* LUCILLE *enters* RIGHT. *[downstairs]. She looks around, sees* HILDE *on the balcony.* HILDE *looks at her blankly.*)

LUCILLE

Is everybody finished with this room?

HILDE

(*Pause.*)

Yes . . .

(*A pause, and then* HILDE *exits into her room, reaching for the switch within. The light inside goes out and the door closes.* LUCILLE *moves* RIGHT, *touches the switch* DOWNSTAGE *of doorway, extinguishing the main lighting. She goes to the piano, turns off work lamp, and then crosses* LEFT *toward portrait. The stage is now in semi-darkness, illumined only by portrait light and offstage lights* RIGHT *of balcony and in downstairs hallway. When* LUCILLE *reaches portrait,* MRS. PRICE *propels herself on from* RIGHT *on balcony.*)

MRS. PRICE

(*Forced sarcasm that doesn't quite cover her unhappiness.*)

Aren't you coming up, Hilde? I didn't think there were a thousand records to file.

LUCILLE

It's me, Mrs. Price.

(*Turns off portrait light.*)

MRS. PRICE

(*A beat.*)

Where are . . . Miss Hahn and Mr. Schildger?

LUCILLE

She's in her room. I guess he's in his.

MRS. PRICE

I didn't hear him go up . . .

LUCILLE

Isn't she going to help you get ready for—

(MRS. PRICE *hears a sound from* HILDE*'s room. She snaps her head around, listening.*)—

What is it?

MRS. PRICE

Shh!

(*She waves* LUCILLE *to silence and leans closer to* HILDE*'s door.* LUCILLE *moves quickly to the foot of the staircase.*)

LUCILLE

(*An anxious whisper.*)

What's wrong? What is it?

(MRS. PRICE *straightens in her chair, her face and body locked in the same tension and fury she exhibited at* PAUL*'s German curse. She gives her chair a single sharp forward* *thrust, bringing it squarely to the head of the stairs.* LUCILLE *gives a sibilant whisper of alarm.*)

Mrs. Price!

(*Frightened,* LUCILLE *mounts a few steps.* MRS. PRICE *stares blindly at her.*)

You scare me! Get back! You're going to hurt yourself!

(MRS. PRICE *is immobile.* LUCILLE *climbs a few more steps, cautiously, like an animal trainer facing a rebellious beast.*)

Get back, honey!

(*A few more steps.*)

Back . . .

(*And another.*)

Back . . .

(MRS. PRICE *draws her chair back from the head of the stairs, turns it* DOWNSTAGE, *staring in anguish beyond the balcony railing.* LUCILLE *comes quickly to her side.*)

You all right, honey? You all right? You scared me so. I feared you was going over! Why did you do that?

(*Pause.* MRS. PRICE *is motionless.*)

You want me to put you to bed? You want me to take nice care of you like I used to?

(MRS. PRICE *nods vigorously, childlike.* LUCILLE *takes hold of the back of the chair.*)

I'm going to fix you some warm milk with a spoon of honey in it. Remember that? And then I'm going to—

MRS. PRICE

Wait!

(*Her eyes clamp tight for a moment, then they open. She raises her head proudly, thinks, and then calls out in a tremulous voice:*)

Hilde! Lucille is going to put me to bed tonight. I won't need you. Lucy will tend me in the morning too. Good night! Good night, Paul!

(LUCILLE *pushes the wheel chair off* RIGHT *as the lights quickly dim out.*)

THE CURTAIN FALLS

ACT TWO

SCENE TWO

When the curtain rises, the lights are up full, a bleak, grayish light that comes through the window with a suggestion of pre-winter coldness.

EVERETT, *in a white mess jacket, has gathered up all the drawing equipment.* HE *crosses and puts it in one of the cabinets at* LEFT. *Records and file cards have already been put away. Caster table and small table stand in same locations as at end of previous scene. Dust-cloth on caster table. Portrait light and piano work lamp are off. A waste basket stands* DOWNSTAGE CENTER. *As* EVERETT *returns to caster table and begins dusting its top,* PAUL *enters* RIGHT. HE *wears slacks, a sport jacket, and an open-collared shirt. His mood is resolute and affirmative, with only the slightest hint of underlying tension.*

PAUL

Good morning, Everett.

EVERETT

Oh, morning, Mr. Schildger. I'll be out of your way in a minute.

(*Pushing caster table up to cabinets.*)

You find your breakfast all right?

PAUL

Yes, I did.

EVERETT

(*Returning to small table.*)

Lucille's taking care of Mrs. Price this morning, so I have to do the cleaning.

(*Emptying ashtray into waste basket.*)

You're in here early, aren't you?

PAUL

(*Taking off his jacket.*)

No earlier than I will be every day from now on. I have set myself a new schedule. I am going to study eight hours each day instead of six.

EVERETT

(*Wiping ashtray.*)

Eight hours? You certainly must love that piano.

PAUL

That is why I am here, Everett. That is why . . .

(*Folds jacket carefully over back of couch.*)

Has Mrs. Price come down yet?

EVERETT

No, sir. She had her breakfast upstairs.

PAUL

And Miss Hahn?

EVERETT

Mrs. Price told Lucille not to bother her. Oh, there's the elevator now.

(*Makes a few quick, final cleaning gestures, picks up waste basket.*)

She isn't sick, is she? Miss Hahn?

PAUL

(*Looking off* RIGHT.)

No. No, she's not.

EVERETT

(*Crossing* RIGHT.)

That's good. I thought maybe she was.

(EVERETT *exits* RIGHT. *During the following offstage dialogue,* PAUL *stands facing* RIGHT, *readying himself for* MRS. PRICE*'s entrance. He tightens his belt, squares his shoulders, etc. Except for one hasty glance at* HILDE*'s door, he seems reasonably self-assured.*)

LUCILLE

(*Off* RIGHT.)

Hold the door, will you, Everett?

EVERETT

(*Off* RIGHT.)

Good morning, Mrs. Price.

MRS. PRICE

(*Off* RIGHT.)

Good morning.

LUCILLE

(*Off* RIGHT, *closer.*)

In we go. I hope Everett cleaned all right.

(MRS. PRICE, *in a green robe, enters* RIGHT. LUCILLE, *a newspaper folded under her arm, is pushing the wheel chair.*)

PAUL

Good morning, Mrs. Price.

MRS. PRICE

Good morning.

PAUL

I was just about to start work.

MRS. PRICE

(*Not looking at him, reining back the fury and frustration which have built up through a sleepless night.*)

I would like to speak to you before you do.

PAUL

(*An agreeing smile.*)

Yes. Yes, I would like to speak to you too.

(*During this,* LUCILLE *has settled the wheel chair in its usual position* CENTER LEFT *and put the newspaper on small table* LEFT *of* MRS. PRICE.)

LUCILLE

You want the rolling table near you? Maybe you'll want to do the crossword.

(*Goes* UPSTAGE *for caster table.*)

MRS. PRICE

Don't bother.

LUCILLE

No bother.

(*Bringing table* DOWNSTAGE.)

As soon as I've straightened your bedroom, I'm going to start right in on lunch, 'cause it's something special today.

(*Puts table* UPSTAGE RIGHT *of wheelchair.*)

You got your cigarettes? Eyeglasses?

MRS. PRICE

(*A brittle smile.*)

Everything. Thank you, Lucy.

LUCILLE

You're welcome. You want anything, just buzz.

(LUCILLE *crosses and exits* RIGHT. *She leaves doors open. Pause.* PAUL *and* MRS. PRICE *look at each other,* PAUL *a bit uncertain as to how to embark on an apology,* MRS. PRICE *still holding back her desperate anger.*)

PAUL

Mrs. Price, I am prepared to apologize for my language of last night. It was stupid of me to lose control of my temper as I did. I am sorry.

MRS. PRICE

Sorry for your language . . . And for nothing else?

PAUL

(*Pause.*)

Tearing the portrait? Of course I'm sorry for that. It was not intentional.

MRS. PRICE

(*Her control beginning to break.*)

And there's nothing else you're sorry for?

PAUL

I don't know what you—

MRS. PRICE

You know! You know what I'm talking about!

(*A beat, as she fights to organize and rationalize the bursting anger.*)

I had a sister, did you know that? A year younger than I. Our mother died when she was born. That was our room; the room where Hilde is now. The only girls, she and I, in this house full of my brothers and my father and my father's friends, this house full of cigar smoke and shouting and Tuesday night poker parties. That room was our haven! We ate there and played there—whispered our secrets in that blue bed. She died! Sixteen years old, rheumatic fever. Last night you—When I put Hilde in that room, I wanted—I did not expect that room to be—cheapened!

PAUL

(*Pause.*)

Nothing was *cheapened* . . .

MRS. PRICE

(*A pained cry.*)

I heard you in there with her!

PAUL

I was in the room. Nothing was *cheapened*.

MRS. PRICE

I did not come down here to argue over words! There must be no repetition of what happened last night. Do you understand?

(*From a greater emotional depth.*)

I don't want it to happen again!

PAUL

(*Vehemently.*)

Are you telling me to go?

(*A beat.* MRS. PRICE *is speechless.* PAUL *turns, starts toward the door* RIGHT. MRS. PRICE *cries out:*)

MRS. PRICE

Paul! I didn't say that! *Paul!*

(*The desperate cry hangs in the air.* PAUL *stops, turns.* MRS. PRICE *averts her face, eyes shut tight.* PAUL *approaches her slowly, wonderingly.*)

PAUL

What kind of woman are you? You say I cheapen your house, you make me pick up papers from the floor, and when I turn my back you cry out like . . .

MRS. PRICE

Paul, I'm sorry about the drawing incident, truly I am, and I swear I won't let myself do *anything* like that again!

PAUL

You swear . . . You have just *done* something like that again; setting yourself up as Hilde's guardian, telling me I dare not—

MRS. PRICE

(*Overlapping.*)

It's the room! I have no interest in Hilde! I told you what the room means to me!

PAUL

I do not believe it! Concern for the room could never have made you so angry! Because Hilde is your employee, you think you can—

MRS. PRICE

Stop speaking of Hilde! Stop . . .

(*A moment of spent silence.*)

PAUL

Mrs. Price . . . we have tried an arrangement, and it has produced only disturbance . . .

MRS. PRICE

No . . . no. I didn't mean to come in here and speak so harshly. I was up all night—

PAUL

Harshly or not, you had no *right* to speak.

MRS. PRICE

No right. Does anyone wait for a "right" to be angry, or a reason? It's true; the significance of the room was only an excuse. The reason for my anger? I don't know. I don't know . . .

PAUL

(*Leaning toward her, as though entreating her agreement.*)

We should go back to the earlier arrangement; I could visit in the evenings and practice . . .

MRS. PRICE

(*Pleadingly.*)

Paul . . .

(*An anxious, at-a-loss pause, and then a tense, desperate smile.*)

Do you know why I was angry? I've found the reason now. Yes, I have. Do you know why I was so upset about your being with Hilde?

PAUL

(*Pause. An edge of wariness.*)

Why?

MRS. PRICE

In the weeks you've been here, Paul, you've displayed so many admirable qualities . . . Oh, I'm afraid that what I'm about to say is going to make you very angry . . . I was upset last night and this morning because—because it pained me most terribly to think of you flying as you did to . . . someone who is . . .

PAUL

(*A beat.*)

Someone who is—*what?*

MRS. PRICE

Someone who . . . is fine, but not fine enough.

PAUL

(*A cold pause.*)

What you *mean* to say is that—the servants' daughter is beneath me.

MRS. PRICE

Servants' daughter?

PAUL

That is the way the same idea was put to me twenty years ago!

MRS. PRICE

Hilde's background had not even entered my mind. Now that you bring it up, I suppose it must count for something. And has she your talent, or sensitivity, or worldliness or wit? Oh, Paul, when I think of the life before you, the doors opening, the honors, the people you'll meet!

PAUL

Stop this, Mrs. Price.

MRS. PRICE

"Cinderella and Prince Charming" is a lovely story, but gifted people should associate with others of their kind!

PAUL

Stop, Mrs. Price!

(HILDE *emerges from her room.*)

MRS. PRICE

As you wish. It's futile to reason with a romantic.

HILDE

(*Uncomfortably, sensing the tension in the room.*)

Good morning . . . Who is a romantic?

(*She starts down the stairs, and* PAUL *starts swiftly up them.*)

MRS. PRICE

Paul is. He doesn't know that in real life, Cinderella's prince wakes up with—

(*Halfway up the stairs,* PAUL *catches* HILDE *in his arms and kisses her soundly.*)

soot on his face!

(MRS. PRICE *starts for the door.* HILDE *struggles in* PAUL*'s embrace.*)

HILDE

Paul! Paul, please! Let go of me!

MRS. PRICE

(*Trying to mask her distress.*)

It's all right, Hilde. I was going out anyway. I have to tell Lucille and Everett about that closet for Paul!

(HILDE *frees herself of* PAUL*'s arms, leans over bannister.*)

HILDE

Mrs. Price . . .

(MRS. PRICE *stops near door.*)

I—I feel terribly guilty about . . . neglecting my duties this morning . . .

PAUL

Hilde!

HILDE

. . . and last night . . .

MRS. PRICE

(*Tensely.*)

Apologies have been flying back and forth in here like pingpong balls. Let's just pretend that we all woke up with amnesia and let it go at that, shall we?

(*Exits* RIGHT.)

HILDE

(*Looking after her, surprised.*)

Yes . . .

(*Turns to* PAUL.)

The two of you . . . apologized to each other?

PAUL

(*Taking her in his arms, a trifle stiffly.*)

Yes.

HILDE

And she said nothing about—?

PAUL

Nothing.

(*Kisses her firmly, then smiles.*)

Good morning. . . .

HILDE

And what is all this about "romantics"? In real life, Cinderella's prince—

PAUL

(*Cutting her off sharply.*)

Nothing! Nonsense, idiotic nonsense. She talks . . .

(*Descends stairs.*)

HILDE

(*Following after him.*)

Why did you make such a display of kissing me, with Mrs. Price sitting right there? It was very thoughtless of you.

PAUL

(*Pause.*)

Thoughtless?

HILDE

Yes. After all, you must have *some* consideration for my position here. I was embarrassed.

PAUL

I wanted to kiss you. It did not seem necessary to ask her permission.

HILDE

(*Teasingly.*)

You might have asked mine. There sits my employer, and you gather me up like—

PAUL

Your employer, not your owner. She is not *your* owner; she is not my owner!

HILDE

(*Moving* DOWNSTAGE, *dismissing the subject amusedly.*)

All right, all right . . . I'm sorry I said anything!

(*She lifts a figurine from table, inspects it, wipes it with her handkerchief.* PAUL *watches her.*)

PAUL

There is no need for you to dust those objects.

HILDE

I told you everything would be patched up in two minutes, didn't I?

PAUL

Everett has already cleaned. There is no need for you to dust those objects.

HILDE

(*Poking at a cranny in the figurine.*)

He didn't make a very good job of it.

PAUL

Then leave it for Lucille! You are not the housemaid!

HILDE

(*Turns, stares in surprise.*)

Paul . . .

(PAUL *turns away.* HILDE *puts down figurine and goes to him. She takes his arm.*)

Paul, what's the matter?

PAUL

Nothing. Nothing is the matter.

HILDE

What did she say to you?

PAUL

Nothing. Nonsense, all sorts of idiotic nonsense . . .

HILDE

Idiotic . . .?

(*A baffled pause.*)

The talk about "Cinderella"? The prince wakes up . . .

PAUL

(*Quickly.*)

The wildest kind of flattery. I am worldly, I have great talent, sensitivity, doors will open for me . . . A whole stream of flattery because I said I might leave!

HILDE

(*Pause.*)

Cinderella's prince wakes up . . . with *soot on his face* . . . You?

(*Pause.*)

And I . . . am Cinderella? Why would . . . she say this?

PAUL

I told you she was speaking nonsense. Ugly, unkind nonsense . . . I hardly remember what she said.

HILDE

(*A faint smile.*)

It is not such nonsense, Paul. I have done housework . . .

(*Pause.*)

How did you answer her?

PAUL

I told her that it was not true. I forbade her to say such things.

HILDE

And did you tell her that even if it *were* true it would make no difference, because you love me?

PAUL

(*Pause.*)

Yes. Yes, I said that too. I said "I love her . . . so even if . . . it were true . . . it would make no . . ."

(*His voice trails off, unable to sustain the lie.*)

Hilde, I *do* love you. . . .

HILDE

And *this* is why I am kissed so soundly when I come down the stairs . . . A demonstration . . .

(PAUL *shifts uncomfortably.* HILDE *inquires sadly:*)

For her or for you?

PAUL

I love you, Hilde . . .

HILDE

(*Nods.*)

Yes . . .

PAUL

What was I to do? Strike her? It wouldn't have stopped her! A flood of nonsense! Nonsense and flattery! I am talented, I am brilliant, I am this, I am that! Puffing up my vanity! I should associate with gifted people, I am—

(*Stops short.*)

HILDE

(*Pause.*)

But you hardly remember what she said . . .

PAUL

Oh, my God!

(HILDE *crosses toward stairs.* PAUL *catches her arm as she passes.*)

Where are you going?

HILDE

Back to my room.

PAUL

Stay here!

HILDE

Let go of me!

PAUL

You stay here!

HILDE

You'll get soot all over you!

PAUL

Hilde, Hilde . . . as God is watching us, I swear by my soul I did not want to listen!

HILDE

But you did listen! The doors weren't locked, your hands weren't tied—but you listened! Just as you used to listen to your mother, when she scolded you for meeting me in the garden!

PAUL

(*A frozen moment, then with cold, tight-jawed anger.*)
What do you mean by that!

HILDE

Mean? I mean what I said! You listened to her just as you used to listen to your mother when she scolded—

(PAUL *slaps* HILDE *sharply across the cheek. She stares at him. His hand falls away from her arm.* HILDE *turns and runs to the staircase with an inarticulate cry.*)

PAUL

Hilde!
(*Runs after her.*)
Hilde, forgive me—

MRS. PRICE

(*Entering* RIGHT.)
What is it? What's happened?
(HILDE *runs up the stairs.* PAUL *charges up after her.* HILDE *exits into her room, shutting and locking the door.* MRS. PRICE *propels herself anxiously* DOWNSTAGE CENTER, *turns* UPSTAGE. PAUL *leans for a moment against* HILDE*'s locked door.*)
What's wrong?
(PAUL *turns away from the door. Pause.*)

PAUL

(*Softly.*)
So many years she waited for me . . . prayed, worked to bring me across . . . What for? For me to strike her? For more waiting while I play my damned scales?

MRS. PRICE

Paul, don't—

PAUL

(*Aware of her now, starting down stairs.*)

You called me a fake the night I came here; you were right, you know!

MRS. PRICE

No, no, I wasn't!

PAUL

No? I shout at *you* when you say she's beneath me, I shout at *her* when she touches an ashtray! Isn't that being a fake? Fake with her, fake with you, with myself, with the piano, with everything! Everything! Scales I play . . . !

MRS. PRICE

It's not your fault that years of your life were wasted!

PAUL

Not my fault! Oh, I tell you something . . .

(*Coming down to face* MRS. PRICE.)

I tell you what a fake I am with my piano . . . In one of the camps was another prisoner who wanted to be a pianist. Do you know what *he* did? Do you know what he did?

(*Drops to his knees.*)

On the *floor* of the barracks, near his bed, he drew with charcoal the keyboard. At night, if there was moonlight, you could hear his fingertips . . .

(*Drums on the floor.*)

I tried it; I drew the keyboard—so, so. I studied—an hour or two, *for two nights.* It was so much easier just to go to sleep! Isn't that being a fake? Isn't it?

MRS. PRICE

(*Moving close to him.*)

Oh, Paul . . . I *know* I'm right about your gifts and your talent! You have a future before you, a bright, bright future! You mustn't lose—

PAUL

No more flattery! No more!

MRS. PRICE

Flattery? Yes, I wanted to calm you—but still I spoke truth, Paul! I swear I did! If it sounded like only empty flattery, then I could say some other things that would sound like anything but that! You're lazy sometimes; I know that. And sometimes pompous. And you have a terrible streak of violence in you. Does that sound like flattery? No, it doesn't—but it's true, just as the other things I said were true! Doors *will* open for you, Paul!

(PAUL *looks at her, wanting to believe.*)

Do you think I would even be speaking to you now if I didn't know you have qualities that far outweigh your faults? You judge yourself too severely!

(MRS. PRICE *is very close to* PAUL *now.*)

Believe in yourself, Paul. I believe in you.

(*A beat, and they both become aware of the closeness.* MRS. PRICE *fumbles in one of the compartments of her chair.*)

May I have my lighter, please?

(MRS. PRICE *takes out a cigarette as* PAUL *rises from his kneeling position and takes a lighter from the small table.* MRS. PRICE *extends her hand for the lighter.* PAUL *stops, looks at the lighter in his hand, looks at* MRS. PRICE. *She is waiting for the lighter.*)

May I?

(PAUL *strikes the lighter.*)

Oh—why, thank you.

(PAUL *extends the flame slowly to* MRS. PRICE*'s cigarette, his eyes on her face. Her hands touch his lingeringly as she accepts the light.*)

Thank you, Paul . . .

(*A beat.* PAUL *closes the lighter, straightens self-consciously.*)

PAUL

I should . . . go to Hilde . . .

(*He puts the lighter on the table and goes slowly up the stairs, his hand trailing along the bannister, his eyes on* MRS. PRICE. *He taps softly on* HILDE*'s door, then turns to it and speaks in gentle, murmuring German. He taps again, and the door opens for him. With a final glance at* MRS. PRICE, *he exits, closing the door.* MRS. PRICE *whirls her chair around to face* DOWNSTAGE. *For a moment she sits quite still, her eyes shut. Then her right hand fists and begins to beat on the arm of her chair in a slow, desperate cadence.*)

THE CURTAIN FALLS

END OF ACT TWO

ACT THREE: DECEMBER

SCENE ONE

The curtain rises in darkness. Snow is seen outside the window, falling against a gray sky. A Christmas tree becomes visible, decorated but unlighted, it stands between the end of the piano and the foot of the staircase, in the place previously occupied by the wing chair, which is now gone. Main lighting dims up gradually. It is late afternoon. Portrait light and piano work lamp are off.

MRS. PRICE, *in a robe of dark blue, sits at* LEFT, *facing* RIGHT. HILDE *stands before the couch, facing* MRS. PRICE. EVERETT *and* LUCILLE *stand* UPSTAGE CENTER. *No one moves. In the frozen tension of the tableau, there is the suggestion of an inquisition. After a moment:*

MRS. PRICE

(*Slowly, intently, as though reasoning with someone wild.*)

Now listen to me carefully, Hilde, and try not to lose control of yourself. . . .

HILDE

(*With an edge of hysteria.*)

I am not losing control of myself!

MRS. PRICE

Listen to me, Hilde . . . The bracelet is *fully covered* by insurance. If you lost it, there is *no harm done.*

HILDE

(*Forcing back the hysteria.*)

I did not lose the bracelet.

MRS. PRICE

There is nothing to be afraid of. To tell the truth, I hope you *did* lose it, because then I'll get a new one which will probably be much, much nicer.

HILDE

I did not lose the bracelet.

(*A pause, then tautly, as though reiterating for the third or fourth time:*)

I went to the jeweler. He fixed the clasp in two minutes. He wrapped the bracelet in the gray cloth. I held it in my hand between there and here. I came into the house, went up the front stairs and into your room. I put—

MRS. PRICE

I didn't hear you come into the room . . .

HILDE

You were asleep! You were taking a nap . . .

(*A pause, then she resumes.*)

I put the bracelet on your dressing table and went out of the room and closed the door. I went into my own room and . . . wrapped the last of my Christmas presents . . .

MRS. PRICE

And when I called you to help me from the bed, there was no bracelet.

HILDE

I left it on the dressing table. Next to the silver-backed mirror.

MRS. PRICE

(*Pause. Wearily.*)

Search the room again, Everett.

HILDE

The room has been searched three times!

EVERETT.

(*Starting to go. To* MRS. PRICE.)

Should I—?

MRS. PRICE

All right, never mind, never mind . . .

(*With sudden impatience.*)

Hilde, just tell me that you lost it and I'll call the insurance agent and that will be that!

HILDE

I did not lose it! Why won't you believe me?

MRS. PRICE

Then where did it go? Did burglars cross the garden without marking the snow, scale the side of the house and enter a locked and shuttered window? Have Lucille and Everett become diamond thieves after twenty-four years of service?

(*Pause.*)

Did I take it? Is that what you think? Did I roll off the bed and somewhere find strength enough to drag myself thirty feet back and forth across the room, and then pull myself up again onto the bed?—all so we could begin the holidays with an afternoon of futile searching? Is that what you think?

HILDE

(*Pause. Slowly.*)

No . . . I hadn't thought that . . .

(*Pause. Quietly.*)

Why does something like this happen on the one afternoon when Paul is out of the house?

MRS. PRICE

You aren't suggesting that he slipped back from whatever mysterious errand he's off on—?

HILDE

No!

(*Pause.*)

I just ask why this happens on the one day he is out. Why did you take a nap this afternoon, when you haven't done so in almost a year? Why was the clasp on the bracelet bent? Why do you keep saying "Admit you lost it," when I have told you that I didn't lose it?

(*Pause.*)

Am I to be accused of thievery?

MRS. PRICE

No one said you took the bracelet!

HILDE

(*Pause.*)
Did *you* take it?

LUCILLE

Don't you get smart with Mrs. Price . . .

MRS. PRICE

Quiet, Lucy; she's upset.

HILDE

Yes, I am upset! Yes! Did you take the bracelet? No one else could have!

MRS. PRICE

You shouldn't be talking this way, Hilde . . .

HILDE

Why are you doing this to me? Is it punishment? Did I disturb the sketching this morning, or the card game last night, or the German lesson yesterday afternoon?

MRS. PRICE

(*Turning away.*)
The bracelet is lost. I will file a claim and—

HILDE

(*Overlapping.*)
The bracelet is not lost!

MRS. PRICE

(*Turns. Pause. Tensely.*)

Are you seriously saying that I took it?

HILDE

Yes, I am!

MRS. PRICE

(*Pause.*)

You're calling me a liar . . .

LUCILLE

Mrs. Price . . . make her go . . .

HILDE

(*A long pause, as the design of the corner into which she has been led becomes clear to her. She smiles. Bitterly humorous:*)

Oh, Lord. Oh, dear, dear Lord. *Now* I understand what has been happening. You take the bracelet; you tell me how you took it; and then, when I charge you with it, you have a reason to send me away.

(*Pause. Gravely.*)

Yes, Mrs. Price. I am calling you a liar.

MRS. PRICE

(*Pause.*)

I'm sorry to have to do this, Hilde, but you haven't left me much choice, have you? . . . Lucille, you and Everett had better go up to Miss Hahn's room. If her suitcases aren't large enough for all her belongings, you can use one of mine.

LUCILLE

Yes, ma'am.

(LUCILLE *starts quickly up the stairs.* EVERETT *follows slowly.* MRS. PRICE *is taking eyeglasses, a checkbook and a pen from compartments of her chair. During the following,* LUCILLE *and* EVERETT *exit into* HILDE*'s room, and* MRS. PRICE *writes a check, using as a writing board a hard-covered book which she takes from the small table.*)

HILDE

I am to be gone before Paul returns; is that what you want? And then you will tell him that your bracelet is lost and that I accused you of hiding it and lying about it. Lucille and Everett will be brought in to confirm the story . . .

MRS. PRICE

(*Writing, not looking up.*)

I—am giving you a check for—more than is customary in a situation like this.

HILDE

Why? So you will feel less guilty?

(MRS. PRICE*'s hand stops, then resumes writing.*)

Do you think he'll stay here when he learns what has happened? He won't, Mrs. Price; he can't have changed *that* much! And I'll tell him! I'll tell him!

(*Bracing herself against any reaction.* MRS. PRICE *tears the check from its stub and holds it out to* HILDE. HILDE *shakes her head.*)

No, no, I won't take it.

MRS. PRICE

It's . . . five hundred dollars . . .

(HILDE *moves away.* MRS. PRICE *follows, the check extended before her in genuine compassion.*)

Take this—not for my sake . . .

HILDE

(*Not taking the check, but crouching down so that her eyes are on a level with* MRS. PRICE*'s. Emotionally.*)

We were such good friends, you and I . . . and now you bring me so much unhappiness . . . ! You gave me the loveliest room in the entire house, you bought clothing for me, and sweet little gifts . . .

MRS. PRICE

(*Pause. Withdraws the check into her lap. Guardedly.*)

I treated you exactly as I would treat any other employee.

HILDE

No, no, we were like sisters. You said it yourself; I was a sister to you . . .

MRS. PRICE

Lucille! Hurry up in there!

(*Withdrawing chair to small table.*)

I never said that. . . .

HILDE

(*Rising from crouching position.*)

A dozen times, you said it!

MRS. PRICE

(*Taking off eyeglasses, putting check, checkbook, etc., on small table. Tensely.*)

If the truth is to be told, Hilde, I have always been—bored in your company. What might have seemed an excess of friendliness was only the—desperation of someone who had been without friends too long.

HILDE

No, those days were happy days, for me and for you too! You said it yourself; the happiest days in your whole life! That's why you were going to draw my picture; to keep the memory of such happy days.

MRS. PRICE

Those days were hateful to me! Dull, unhappy and hateful! Those were the days that drove me to swallow the sleeping pills! Was that a sign of happiness?

HILDE

(*Turning away despairingly.*)

Dear God! I don't understand *you*, I don't understand *him* . . .

MRS. PRICE

Lucille! Get her out of here as soon as you're done! I want her out!

HILDE

I will wait for Paul!

MRS. PRICE

She'll wait for no one! Pack her things and get her out! I'm going up to my room!

(MRS. PRICE *turns her chair toward door* RIGHT. HILDE *takes hold of the chair, stopping her.*)

HILDE

I will wait for Paul!

MRS. PRICE

(*Coldly, in fright and anger.*)

Let go of this chair.

HILDE

I'll tell him what you have done to me!

(HILDE *turns the chair swiftly toward herself, holds it by both its arms.*)

MRS. PRICE

Let go of me, Hilde . . .

(*Puts her hands around* HILDE*'s wrists, attempting to force them from the chair-arms.*)

HILDE

I am no longer employed here; I don't need to obey you! I am nothing in this house!

MRS. PRICE

I tell you—let go—

HILDE

I will not leave until I see Paul!

MRS. PRICE

(*Straining against* HILDE*'s wrists.*)

You'll wait for him outside!

(MRS. PRICE *thrusts* HILDE*'s hands away from the chair triumphantly.* HILDE *looks down at her hands, then looks at* MRS. PRICE.)

HILDE

There is *great* strength in your arms . . .

(MRS. PRICE *turns chair* RIGHT, *and with several powerful thrusts, propels it to the door.* HILDE *calls out* LEFT.)

Did it hurt very much?

(MRS. PRICE *stops.*)

Did it hurt, Mrs. Price?—dragging yourself back and forth across the room to get the bracelet, and then pulling yourself up again onto the bed?

MRS. PRICE

(*Turns toward* HILDE. *Pause. Hating her, fearing her:*)

Get—out—of my—house . . .

(MRS. PRICE *exits* RIGHT. LUCILLE *enters from* HILDE*'s room, carrying* HILDE*'s coat and purse.* EVERETT *follows with two suitcases, from one of which a fold of cloth protrudes.*)

LUCILLE

(*Descending stairs, calling after* MRS. PRICE.)

She'll be gone in one minute, Mrs. Price.

(HILDE *looks from the doorway to* LUCILLE, *then goes quickly to piano.*)

Come on, Everett . . .

(HILDE *takes up a pencil and begins writing hastily on a pad of music paper.* LUCILLE *crosses to within a few feet of her. Contemptuously.*)

Here's your coat.

HILDE

(*Not looking up from her writing.*)

Put it on the couch.

LUCILLE

(*A beat.*)

Don't you tell me what to do.

HILDE

(*Looks up. Pause. great strain.*)

I am writing a note to Mr. Schildger. When I have finished I will—

LUCILLE

(*Over* HILDE*'s last few words.*)

Mrs. Price said you go when your clothes are packed and they're packed now!

EVERETT

(*At foot of stairs, the suitcases in his hands.*)

For pity's sake, Lu, let her write a note if she wants.

LUCILLE

(*Thrusting coat and purse into* HILDE*'s arms.*)

Here's your coat! You go now, like she said! You don't wait for anybody and you don't write any letters!

(*Snatches pad from piano, holds it defiantly.*)

EVERETT

(*Under his breath, tiredly.*)

Ah, Lu . . .

HILDE

(*Barely keeping control of herself.*)

Give me that pad, Lucille . . .

(*Lets coat and purse drop to piano bench.*)

LUCILLE

(*Backing a step* LEFT.)

Get out! Always telling me what to do . . . Now *I'm* going to do some telling!

HILDE

(*A step toward* LUCILLE. *Near the breaking point.*)

I want that pad . . .

PAUL

(*Entering* RIGHT.)

The snow has stopped! The world is perfectly white!

(HILDE, LUCILLE *and* EVERETT *stare at him. He is wearing a Chesterfield and a white muffler, and carries his hat and a red and green paper shopping bag filled with gift-wrapped packages. The stares with which he is met cut through his jubilance.*)

What is it? What's wrong?

(*An anxious step forward.*)

Has something happened to Mrs. Price?

HILDE

(*A pause, then she cries out:*)

To me! Something has happened to me! I've been dismissed! Made to go through a—a court-room trial—a—

LUCILLE

(*Overlapping, starting on "been."*)

Called Mrs. Price a liar to her face! She's supposed to leave right now!

PAUL

What? What?

HILDE

Dismissed!

(*Pointing at* EVERETT.)

My clothes are packed, money is offered to me—

LUCILLE

(*Overlapping, starting on "clothes."*)

She goes right now! Mrs. Price's orders!

PAUL

Dismissed?

HILDE

Yes! Yes!

LUCILLE

Called her a liar!

PAUL

What kind of ludicrous—Where is Mrs. Price?

LUCILLE

In her room and not going to be disturbed!

HILDE

(*Overlapping, starting on "and."*)

Oh, yes, locked away and safe in her bedroom!

PAUL

(*In exasperation at the confusion.*)

God Almighty!

HILDE

(*Pause.*)

She *wanted* me to call her a liar . . .

PAUL

(*To* LUCILLE *and* EVERETT.)

Leave us alone, please.

(*Puts shopping bag and hat on couch.*)

LUCILLE

Mrs. Price said she goes right now!

(EVERETT *crosses* RIGHT *with suitcases.*)

PAUL

Leave us, please, Lucille.

(*To* HILDE, *indicating suitcases.*)

Your things?

(HILDE *nods.*)

Everett! Put those in the corner there.

(PAUL *takes off his coat.* EVERETT *puts suitcases down* DOWNSTAGE RIGHT *by telephone table.*)

LUCILLE

She's supposed to go right now.

PAUL

(*Tosses coat over back of couch.*)

I asked you to leave us alone.

EVERETT

(*By door* RIGHT.)

Lucille . . .

LUCILLE

(*Facing* PAUL *adamantly.*)

I take my orders from Mrs. Price.

PAUL

(*Pause. Slowly, firmly.*)

You take this order from me, Lucille. Leave this room and go about your work.

(*Pause.* LUCILLE *puts the music pad scornfully on the piano, crosses to the stairs and starts to climb them.* EVERETT *exits* RIGHT.)

LUCILLE

(*Contemptuously, as she mounts.*)

I've got to straighten up in there.

PAUL

Close the door.

(HILDE *moves to the hassock and sits tiredly.* PAUL, *by the piano, watches as* LUCILLE *exits into* HILDE*'s room. Pause. The door closes.* PAUL *sighs and shakes his head. He picks up the music pad, glances at it.*)

HILDE

(*Drained.*)

I was writing you a note. She grabbed it from me.

PAUL

(*Reading.*)

"*She* took the bracelet."

(*Looks up.*)

Who? What bracelet?

HILDE

Mrs. Price.

PAUL

Mrs. Price—?

HILDE

She sent me out with a bracelet to be repaired. I brought it back and left it in her room. She hid it, so that I would accuse her of hiding it.

PAUL

(*Incredulously.*)

What?

HILDE

This gave her an excuse for dismissing me.

PAUL

She hid the bracelet so that—

HILDE

(*Overlapping.*)

So that I would accuse her of hiding it. She pretended I had lost it.

PAUL

(*Pause.*)

There has been—some kind of ridiculous misunderstanding here. I will have it put straight in five minutes.

HILDE

(*Rises.*)

She won't see you! She won't see anyone until she is well prepared for it!

PAUL

(*Stops, turns.*)

She would never stoop to such deceit! I could never believe it!

HILDE

She wants me out of here—doesn't she?

PAUL

(*A beat.*)

No. No, she doesn't.

(*Returning to* HILDE.)

So she thought you lost her bracelet . . . Is that any reason to accuse her of taking it? Allowances must be made for her, because of her condition; you told me that, didn't you?

(*Pause.*)

At times during the past weeks, I have felt that . . . I should be attending more to my studies and less to her . . .

(*Drawing himself up.*)

But then I remind myself of the brutal way in which she was injured—

HILDE

She is a liar. She could lie about anything. Maybe—maybe that story was another lie, to win your sympathy!

PAUL

What?

HILDE

Maybe there was no boat and no crash. Maybe the condition came from an illness!

PAUL

You're speaking nonsense! Your anger has upset you!

HILDE

After what she has done today, I put no lie beyond her!

PAUL

It's not possible! She could not have invented such a fearful story! No one would lie about so important a—No, no, you—you try to discredit her with no evidence whatsoever. It's shameful of you!

(*Puts music pad on end table.*)

She deserves our compassion . . .

HILDE

(*Pause.*)

When you came in here just now, and I told you what had happened, I thought you would say—we should both leave.

PAUL

I see no reason for us to leave once this bracelet nonsense has been set straight. There—there is my *work* to think of!

HILDE

Your work? Card games? German lessons? The piano yesterday was played for less than two hours.

PAUL

I can't play all day every day! I'm not a robot, you know!

HILDE

Mrs. Price said that once; has she said it again?

PAUL

No, she hasn't!

HILDE

Oh, Lord, this is all my fault for bringing you here!

PAUL

There is no need for you to carry on as though you had sent me back to the prison camps! You'll see; the bracelet will be found, you'll apologize to her, and she will end up rehiring you with extra wages in the bargain. She needs you *much more* than she does Lucille and Everett.

(*A pause, and then* HILDE *goes to the piano bench and takes her coat.*)

Where are you going?

HILDE

(*Putting on coat.*)

Out of here.

PAUL

This is ridiculous! Wait until I have talked with her!

HILDE

(*Slings purse-strap over her shoulder.*)

I have been ordered to leave. I do not intend to stay. I think I have found a little of that pride of yours.

(*Moves* DOWNSTAGE RIGHT.)

PAUL

But—where will you go?

HILDE

A hotel, a rooming house . . .

(*Lifts the suitcases.*)

PAUL

(*Going quickly to her.*)

You are not going to go out this way! Put them down . . .

(*Tries to wrest suitcases from her.*)

HILDE

(*Fighting the urge to cry.*)

I am not going to stay!

PAUL

You'll be coming back here later tonight!

HILDE

Never, no, no . . .

PAUL

(*Removes his hands from hers. Pause.*)

Very well; if waiting here is so difficult, go have a quiet dinner some place and walk about the park; calm yourself and get a clear perspective on this whole matter. You must telephone in a few hours, when I've had a chance to talk with her.

HILDE

Talking will not change things.

PAUL

(*Softly but firmly.*)

Put down those suitcases and do as I ask. Please . . .

(*Pause.* HILDE *puts down the suitcases. Silently she buttons the collar of her coat. Her gaze falls on the shopping bag on the couch.*)

HILDE

(*Wryly.*)

Is that where you were this afternoon—buying Christmas presents?

PAUL

(*Forcedly.*)

You'll see; later tonight we'll be putting them under the tree, just as though nothing had happened.

HILDE

I wish I were as certain of that as you are. Suddenly it is twenty years ago. You are *inside* the house again, and I am outside, watching from the garden.

(*Moves to door* RIGHT.)

PAUL

(*Pained.*)

Hilde . . .

HILDE

(*At the door, ruefully.*)

There is a terrible joke here some place; we come to America, a New World, and we bring an old world inside us.

(*She goes out.* PAUL *stands for a moment, somber, disturbed. The light outside has dimmed during the latter part of the scene, and it is now the time when lamps should be turned on.* PAUL *moves to the end table, picks up the music pad, taps it on his hand a few times, then re-reads what* HILDE *has written. He tears off the top page and reads it again, putting pad absently on table.* LUCILLE *emerges from the room on the balcony, her arms laden with bed-linens. She comes to the railing, surveys the room, gives a satisfied nod and exits* RIGHT. PAUL *turns.*)

PAUL

Lucille.

(LUCILLE *re-appears on the balcony, still holding the bed-linens. She eyes* PAUL *impassively.*)

Tell Mrs. Price that I am waiting to speak to her.

LUCILLE

Mrs. Price is going to rest a while, and then I'm going to bring her supper on a tray, like I used to.

PAUL

When you do so, tell her please that I am waiting to speak to her.

(*Lucille starts to go.*)

Lucille . . .

(*She stops, turns again.* PAUL *moves* UPSTAGE, *studying the sheet of music paper. He looks at* LUCILLE.)

I'm sorry I spoke sharply to you before.

LUCILLE

(*Grudgingly.*)

Oh . . . that's all right . . .

PAUL

I admire your devotion to Mrs. Price. You have been with her for many, many years, haven't you?

LUCILLE

(*Pause.*)

Twenty-four . . .

(*Coming to front of balcony, warming gradually.*)

Twenty-five, come next August. She was still in school when I come here.

PAUL

When she married, I suppose you went with her and her husband on their vacations?

LUCILLE

To the lake, and the place in Virginia, once Palm Springs . . .

PAUL

(*Slowly.*)

You were present at the lake on the . . . day of the . . . speedboat crash—weren't you?

LUCILLE

(*Pause.*)

There was never such an awful day in my whole life. That poor woman, with her middle all crushed . . . Two hours till they found a doctor to put a needle in her, and all that time I was the only one could come near her and try to soothe her.

(PAUL *tears the sheet of paper in half.*)

She screamed so awful . . .

(*Pause.*)

I forgive her everything. Sometime she talks real mean to me, wants things done just so. I forgive her.

(PAUL *is tearing the paper into smaller pieces, standing self-assuredly now.*)

Anything she does now, she paid for a thousand times that day; her legs all twisted, her husband thrown out like a broken ragdoll . . . How could God allow such an accident? That boat come smashing straight into shore full-speed, like it was aimed from a gun!

PAUL

(*Has stopped tearing the paper.*)

I thought—Mr. Price died *in* the boat.

LUCILLE

(*Shaking her head.*)

Thrown out like a rag-doll. Killed when he landed.

(*Starts to go.*)

PAUL

Lucille! Where—was Mrs. Price?

LUCILLE

Caught there, behind the steering wheel.

(*Touches the balcony switch, flooding the room with sudden light.*)

Such an awful accident . . .

(LUCILLE *exits* RIGHT. *as* PAUL *turns toward* MRS. PRICE*'s smiling portrait, his hands fisting at his sides. The lights immediately fade to black, light on* PAUL *and the portrait going last.*)

THE CURTAIN FALLS

ACT THREE

SCENE TWO

PAUL*'s nocturne is heard in the darkness. The curtain rises on the fully-lighted set.* PAUL, *wearing the same suit as in the previous scene, is seated at the piano, playing softly, quite relaxed. The brandy decanter, about one-third full, stands on the* DOWNSTAGE *corner of the piano, along with a partially filled snifter. Portrait light and piano work lamp are on. The drapes are opened, there is darkness outside.* PAUL*'s coat, hat and shopping bag are still on the couch, the coat now neatly folded.* HILDE*'s suitcases still stand* DOWNSTAGE RIGHT. *The door of the cabinet in which the brandy is usually kept stands open. After a moment,* EVERETT *enters* RIGHT, *carefully dressed in a navy blue suit. He crosses to the foot of the staircase.*

EVERETT

(*As he crosses.*)

She's coming down now.

(EVERETT *draws drapes across window,* PAUL, *having finished the nocturne, takes a sip of brandy.* EVERETT *turns to the Christmas tree and touches a switch at the base of it. A dozen tiny lights appear in its branches.* EVERETT *backs* DOWNSTAGE *admiringly.*)

Isn't that pretty?

PAUL

Most pretty . . .

EVERETT

She's had some of those trimmings ever since she was a little girl.

(*Shuts cabinet door, disclosing an old suitcase to which books and sheet music have been tied.*)

Mr. Schildger . . . are you leaving too?

PAUL

(*Sardonically, emphasizing his words with piano chords.*)

Yes, Everett—I—am—leaving.

EVERETT

I'm sorry to hear that.

(*Pause, then crosses* RIGHT.)

She shouldn't have fired Miss Hahn. That poor girl was so upset, she didn't even know what she was saying.

PAUL

(*Rising.*)

Everett.

(EVERETT *stops in doorway.* PAUL *goes* DOWNSTAGE *to couch.* EVERETT *moves closer.*)

Wait a moment, please. I have something . . .

(*Burrows in shopping bag, then upends it, spilling out four wrapped boxes. Selects two of them that probably contain ties and handkerchiefs.*)

Here. This one is for you, and this one is for Lucille. Merry Christmas.

EVERETT

(*Taking the boxes.*)

Why, thank you, Mr. Schildger. Merry Christmas to you! We'll open them the minute we get back from church. Thank you very much!

(*Impulsively offers his hand.*)

PAUL

(*Taking it warmly.*)

You are most welcome!

EVERETT

(*Backing to door.*)

This is awfully nice . . . You tell Miss Hahn "Merry Christmas" too, will you?

PAUL

I will.

EVERETT

Thank you. Good-bye, Mr. Schildger.

PAUL

Good-bye, Everett.

(EVERETT *exits* RIGHT. PAUL, *looking pleased, takes up one of the two remaining boxes—a small, squarish one—and moves* DOWNSTAGE. *He puts it on one of* HILDE*'s suitcases and returns to back of couch. He takes up the empty shopping bag, folds it and drops it on couch beside the fourth gift, at which he smiles wryly. It is an oblong box, wrapped in white paper and elaborately tied with white satin ribbon.* PAUL *goes* UPSTAGE *to piano and pours brandy* *into snifter. As he takes up the glass,* MRS. PRICE *enters* RIGHT., *with* LUCILLE *pushing the wheel chair.* LUCILLE *is wearing a hat and her church-going dress.* MRS. PRICE *is in her loveliest gown: cloud-pink, festive, a shade too girlish. She is armored with many diamonds, the cigarette holder and the earrings which she wore in Act One, Scene One. Her lips and nails are very red. She is armored too with an effusive show of femininity and charm, but beneath it can be sensed a tight core of anxiety.*)

MRS. PRICE

Good evening, Paul.

PAUL

Good evening, Mrs. Price.

MRS. PRICE

(*Quickly.*)

Oh, how lovely the tree looks! Lucy, look at it. Isn't it lovely?

LUCILLE

(*Pushing chair to* CENTER LEFT.)

Just perfect, Mrs. Price. Just perfect!

(PAUL *watches with almost casual detachment as* MRS. PRICE *is settled in her place and made comfortable by* LUCILLE. *His unsuspected knowledge gives him an air of assurance and superiority which he has never had in previous encounters with* MRS. PRICE, *but in him too there is a small inner tension running counter to the outer show.*)

PAUL

(*A tinge of cynicism.*)

You are looking especially . . . attractive this evening, Mrs. Price.

MRS. PRICE

Thank you, Paul; that's as nice as the music you produce on the piano!

LUCILLE

(*Arranging* MRS. PRICE*'s skirt.*)

We fixed her up pretty, didn't we? It's the holidays; people should be prettiest on holidays.

MRS. PRICE

I'm just *liable* to keep that tree burning all year!

(PAUL *sips his brandy, watching.*)

LUCILLE

You comfortable now?

MRS. PRICE

Yes, dear. Thank you.

LUCILLE

We'll get back as quick as we can.

(*Moving toward* RIGHT.)

MRS. PRICE

I trust you'll explain to God why I can't be present.

LUCILLE

(*Stops, turns.*)

You shouldn't talk blasphemous, Mrs. Price. Especially not on Christmas Eve.

MRS. PRICE

I'm sorry, Lucy.

(EVERETT *appears at door* RIGHT. *wearing an overcoat and holding* LUCILLE*'s coat.*)

Lucy . . .

(LUCILLE *returns to* MRS. PRICE, *who has taken a wallet from a compartment of the chair. Giving bills to* LUCILLE.)

Here. Put this in the collection for me.

LUCILLE

(*Looks at bills.*)

Oh, my . . . God bless you, I certainly will! Merry Christmas! Merry, merry Christmas!

MRS. PRICE

Merry Christmas, Lucy. Everett . . .

EVERETT

Merry Christmas, ma'am.

LUCILLE

(*Crossing, overlapping* EVERETT*'s line.*)

Merry Christmas, Mr. Schildger.

PAUL

Merry Christmas, Lucille.

LUCILLE

(*At door, holding bills.*)

My friends are going to think I'm Mrs. Rockefeller!

(EVERETT *gives* LUCILLE *her coat as they exit* RIGHT. MRS. PRICE, *smiling, replaces her wallet in chair.*)

MRS. PRICE

It's like a wedding; if you can't go, you should still send a gift.

(*There is a moment of silence, during which* MRS. PRICE *adjusts her jewelry a trifle self-consciously. SOUND: A door closing in the back of the house.* MRS. PRICE *steals a sidelong glance at* PAUL. *He is leaning against the curve of the piano, glass in hand, watching her. He gives no evidence of intention to speak. She holds her cigarette holder in her lap, looks at it, then speaks. This speech has been rehearsed:*)

I know you must be terribly distressed about Hilde's departure, and I'm sorry to have kept you waiting so long to discuss it. It's taken me all this time to compose myself after the unpleasantness she put me through.

(*Pause.*)

I understand she saw you before she left. I don't know what . . . wild accusations she may have made against me, but I assume they included her—fantasy about my dragging myself thirty feet in order to steal my own bracelet and make her seem a thief. Panic, no doubt, inspired the fantasy; missing jewelry is a servant's nightmare. But why she clung to the story I can't explain, except in the light of—jealousy of the time you and I have spent together.

(*She glances at* PAUL. *He sips his brandy. She returns her gaze to the cigarette holder.*)

At any rate, when I denied the charge, she called me a liar; not once, but several times. Lucille and Everett will bear me out on this. I had no choice but to ask her to leave. And that is the complete truth; I give you my word on it.

PAUL

(*The slightest hint of sarcasm.*)

You . . . give me your word . . .

MRS. PRICE

I do.

(*Puts cigarette holder on small table.*)

What I resent most bitterly is not her ingratitude toward me, but her absolute lack of consideration for you and your work. To provoke a situation like this, just when you are making real progress, is unforgivable. But she *has* made the break that your sense of honor would have prevented you from making, and I truly think it's all for the best. I know it's difficult for you to accept that now, but in a day, or a week, or a month, believe me, you will see that it's so.

PAUL

Do you give me your word on the truth of that, also?

MRS. PRICE

(*Pause.*)

Yes, I do.

PAUL

(*Pause.*)

What is the value of your word, Mrs. Price?

MRS. PRICE

(*An uncertain pause, then a smile.*)

I suppose that is something that you must decide.

PAUL

Yes . . .

(*Picks up decanter. Musingly.*)
What is the value of the word . . . of an habitual liar . . .

(MRS. PRICE *stares at him. He pours brandy into the snifter.*)

MRS. PRICE

(*Pause. Not quite covering her fear:*)
How many drinks have you had?

PAUL

(*Transfers decanter to left hand, lifts glass.*)
Your health.
(*Sips brandy.*)

MRS. PRICE

I think you have had enough brandy!

PAUL

You tell me how much I may drink?

MRS. PRICE

If you wish to become drunk and insulting, please don't do it on my brandy.

PAUL

Very well, Mrs. Price. No more of your brandy.

(*He lifts the decanter outward, then swings it back, smashing it against the side of the piano. Dropping the neck of it, he places his snifter carefully on the corner of the piano.*)

MRS. PRICE

That was the action of a fifteen-year-old boy.

PAUL

Thank you. I am feeling very youthful this evening.

MRS. PRICE

(*Propelling chair toward* RIGHT.)

Then we had better continue our discussion in the morning, when you are a little more mature.

PAUL

I shall be gone in the morning!

(MRS. PRICE *stops, turns chair.* PAUL *moves* UPSTAGE LEFT.)

I am leaving!

(*Kicks suitcase.*)

I wait only for Hilde's telephone call to tell me where she is.

MRS. PRICE

(*The armor disintegrates.*)

You're . . . going away?

(*Propels chair to* CENTER STAGE.)

PAUL

(*Going to her.*)

Do you think I can remain here? I have learned something, Mrs. Price!

MRS. PRICE

What else did she tell you? What filthy lies? I know her type; I roomed with one at college! Foul slanders!

PAUL

(*Over her.*)

She did not tell me; she only suggested! It was *Lucille* who told me!

MRS. PRICE

(*Completely lost.*)

Lucille . . . told you . . .

PAUL

That you have lied to me from the very first moment! About the boat!

MRS. PRICE

The boat . . . the . . .

(*Moves chair* DOWNSTAGE *toward* LEFT.)

What did Lucille tell you . . .

PAUL

The boat in which you crashed.

(*Moves toward her.*)

Who was driving the boat, Mrs. Price?

MRS. PRICE

(*Pause.*)

He was . . .

PAUL

(*Moving closer.*)

Lucille says it was he who was *thrown* from the boat, not you. Lucille says it was you who were driving the boat, not he.

MRS. PRICE

(*Pause. Weakly.*)

Her memory was never too good . . .

PAUL

Her memory is *very* good. *You* were driving the boat. You killed him.

MRS. PRICE

(*Moves chair evasively toward* RIGHT, DOWNSTAGE.)

It was an accident . . .

PAUL

So your brothers told the police, but I am not gullible or bribable, nor am I like Lucille, loving and trusting!

(*Pause.*)

Why did you kill him, Mrs. Price? I am most curious . . .

MRS. PRICE

(*Sending chair swiftly toward doorway.*)

You should have broken that decanter half an hour ago! You're drunk!

(*Crossing quickly* UPSTAGE *of couch,* PAUL *reaches the doorway before* MRS. PRICE. *He slides the doors closed.* MRS. PRICE *stops a few feet short of him.*)

Open that door!

PAUL

(*His back to the door.*)

I am perfectly sober! I have a—slight sharpness, that is all.

(*Pause.*)

Why did you do it?

MRS. PRICE

(*Pause.*)

Open that door, Paul. Let me out of this room.

PAUL

Why did you crash the boat?

(MRS. PRICE *turns chair, heads blindly for foot of staircase.* PAUL *follows.*)

Perhaps I can guess . . . You said you were leaving him; was that reversed too? Was it he who was leaving?

(*Helpless at the foot of the staircase,* MRS. PRICE *moves her chair a few feet* DOWNSTAGE *and sits with her hands clenched, her jaw set, her eyes blazing.* PAUL *moves about near her, but never touches the chair.*)

It was he who was leaving!

(MRS. PRICE *averts her face sharply from his direction.*)

Why, Mrs. Price? Why was he going? Why was he leaving you?

(*Leans closer. Intently.*)

Why, Mrs. Price? What was his reason?

MRS. PRICE

(*Her eyes are closed. She has salvaged some control. Somnambulistically.*)

Get out of here. I don't want to speak to you.

PAUL

Answer me . . .

MRS. PRICE

Go to your Hilde. Get out of this house.

PAUL

Answer my question! Why was he leaving you?

(*A futile, hateful pause, then he backs* LEFT, *staring at her, his eyes narrowed.*)

You are . . . exactly like my mother . . . So *she* would sit when someone displeased her. Her eyes shut, a wall built around her . . .

(*Pause. Feeding his anger.*)

Liar . . . murderer . . .

MRS. PRICE

(*Immobile as a statue.*)

Go to your Hilde.

PAUL

You took the bracelet! To make her accuse you!

MRS. PRICE

(*Eyes opened. Flatly.*)

If you do not leave now, tomorrow morning I will speak to the immigration authorities.

PAUL

(*Pause. The anger focused into cold intensity.*)

Is the bracelets in your chair, Mrs. Price?

(*Takes a step toward her.*)

MRS. PRICE

Don't you come near me.

PAUL

I must find the bracelet, mustn't I? To vindicate Hilde?

(*Moves closer.*)

MRS. PRICE

Paul . . .

(*She attempts to retreat, but* PAUL *has got hold of the chair arm.*)

PAUL

(*Indicating compartment.*)

This side or that side?

(*A defensive movement from* MRS. PRICE *betrays it.*)

This side . . .

(*He opens the compartment on the inside of the nearer chair arm, his eyes not on his hands, but on* MRS. PRICE. *She grabs his wrists.*)

MRS. PRICE

Take your hands out of there!

PAUL

(*Through his teeth.*)

Make me do it . . .

(*Her hands fly to his face. He catches her up by the arms, lifts her to a semi-standing position, stares into her face for an instant, whispers a curse—*)

Damn you!

(*—and flings her forward. She falls to the floor, breaking the fall with her hands and crying out in pain.* PAUL *glares at her for a moment in triumphant fury, and then reminds himself:*)

Bracelet . . . I will find the . . .

(*He pulls the empty chair* UPSTAGE LEFT, *away from her feet and bends over it, digging in the compartment.* MRS. PRICE *grits her teeth, keening in agony. She is resting on one hip, supporting herself on her hands, facing* DOWNSTAGE. PAUL *holds up a glittering bracelet.*)

Here is your bracelet! Lügnerin! Weibsbild!

(*Hurls it at her.*)

Now call your Brownshirts! Have me arrested!

(*He stands over her, catching his breath, his hands fisted at his sides. She swallows her pain.*)

MRS. PRICE

I did it for you! For *you* to be free! She's been like a ghost on that stairway; watching, reminding . . . I wanted her gone!

PAUL

(*Contemptuously.*)

When you want someone gone, it happens, doesn't it? Through lies. Or through murder! You killed your husband, didn't you!

MRS. PRICE

No! He forced me to do it! Said he was leaving, said I didn't love him, couldn't love any man! Foul accusations—Oh, God, God, God—*what made me marry a man so easy to despise?*

PAUL

You wanted him gone . . .

MRS. PRICE

(*Shaking her head wearily.*)

No . . . no . . . no . . . "Jump," I said, "jump"—but he wouldn't let go of me . . .

PAUL

You were trying to kill him!

MRS. PRICE

Not him! Myself!

(*A long despairing moan.*)

Myself . . .

(*She cries; all the tears that haven't been cried in a lifetime, repetitions of the word "myself" buried among them.* PAUL *watches, his fury subsiding. He breaks away, going* UPSTAGE LEFT, *picks up his suitcase, brings it briskly* DOWNSTAGE RIGHT *and stands it between* HILDE*'s two suitcases.* MRS. PRICE *is still crying.* PAUL *glances at his watch. He stands before the telephone, his back toward* MRS. PRICE. *She cries out:*)

Twice I've tried; the boat, the sleeping pills . . . There must be an end! Doubting, loathing . . . The third time is lucky! The third time! A third time . . .

PAUL

(*Firmly, not turning to her.*)

You will not win pity from me by speaking of suicide.

MRS. PRICE

Pity! You think *pity* is what I want from you? Do you think *pity* is enough to make my life bearable?

PAUL

(*Turning swiftly toward her.*)

What *do* you want then? Why did you *lie* to get me here and *lie* to keep me here and *lie* to fire Hilde?

MRS. PRICE

(*Sobs for a moment.*)

I wanted you to . . . serenade me . . . write a nocturne and dedicate it to me . . .

(*Smiling through the tears, as over a sweet, lost dream.*)

I wanted you to talk with me, and compliment me occasionally, always be near . . . Those are the things that all women enjoy, and I enjoy them too. *I am no different* . . . I wanted *you* here, not Hilde. Only you! I did! I did!

(*The tears have slowed.*)

Our hours together were so wonderful . . . I *enjoyed* them . . .! I did.

PAUL

(*Moving toward her, soothingly.*)

I know, I know . . . I enjoyed them too . . .

MRS. PRICE

(*Turning to him.*)

You . . . did?

(*Pause.* PAUL *crouches down beside her.*)

Go to Hilde, Paul . . . Yes, go! For God's sake, don't wait! Go now! Go to her!

PAUL

I must wait till she calls me . . .

MRS. PRICE

(*Almost a whisper.*)

Don't wait . . .

(PAUL *puts one arm under her legs, the other about her waist. She winds her arms around his neck. He lifts her from the floor.*)

I told you to go look for her, Paul. I did. I told you to go . . .

(PAUL *places her carefully in the wheel chair.*)

PAUL

(*Pause. Awkwardly.*)

I'm—sorry I did that. This happens to me; part of me strikes out at someone while—another part watches, not wanting to . . .

MRS. PRICE

I know, Paul. I know . . .

(*They look at each other, a long look.* PAUL, *embarrassed, goes* DOWNSTAGE RIGHT *and sits on the arm of the couch, facing the telephone, his back toward* MRS. PRICE. MRS. PRICE *sits with her hands clenched in her lap, her eyes shut, a battle going on within her. When she finally opens her eyes and speaks, every word is expelled against great resistance.*)

Are you going back to—your bakery?

PAUL

(*Lowers his head, is silent for a moment.*)

I doubt it. I said some foolish things the day I left.

MRS. PRICE

(*Pause.*)

I suppose there are—other bakeries.

(PAUL *is motionless, silent.*)

Will you and Hilde—marry right away? Or will you wait until you—you can afford the sort of apartment you would like? You have—expensive tastes, you know.

PAUL

We will wait, I suppose . . . A little while . . .

(*Pause.*)

I will study very hard . . .

MRS. PRICE

(*Pause. Genuine pain.*)

Paul, Paul . . . Don't force me to . . . confess *all* my lies this evening . . .

(*Pause.*)

You said pleasant things to me, so I said—pleasant things to you.

PAUL

Pleasant things?

MRS. PRICE

About your—piano-playing . . .

(*Pause.*)

A man of thirty, Paul—still "preparing"?

(*Pause.*)

You've heard all my records: Backhaus and Rubinstein, Firkusny, Gieseking, Horowitz, Arrau . . . Do you honestly think that—*you* are what they are?

PAUL

(*Pause.*)

I think . . . I might be . . . some day . . .

MRS. PRICE

But when, Paul? When? At—sixty?

PAUL

(*Rises, faces her.*)

The professors last winter . . . They said I showed promise . . .

MRS. PRICE

But they offered no fellowship, did they?

PAUL

Because I am not a citizen!

MRS. PRICE

Maybe that saved them from having to name a more unpleasant reason!

(*Pause.* PAUL *stands tensely.*)

A medal at school is—no guarantee of later prizes.

PAUL

No, but . . . it has a significance . . . An indication of . . . They call it "The Wagner Medal." It is awarded only in exceptional instances, not every year like . . . other medals . . .

(*Pause.*)

Foolish, of course; Wagner and a schoolboy . . . But it has a significance . . .

(*An empty pause. He turns away from* MRS. PRICE.)

MRS. PRICE

Oh, Paul . . . Your chances for success are so *very* slender even in the best of circumstances! In the worst, working all day in a bakery and studying at night on a secondhand upright—they're nonexistent.

PAUL

No . . . no . . . I can *do* it, I can, I can, I can . . .

MRS. PRICE

You can't, Paul. *I* know it, and you know it even better than I do.

(*Pause. Her chair moves forward slightly. It is difficult for her to keep the anxiety out of her voice.*)

You do have *one* chance, Paul . . . One chance to make yourself into the man you were meant to be . . .

(PAUL *turns toward her.*)

A small chance, but not one to toss away . . .

(*Leaning toward him.*)

If you were to devote your full time to studying . . . *if* it were possible to obtain a *very fine teacher* for *as many hours a week* as you felt necessary . . .

PAUL

(*Stares at her wonderingly.*)

You . . . still want me here . . . after . . .

(*A gesture toward the floor.*)

after I hurt you . . .

MRS. PRICE

(*Pause.*)

I forgive you for hurting me. I forgive you, Paul . . . And I do still want you here.

(PAUL *stares at her. SOUND: Telephone rings.* PAUL *doesn't move.*)

Don't answer it, Paul. Please don't.

(*SOUND: Telephone rings second time.* PAUL *begins backing slowly toward telephone, his eyes riveted on* MRS. PRICE. *Her tone begins growing more urgent, the sentences come faster.*)

Please, Paul. For your sake, for my sake—for her sake too. It's your only chance. This is where you belong. Stay here, stay here with me! You know that you want to!

(*SOUND: Telephone rings third time.* PAUL *is closer to it, his eyes still locked with* MRS. PRICE*'s.*)

Don't throw your life away! You weren't *meant* for shabby clothing and rented rooms!—You know you couldn't bear it after what you've had here! Please, Paul, don't do it!

(SOUND: Telephone rings fourth time. PAUL *is by the telephone, his right hand groping for it, his eyes still on* MRS. PRICE.)

Please, Paul, don't . . . don't go 'way . . . Don't, Paul . . . Please don't . . . Please . . . Don't . . .

(SOUND: Telephone rings fifth time. PAUL *lifts the receiver in midring. Still staring at* MRS. PRICE, *he brings the receiver very slowly to his ear.* MRS. PRICE *watches him fearfully.)*

PAUL

(With effort.)

Hilde . . . Hilde? Yes . . . this is Paul . . .

MRS. PRICE

This is Paul . . .

(Sits back bitterly.)

Go ahead. Go to her. Go to your Hilde, your mended clothing, your rented piano . . .

PAUL

Hilde . . . where are you?

MRS. PRICE

(Louder.)

Where are you, Hilde? Where is the bakery? Where is the rooming-house?

PAUL

(Turning DOWNSTAGE, *his left hand over his ear.)*

Hilde . . . I cannot hear you. Speak louder, Hilde!

MRS. PRICE

(*Shouting.*)

Where is the bakery? Where is the rooming-house?

PAUL

(*Covering mouthpiece with his hand, whirling at her.*)

Stop it! Stop! For the love of God! Please! Stop. Please . . .

(*Their eyes are locked again. A frozen moment.* HILDE*'s voice is heard, a tiny sound in the silence.*)

HILDE

(*On phone.*)

Paul?

MRS. PRICE

Stay, Paul! Stay! You know this is where you want to be! I forgive you for hurting me! I deserved it for lying! Only stay, stay with me! Your work is the reason!

(*Pause.*)

You and I need each other!

(*A long pause.* PAUL *is motionless.*)

HILDE

(*On phone.*)

Hello, Paul? Are you there?

MRS. PRICE

Your work is the reason . . .

(*SOUND: Clicking on the other end of the line, then sound of receiver being hung up.* PAUL *stares at the dead receiver in his hands, at* MRS. PRICE, *at the receiver again.*)

PAUL

(*Halfway between sadness and amusement.*)

She was . . . just at the corner . . .

(*Slowly he turns and replaces the receiver on the telephone.* MRS. PRICE *brings her chair quickly* DOWNSTAGE CENTER, *closer to him.*)

MRS. PRICE

You must stay here and study; in earnest, this time! The things I said about your playing—I exaggerated, because I feared you would leave. Staying here, you'll have more than a slender chance of success. You'll have a *good* chance!

PAUL

(*Pause.*)

If . . . I were to stay here . . . I would have to work . . . truly hard . . . Not like before . . .

MRS. PRICE

No card games, no records, no reading aloud! We'll guard ourselves and see that you study. I'll stay out of this room whenever you're working! I promise! I'll stay out!

(*Pause.* PAUL *crosses toward her.*)

PAUL

And you are not afraid that . . . some day I might . . . hurt you again?

MRS. PRICE

No, I am not afraid.

(*Pause.* PAUL *picks up the bracelet from the floor. He holds it for a moment, looking at it.*)

This evening must be wiped completely from our minds. It can be done!

(PAUL *hands the bracelet to* MRS. PRICE. *She puts it quickly into one of the compartments of her chair as she speaks.*)

Push it into the farthest compartment, wall it over and never look back. That's what the New Year means: forgiving, forgetting, resolution, change . . .

(*Pause.* PAUL *picks up the white-wrapped gift from the couch. He turns it aimlessly in his hands—the stance of an awkward schoolboy.*)

A new beginning . . .

(PAUL *offers the box expressionlessly to* MRS. PRICE. *She takes it with unbelieving delight.*)

Oh . . . ! Oh!

(*She looks at him gratefully, then attacks the wrappings.*)

It's been so many, many years since I . . . What is it? No, don't tell me!

(*She passes the wrappings to* PAUL, *he takes them automatically.*)

Let me see for myself!

(*Hesitates for a delicious moment, then opens the box.*)

Oh . . . ! Beautiful . . . beautiful . . .

(*Unfolding a long, flower-embroidered stole of sheerest white lawn.*)

Beautiful . . .

PAUL

(*Her enthusiasm warming him a bit.*)

It is imported fabric . . . woven in Sweden . . .

MRS. PRICE

It's just lovely! So fine, so delicate . . . !

PAUL

(*Taking hold of a corner of the stole.*)

Such a scarf was worn by—women in—Stuttgart . . .

MRS. PRICE

It's the perfect gift! I couldn't be hap—

(*She stops short as the doors of the room open.* HILDE *stands* RIGHT, *surveying the tableau of* PAUL *and* MRS. PRICE *and the white stole joining their hands.* PAUL *and* MRS. PRICE *look away. They remain motionless.* HILDE *steps into the room.*)

HILDE

Here are the keys. I have come to take my suitcases.

(*She puts a ring of keys on the end table, then moves* DOWNSTAGE *to her suitcases. She picks up the gift box which* PAUL *put there. She holds it for a moment in both hands, reading the label attached to it.*)

You told me before to find a clear perspective, Paul. That isn't easy to do, not when one has loved as long as I have . . . But now, now I am finding the clear perspective . . . All my life I have been loving an imaginary Paul. You were like him for a while—you were!—but now . . . I don't know you.

(*She puts the gift box on the couch.*)

I have changed my mind, Mrs. Price. I am going to take that check you offered me.

(*Crossing* RIGHT *to small table.*)

It was childish of me to refuse it before. I can make good use of it.

(*Takes check from table, folds and pockets it. Crossing* LEFT *to suitcases.*)

I must buy new clothes and find a new job, and find a new place to live . . . and new people.

(*She takes up her suitcases, hesitates for a moment at the sight of* PAUL'S *suitcase, then goes* UPSTAGE *to door. She stops, turns, puts down her suitcases, and unfastens the gold chain from about her wrist.*)

Your medal . . .

(*She puts the medal and chain on end table.*)

I am rich. I have five hundred dollars. I no longer have need of luck charms.

(*She takes up her suitcases and goes out* RIGHT. *There is a long pause. SOUND: The front door closes. Another moment of silence, and then* MRS. PRICE, *with desperate gaiety, drapes the white stole about her head and shoulders.*)

MRS. PRICE

Oh, Paul, this is the loveliest gift I have ever been given in my entire life! I couldn't be happier! I shall wear it forever!

(*A beat.*)

And now—you must wish me a merry Christmas and kiss me once upon the cheek!

PAUL

(*Pause.*)

Merry Christmas, Mrs. Price . . .

MRS. PRICE

(*Lightly, with a lilt of coyness.*)

Jeanette. Jeanette is my first name.

PAUL

(*Pause.*)

Jeanette . . .

(*He bends slowly and kisses* MRS. PRICE *on the cheek.*)

MRS. PRICE

Danke schon, Paul. Du bin sehr gütig!

PAUL

(*Automatically correcting her.*)

Du *bist* sehr gütig. Ich bin, du bist, er ist.

MRS. PRICE

(*Repeating imperfectly.*)

Ich bin, du binst, er—

PAUL

(*Amused now, a faint smile.*)

Nein, nein. Ich bin, du bist, er ist. Ich bin . . .

MRS. PRICE

Ich bin.

PAUL

Du bist . . .

MRS. PRICE

Du bist.

PAUL

(*Sitting on hassock.*)

Er ist . . .

MRS. PRICE

Er ist.

PAUL

Wir sind . . .

THE CURTAIN FALLS

THE END

DR. COOK'S GARDEN

(1967)

INTRODUCTION

(*DR. COOK'S GARDEN*)

Ira Levin wrote *Dr. Cook's Garden* just after completing his 1967 novel *Rosemary's Baby.* So it's notable that both works feature shall we say, *unorthodox* physicians—previously, *Dr. Sapirstein*; now, the titular *Dr. Cook.* There's no tannis root in this garden, however; as with *Interlock*, the issues and conflicts at hand are purely of the earthly, human realm. (And doctors simply make good villains—see Levin's incorporation of real-life Dr. (Josef) Mengele in *The Boys from Brazil.*)

This is the tale of young doctor Jim Tennyson, who's returned home for a brief visit, but finds himself enmeshed in the affairs of his mentor, the senior *Cook.* The work's partial focus on *bioethics* presages both *The Boys from Brazil* as well as Levin's 1970 novel *This Perfect Day.* And as usual, an air of moral ambiguity hovers over the proceedings, with Levin presenting all sides of the matter, but leaving it to us to decide for ourselves where our sympathies lie—no easy task, given how masterful his case-making can be.

Between *Interlock* and *Dr. Cook's Garden*, Levin had written a genre-hopping succession of plays: a comedy (*Critic's Choice*), a classical drama (*General Seeger*), and a musical (*Drat! The Cat!*) This period was to constitute one of two such elongated stretches during which he took a hiatus from novel writing to focus on his stage work. (The second such novel-writing interregnum would yield *Deathtrap* and *Veronica's Room*, among others.)

Though Levin's trademark humor is not entirely absent in *Greenfield Center*, it is—as befits the countrified setting—of a slightly more down-home nature than the urbane *Interlock* and *Critic's Choice*—knowing eye-rolls over this or that neighbor's irksome-but-beloved idiosyncrasies, and the like. But as *Deathtrap* would have it, those jokes come only *"in the right places"*—e.g. in service of the broader narrative. The opening scene's humor isn't mere glad-handing; it's introducing needed expository information, while planting seeds for later dramatic germination. (Apologies for the unintentional gardening metaphor.)

And again, as in so many Levin works, there's an autobiographical thread present, vis à vis the play's Vermont setting. Levin's father Charles was born in Burlington—the family having settled there after emigrating from Russia in the late 1800s. Also, Levin wrote *Cook* while living in still partly rural Wilton, Connecticut. Some observers note a possible overlap between *Cook*'s Greenfield Center and Levin's later *Stepford* (which was loosely modeled on Wilton), both locations being bucolic idylls of "perfection."

Dr. Cook's Garden was the last of Levin's plays to employ the classical three-act structure. He was (along with popular entertainment in general) moving towards a more "naturalistic" presentation. In keeping with that trend, whereas *Interlock*'s events played out over the course of three consecutive months (one per act), *Doctor Cook's Garden* tightens up the timeframe, with all of its action happening in virtual real time over the course of Jim's visit. (Only two brief stretches transpire offstage, one for each of its two intermissions.) Levin's next play, *Veronica's Room*, unspools in *actual*... well—you'll see.)

"The domestics" last seen in *Interlock* (Lucille and Everett) return anew, in slightly more contemporary dress—here as Dora (Cook's faithful housekeeper) and Elias (his moonlighting gardener.) And they'll return again (with a twist) in *Veronica's Room.* Just as doctors make good villains, *domestics* were convenient dramatic facilitators of the day—a facile arrangement Levin lampooned himself in his 1960 comedy, *Critic's Choice* (as featured in Blackstone's companion volume of Levin's *comedies*).

While George C. Scott had been hired to direct the Broadway premiere of *Dr. Cook's Garden*, he quit his post a week before opening night over issues with the show's star, telling the *New York Times*: *"I wanted to get rid of Burl Ives and I couldn't get rid of him, so I got rid of myself."* Levin was left to finish directing the show himself—his one and only such turn.

Levin had his own misgivings about Ives' casting, relating in 1997 *"I had* [imagined] *an intense, driven actor—in my wildest dreams, perhaps Fredric March. Instead we got Burl Ives, who was so laid-back and so folksy. We needed someone demonic or satanic, really!"* Ives did have a markedly benign persona. How benign? That's him voicing (and singing) the role of plaid-vested *Sam the Snowman* in the stop-motion classic *Rudolph the Red-Nosed Reindeer.*

Appearing as the idealistic Jim—without issue—was Keir Dullea, who'd star the following year in *2001: A Space Odyssey*, and who'd two years earlier starred in *Bunny Lake Is Missing*—a film Levin was originally hired to adapt to screen (a matter unto itself).

Paramount Pictures, having produced the 1968 screen adaptation of *Rosemary's Baby*, scooped up the film rights to *Dr. Cook* well in advance of its opening, and a television adaptation was produced in 1971, with casting (Bing Crosby) that again leaned more *singerly* than satanic.

But back to *Greenfield Center*—and the return of a certain newly-minted physician.

Nicholas Levin
January 2025
New York City

DR. COOK'S GARDEN

CHARACTERS

Dr. Jim Tennyson
Bea Schmidt
Dora Ludlow
Elias Hart
Dr. Leonard Cook

This action takes place in the home and office of Dr. Leonard Cook, in the village of Greenfield Center, Vermont.

The time is a Friday in the fall of 1966.

ACT ONE: Late Afternoon
ACT TWO: Ten Minutes Later
ACT THREE: Half an Hour Later

NOTE: What in Vermont is called a town is in other states a township; an area roughly six miles square containing several separate communities. Greenfield Center, the village in which the play is set, is in Greenfield Town, which also encompasses the village of South Greenfield ("South Green") and Hart Mills; and that is what the characters mean by the word "town"—the three villages and the farms surrounding them.

SETTING

Dr. Cook, a bachelor, lives in a small, old, comfortable, two-story house, the ground floor of which he has given over almost entirely to his medical practice.

At the center of the stage, and occupying most of it, is his office, originally the house's living room. There are a rolltop desk and a swivel chair, a sagging davenport, another chair or two, a small table, file cabinets, and bookcases full of medical books. DOWNSTAGE RIGHT, closed sliding doors to an inner examining room, originally the dining room. Certificates on the walls, and a framed cover of *Flower and Garden* magazine. Perhaps a fireplace or stove.

At LEFT, the front door of the house and a small foyer, with a hallway UPSTAGE to the kitchen area. Between the foyer and the office, the lower part of the enclosed winding stairway to the second floor.

Also at LEFT, part of the waiting room, and a reception desk.

The office is orderly but holds several decades' accumulation of records and journals. The general effect is one of comfort and old-fashioned dependability.

ACT ONE

AT RISE: DR. JIM TENNYSON, *a likeable-looking young man in a topcoat, is bugging* BEA SCHMIDT, *a middle-aged woman wearing a sweater over a white uniform. They are in the office near the foyer. Late-afternoon sunlight pours through the* LEFT *window, shafting horizontally across the office. A suitcase stands by the front door.* DORA LUDLOW, *an elderly woman in a house-dress, hurries in from the kitchen.*

JIM	BEA
You haven't changed a bit! Not a hair, Bea! You look exactly the same!	Look at you! Just look at you! I wouldn't have known you! I swear I wouldn't have!

DORA

Jim? Is he here? Jim?

JIM

Dora!

DORA

Oh my land.

BEA

Look at him!

(JIM *relinquishes* BEA *and hugs* DORA. BEA *digs in her pocket, teary-eyed.*)

DORA	JIM	BEA
What a big tall handsome *man* you are.	Dora! Oh, it's so good to see you again!	Oh, I never saw such a change in a person . . .

(ELIAS HART, *a middle aged man in work clothes, enters* LEFT *and comes through the waiting room.*)

DORA

Wait till Doc sees you! He's just going to pop with pride!

JIM

Is he in?

BEA

(*Wiping her eyes with a handkerchief.*)

He's in South Green. Oh, and he wanted to *be* here!

JIM

The plane was early into Burlington, so I got the one o'clock bus. What are you *crying* for?

BEA

I can't *help* it!

JIM

Elias!

ELIAS

Hello, Jim. I saw you crossing the road.

JIM

(*Going to him and taking his hand.*)

How *are* you?

ELIAS

Fine, thanks.

JIM

Congratulations! Doc wrote me!

DORA

I'm going to cry too.

ELIAS

Oh, it's nothing important.

JIM

What do you mean? Town constable is tremendously important! You're the force of law and order, aren't you?

ELIAS

Say, we have to call *you* Doc now too. He's Doc now too.

JIM

Don't you dare! Doc is Doc. I'm Jim, that's all.

ELIAS

A bigger and finer-looking Jim than set out from here, that's for sure.

JIM

(*Looks about, at* ELIAS *smiling, at* BEA *and* DORA *wiping their eyes.*)

Well. It's a pleasure to be back in Vermont, where everyone is so cold and unemotional.

(*They all smile.* BEA *and* DORA *pocket their handkerchiefs.*)

BEA

Take your coat off.

ELIAS

How long are you here for?

JIM

Just the weekend.

BEA AND DORA

Ahh, no . . .

JIM

I have to be back in Chicago Tuesday morning.

(BEA *takes his coat.*)

DORA

There's a party for you tomorrow night.

JIM

I know.

BEA

Ray and Jean Higley.

JIM

I know. I stopped off at the cemetery and Essie Bullit was there; she told me all about it.

DORA

(*Taking the coat from* BEA.)

Here, I'll hang it up. Would you like some coffee?

JIM

I'd love some.

DORA

Bea? Elias?

BEA

Yes. Please.

ELIAS

None for me, thanks. I'm in the middle of moving some azaleas. I have to go right out again.

(DORA *goes into the foyer.*)

JIM

I'm surprised that you're still gardening.

ELIAS

Only for Doc, none of the others. Whenever I have an hour or two I stop by. We're getting to be famous; look at that *Flower and Garden* there.

(DORA, *having hung* JIM*'s coat on a rack by the front door, exits to the kitchen.*)

JIM

Doc sent me a copy when it came out. It's great.

ELIAS

Vermont Life took some pictures too, but they haven't used them yet.

BEA

People have been coming just to see. We had a whole group from Fitchburg, Mass.

JIM

Really?

(*Moves* LEFT, *looking out the window.*)

ELIAS

Now it's nothing. You should have been here last month; pom-poms and crocuses all around behind the birches there . . .

JIM

I wish I *could* have been here.

ELIAS

(*Moving to the rear door.*)

I'll see you later, all right?

JIM

Right. How's *Mrs.* Hart?

ELIAS

Fine. She ran into Earl Booth's delivery truck last winter, but Doc fixed her up good as new. Better than Rudy fixed the Jeep, anyway.

(*He exits.* JIM *and* BEA *smile at each other.*)

JIM

How's *your* family?

BEA

Fine. You'll see them all tomorrow night. May is pregnant.

JIM

Wonderful! When is she due?

BEA

In January.

JIM

That's great!

(*He moves back toward the* CENTER *of the office.* BEA *follows along.*)

BEA

Was it as hard as they say it is, your internship?

JIM

Mmm, no, not really. I'm glad it's over with, though.

(*Looks about.*)

Oh, it's really something to be here again, and to look at Doc's books—which always seemed to me to be about on a par with the sacred secret tablets of God—to look at them and to think, "Glory be, I know what's in them!" When I left, all I knew was where the naked women were.

(*Goes and puts his finger on the right books.*)

There's one in here, on page two-hundred-and-something . . .

and there's a *great* one in here. Has her legs WI-I-I-IDE open!

BEA

You've been in Chicago, all right.

JIM

That was right back here in little old Greenfield Center. Behind all the gee-Doc-can-I-carry-your-bag-for-you. I was really Dirty Jimmy, the young picture-looker-atter.

BEA

You sure fooled me.

JIM

Say, that elementary school is *beautiful!*

BEA

You saw it?

JIM

You can't very well miss it. Good Lord! Davistown must be green with envy. Was somebody being sarcastic, naming it for Lloyd Zachary?

BEA

No, that was Doc's idea.

(*The telephone rings.* BEA *goes to reception desk.*)

He said we should forgive the old buzzard.

JIM

Leave it to Doc.

BEA

Dr. Cook's.

(DORA *enters* UPSTAGE LEFT *with three mugs of coffee.* JIM *goes to take one.*

JIM

Hey, those yellow mugs.

DORA

The last three. I put in cream and sugar; is that okay?

BEA

Hi, Helen. Oh, *good.* I will; he'll be glad to hear it. Yes, I think you should. At least till tomorrow.

JIM

Perfect.

(DORA *brings a mug to* BEA.)

BEA

He's here now. He's six-foot-two and so handsome you could die.

(JIM *shies and winces.*)

I will, dear. Good-by.

(*Hangs up.*)

Helen Scoville says you're to drop by.

JIM

I'm six-foot-one.

DORA

(*Sitting* RIGHT *with her mug.*)

How's Pete?

BEA

All better.

DORA

Thank the Lord.

JIM

What was wrong with him?

BEA

A stomach ache, but Doc was afraid it might be hepatitis.

DORA

Thank the good Lord it's not.

(JIM *sits, they all sip their coffee.*)

JIM

Well? Who's married and who's dead?

DORA

Oh, where to begin, where to begin . . .

BEA

You know about Fran Scudder and Bobby Arvold . . .

JIM

Mm-hmm.

DORA

Alice Hart and Roy Bullit?

JIM

Married or dead?

DORA

Married! They've got two little girls already!

JIM

My God, they *hated* each other!

BEA

Carol Zachary and Ab Sanford—

JIM

No.

DORA

And *Jean* Sanford and Charley Rausch—

JIM

No!

DORA	BEA
Oh, yes.	That's right.

JIM

What happened to Barbara Barnum?

DORA	BEA
Moved away to New York.	She went to New York.

JIM

And Barbara Rousseau?

(*A pause.*)

BEA

She's married to Perry Booth. They had a little girl that was—mentally retarded, but she died. The summer before last. Now Barbara's pregnant again, and worried to death, poor thing.

DORA

Dick Scudder is in Washington, in the Health, Education, and Welfare Department.

JIM

Great.

DORA

The Lick boys and George Rousseau are in Vietnam.

BEA

And Ray Allbright.

JIM

That many?

DORA

Jim Rausch is a prisoner.

JIM

Oh God.

BEA

And who's dead: there's—

DORA

Darryl Maxim—

BEA

Yes, and—

JIM

Who? Darryl who?

DORA

Darryl Maxim; the constable before Elias.

JIM

I didn't know him. Ted Ruth senior was constable when I left.

DORA

And *he* died and then it was Darryl Maxim.

BEA

From Hart Mills.

DORA

Lloyd Zachary's dead and got the new school named for him.

JIM

I know; I thought I was seeing things.

BEA

George Suggs.

JIM

Old Man Beecher must be gone.

BEA

No, he isn't; he's a hundred and eight years old!

DORA

And walks as smart as a rooster—at least when he knows you're watching him.

BEA

The births and the moving-ins have kept ahead of the deaths and the moving-aways, and we're up to fourteen hundred and forty-four.

DORA

Forty-five when Mrs. John Forrest has her baby. She's a week late.

JIM

And still the same contentment everywhere. I felt it the minute I stepped off the bus.

DORA

We're blessed, although what we've done to deserve it is more than I can see.

BEA

I was talking to Ruth Scudder the other day and she said that Ann Fletcher is—

(DR. LEONARD COOK *enters* LEFT. *He is near seventy, energetic and pre-occupied, wearing a car coat over a wool shirt and taking off a peaked cap. He is almost at his desk before he becomes aware of the women and* JIM. JIM *smiles.* DOC *stares at him, automatically putting his bag on the corner of the desk.*)

DOC

Jimmy . . . !

JIM

Hello, Doc.

(DOC *smiles, then beams. He goes to* JIM, *looks him up and down, and takes his outstretched hand with a joy beyond words. He pokes* JIM*'s shoulder and then, overwhelmed, embraces him.* DORA *rises.* DOC *draws back and looks again at* JIM, *shaking his head marvelingly.*)

DOC

My God, my God!

JIM

The plane was early, so I got the one o'clock bus.

DOC

(*To* DORA.)

Will you look at him?

JIM

Look at you; you look wonderful.

DOC

(*Taking off his coat.*)

Dr. Tennyson!

JIM

(*Smiling, bowing his head.*)

At your service, Dr. Cook.

BEA

We're having a coffee clatch.

DORA

(*Reaching for* DOC*'s cap and coat.*)

Would you like a cup?

DOC

No, I had some with Jack Brenner. Oh thanks, thank you, Dora.

JIM

They're filling me in on all the vital statistics.

(DORA *goes to the foyer coat rack.* DOC *takes another look at* JIM.)

DOC

Your mother would have been so proud of you, Jimmy. And your father too, of course; he would have been too. How long are you staying?

JIM

I have to be in Chicago Tuesday morning.

DOC

Tuesday? Why, that's no visit, just a weekend; how are you going to see everybody? You stay longer, stay the week!

JIM

I wish I could, Doc, but I can't.

DOC

Did they tell you about the party tomorrow night?

(JIM *nods.*)

And Mary Broom and the Reverend want you for Sunday dinner.

DORA

(*Taking* JIM*'s mug.*)

You won't *know* the inside of the church; carpet, new pews; was the new organ while you were here?

JIM

Sure it was.

DOC

(*To* BEA.)

How many are waiting?

(DORA *takes* BEA*'s mug.*)

BEA

Not a one. I put everybody off till tomorrow and Monday, so you could be free for Jim.

DOC

Good. That's wonderful.

(*To* DORA.)

You made up the bed, didn't you?

DORA

Yes, and I'm setting the table too. The *table*, not the desk.

(*To* JIM.)

You see that he feeds you at the table tonight.

JIM

I'll do what I can.

DORA

Tomorrow morning I want to see *spots* on the tablecloth.

(*Exits to the kitchen.*)

BEA

Helen Scoville just called.

DOC

She did?

BEA

Pete's stomach ache is completely gone.

DOC

That's a relief.

(*To* JIM.)

It looked a little like hepatitis. With the one central school that could be terrible.

JIM

At least the old schools kept us in three separate bunches.

BEA

That's the only good thing you can say for them.

DOC

(*Taking a long printed form from his desk.*)

What's this, Bea?

BEA

I filled it in; you just have to sign.

DOC

(*Looking it over.*)

Damn insurance companies . . .

JIM

I *saw* the school; it's beautiful.

DOC

(*Taking out his pen and signing the form.*)

It's worth all the fights and maneuvering. I'll show you the inside of it tomorrow.

(*Giving the form to* BEA.)

Mary Ann Forrest didn't call?

BEA

No.

DOC

(*Sitting at the desk.*)

I'll be with you in one minute, Jim. I just want to get my notes down while they're fresh in my mind.

JIM

Sure, go ahead.

DOC

Put these over there, will you?

(*He gives* JIM *two or three 5x7 file cards.*)

JIM

Sure.

BEA

(*About to go out, turns.*)

I'll file them.

JIM

It's all right, I remember the system.

(DOC *takes another card from a file drawer,* BEA *goes into the waiting room,* JIM *begins filing the cards.* DOC *writes,* BEA, *sitting at the reception desk, folds the form and puts it into an envelope,* JIM *files.*)

DOC

(*While he writes.*)

Always get your notes down the first chance you get. The next chance may not come until God-knows-when.

JIM

(*Smiles tolerantly at him.*)

That's good advice, Doc.

(DOC *replaces the card, selects another one, and writes more.* JIM *speaks softly.*)

Shall I bring in some firewood for you?

DOC

No, you go on home now, Jimmy. Your mother's going to give me holy hell as it is.

(DOC *goes on writing,* JIM *grins, and then* DOC *realizes he's been had. He covers his eyes and groans, then laughs with* JIM.)

I walked into *that* one all right, didn't I?

JIM

You sure did.

DOC

You're a tricky young fellow!

JIM

You're an easy fellow to trick!

DOC

I'm almost done now.

JIM

That's all right, go ahead. It's nice to look at everything again.

(DOC *resumes writing.* JIM *browses, looks toward* LEFT *window.*)

That's not bad, having the town constable for your gardener.

DOC

Is he here now?

JIM

Yes.

DOC

(*Finished, re-filing the last card and closing his pen.*)

Good; I've got a sack of Darwin tulips that should have gone in days ago. Is that what he's doing, planting bulbs?

JIM

He's transplanting azaleas.

DOC

(*Rising, going* LEFT.)

I hope he puts the bulbs in . . .

(JIM *steps back,* DOC *goes to the window and looks out.*)

Mm, yes, I can see where—good. Yes, before I put him up to the other selectmen—

(*Turning to* JIM.)

—I made him promise that come what may he'd go right on taking care of the garden. Green all ten fingers, that's what Elias has.

(*Pointing at the* Flower and Garden *cover as he goes back to the desk.*)

That cover is his doing, not mine.

JIM

You're the one who plans everything.

DOC

(*Sitting, calling.*)

Bea! Go on home!

BEA

(*Looking up from writing, calling back.*)

And help with the cooking? No, thanks, five on the dot is when I leave!

(DOC *swivels to face* JIM. *They exchange smiles.*)

DOC

Jim, Jimmy, Jimmy!

JIM

Hi, Doc.

DOC

It's about time you kept your word, you ungrateful son of a gun.

JIM

Every summer I planned to come and every summer there was a chance to earn some money or get half a year ahead. And then *after* school—

DOC

That's all right, that's all right. I know.

DOC

I know, I know. I'm glad you're here now. You can't *possibly* stay the week?

JIM

No, I can't. I wish I could; I'd forgotten what it's like here, how peaceful and serene everything is.

DOC

It's not completely idyllic, don't kid yourself. We had a terrible brush fire in South Green two weeks ago.

JIM

Mmm. In Chicago they've got things called "crime" and "violence" that—well, you wouldn't believe me if I told you.

DOC

(*A smile and a moment of silence.*)

You're all ready to set up shop?

JIM

Mm-hmm.

DOC

And you're definitely not going to specialize.

JIM

Definitely not.

DOC

It's a shame; a boy as good-looking as you could make a fortune in gynecology. Where do you stand with the draft?

JIM

I'm not sure; that's why I have to be in Chicago Tuesday morning. I've asked to be reclassified 4F because of my arm.

DOC

Has it been giving you any trouble?

JIM

No, it hasn't. I'm not completely convinced that we belong there—in Vietnam. That we're going to stop Communism or that we should even *try* to stop it by dropping bombs and shedding blood.

DOC

You would be doctoring, not dropping bombs.

JIM

I'd be cooperating, though, doing my bit to help . . .

(*He sits on the davenport and thinks,* DOC *watches him.*)

DOC

Do you want my old X-rays of your arm? Or a letter from me?

JIM

No, Doc, I came here to visit; I didn't come to get anything. The doctors at the hospital gave me enough X-rays to paper a room with.

DOC

(*Rising.*)

Take the original ones too; it's a good idea. I know the way draft boards think; I'm on one, don't forget.

(*Looks over a dozen accordion files stacked on bookshelves in an out-of-the-way corner.*)

JIM

I honestly don't think that it's necessary, Doc.

DOC

I've got enough of my boys getting shot at over there. Both of the Lick boys, Ray Allbright; Jim Rausch has been taken prisoner. There it is, R through Z. Can you reach this file for me?

JIM

(*Hopping up.*)

Sure thing.

DOC

The one in the corner, R through Z.

(JIM *gets it.*)

I *think* they're in here. Thank you. Mmh!

(*That at the sight of dust. He blows it from the top of the file.* JIM *brushes his hands.* DOC *puts the file on the nearest convenient resting place and unties it.*)

Where are you going to practice? Have you decided?

JIM

No, that's something else that's up in the air. After Tuesday, if I get the reclassification, I'll make up my mind. There's a girl who might have a say in the question too.

DOC

(*Looking up.*)

Is there?

JIM

(*Nodding.*)

We're about ready to take the plunge. This weekend apart is to help us make up our minds.

DOC

That's wonderful news!

JIM

(*Taking out his wallet.*)

Her name is Elizabeth Rodseth. She works at WBKB, a television station.

(DOC *brushes his hands and takes the snapshot* JIM *offers.*)

DOC

Oh, isn't she lovely! Isn't she a lovely looking girl! Is she an actress?

JIM

No, no; she does research for a news show. I knew her at Northwestern.

DOC

(*Returning the snapshot.*)

She's beautiful; don't you let her get away.

JIM

That's what she says.

(*Gets lost in the snapshot.*)

DOC

(*Waits, smiles, cues him.*)

And you haven't decided where you would settle . . .

JIM

I'm for staying right in Chicago, but Liz wants to get back to small-town life. She's from a place in Michigan that's even smaller than Greenfield.

(*He puts the snapshot back in his wallet.* DOC *resumes looking through the file.*)

I'd hate having to drive as far to a hospital as you do, though, and I want plenty of other doctors around, for consultations and just to talk with.

(*Puts away his wallet.*)

DOC

Here they are.

(*He draws two X-ray pictures from the file, glances at them against the light, and passes them to* JIM. JIM *holds one up, looks at it, and draws breath hissingly between his teeth.*)

JIM

Ooh! Poor little me. Whew! That bastard really clobbered me, didn't he.

(*Looks at the second picture.*)

It's funny to think I'm holding it with the same arm. Funny, hell; it's miraculous.

DOC

You were young.

JIM

I had a good doctor.

DOC

(*Smiling, gesturing for the pictures.*)

I'll put them in an envelope.

(JIM *gives* DOC *the pictures,* DOC *takes them to the desk, rummages among the papers there.*)

JIM

Shall I put this back on the shelf?

DOC

Would you, please?

JIM

Sure.

DOC

I felt the same way you do when I first came here.

JIM

(Tying the file.)

Then why did you come?

DOC

For a very good reason. I was starving. It was the middle of the Depression and doctors in the cities weren't making a nickel a week. Not the young ones, anyway.

(He finds an envelope and begins putting the picture into it. JIM *returns the file to its place on the shelf.)*

Greenfield had an ad in the *Journal*, and I figured that country people would at least pay with food if they couldn't pay with cash.

JIM

You were right about that.

DOC

I didn't look forward to being the only doctor, but after a while my feelings changed, and yours would too, Jimmy. I'd fight like hell now if someone else wanted to come near.

(Gives JIM *the closed envelope.)*

Having a whole town in your care is completely different from being a city doctor. You know each and every person in the place, know them better than anyone else does—

JIM

Better than the Reverend?

DOC

Sure, better than the Reverend! He knows the women, some of the kids; the men don't open up to him the way they do to me. He doesn't know *me*, but I know *him*. He's scared to death he's—well, I mustn't say. In the city your patients are—disconnected. You've got a man but not his wife, somebody else's friend, another man's sweetheart. All separate. But in a town like this, a one-doctor town, you've got them all—the wife, the husband, the friend; the sweethearts, the children—all of them tied together, all *involved* with each other. So *you* get involved. You find that you can't take vacations, because every day's a day one of them wants you, and that one is connected to six others, and those six connected to six *times* six.

JIM

It sounds even worse than I thought it was.

DOC

There are *rewards*, Jimmy, wonderful rewards! Looking into a classroom full of kids—a *greenhouse* full of opening flowers!—and you're the one who delivered every last one of them! And delivered most of their mothers and fathers too! Keeping up with what's new because you don't have specialists handy to lean on; studying, and knowing you're ahead of most other doctors. Preserving an Old Man Beecher—he's sound as a bell, would you believe it? Spotting a Dick Scudder, a Jim Tennyson, a Eunice Wilcox; seeing that they're encouraged, given room to spread and blossom . . .

(*A thought checks him.*)

Well, maybe it's not for you; you've got a girl and you'll have a family. Find your own answer, Chicago or someplace in-between size; don't be swayed by me. I hated all cities, if you want the truth. The noise and the people close around made me jumpy as a cat.

(*The telephone rings.* BEA *answers it and* DOC *goes quickly to his desk.*)

BEA

Dr. Cook's. Is it anything urgent? Because if it—

DOC

Hello? Yes. Who's this?

(BEA *hangs up with an air of "I tried."*)

Oh? Hm, that doesn't sound like Frank at all. Have you got him in bed?

(*He opens a file drawer, finds, takes out, and scans a card, listening as he does so.* JIM *watches him.*)

No, I don't think it would be that. Just a minute.

(*Covers the mouthpiece.*)

You want to unpack, don't you; make some phone calls?

JIM

Yes.

DOC

(*Into the phone again.*)

Sharon? It's quiet here now, so I'll come over and take a look at him.

(BEA *rises and comes to the waiting room doorway.*)

Of course it isn't. I'll be there in ten minutes.

(*Hangs up, puts down the card.*)

Frank Prugo. Hasn't been sick a day since June, 1939, when he had the measles. Threw up and has a-hundred-point-four.

JIM

Flu?

DOC

Maybe.

(Going to the coat rack.)

You make your phone calls. I'll be back in half an hour.

JIM

You know, Doc, there's one new thing in medicine that you haven't kept up with.

DOC

(Getting into his coat.)

What's that?

JIM

It's called Not Making So Many House Calls.

BEA

I've been telling him about that for fifteen years.

JIM

It works wonders. The doctor gains weight, his color improves . . .

DOC

(At the desk again, picking up his bag.)

While I'm on my way I'll think of something funny to say back to you. See you tomorrow, Bea.

BEA

Good night.

DOC

Tell her about your girl friend—Bob Hope.

(*He goes out.* JIM *takes out his wallet.* BEA *goes to him.*)

JIM

Her name is Elizabeth Rodseth—

BEA

And she's from a small town in Michigan; I know. Let me see.

JIM

Did you ever think of just cutting a little peephole?

(*Gives her the snapshot.*)

BEA

Oh, isn't she a beautiful girl! Congratulations.

JIM

Don't rush me.

(*Takes the snapshot and puts it back in his wallet.*)

BEA

Will you bring her here so we can meet her?

JIM

If we—

BEA

I'll bet she'd like it here!

JIM

(*Looking about, pocketing his wallet.*)

Yes, she would. I know she would.

BEA

(*A suppressed tension becoming evident.*)

Are you *sure* you don't want to live in a small town again? In *this* town?

JIM

What's wrong, Bea?

BEA

Doc isn't well. I think he's had a heart attack.

(*They are motionless for a moment.*)

JIM

When?

BEA

In August. He stayed in his room all one morning—said he was catching up on magazines—and when he came down in the afternoon he was gray, and so tired looking. That's why I wrote you and reminded you to come see us. He'll let *you* examine him, I'll bet, but he won't go *near* the new doctor in Davistown or Nat Crumley in Hardwick.

JIM

I'll do an EKG on him this evening.

BEA

Don't you let him talk you out of it.

JIM

I'll tie him down if I have to.

BEA

Good!

JIM

But if it *was* a coronary, Bea, all I can do is tell him to take it easy. You know how much good *that's* going to do.

BEA

He would take it easy if—you came in and shared the practice with him, and eventually took it over . . .

JIM

(*Shakes his head.*)

He doesn't want that. It's his town. He just said it; he'd fight if any other doctor tried to move in.

BEA

Not *you*. You're almost his son. He'd love to have you!

JIM

I'm not so sure. He'd have dropped a hint just now, or come right out and asked me. And it wouldn't be right; two doctors here, when there are towns around with none at all. I'll talk to him. Maybe I can get him to say no to a couple of his midnight calls. Even if it wasn't a coronary. It may not have been, you know.

BEA

I've been worrying about him so.

(*She turns a light on, for the room has grown shadowed.*)

I think of poor Darryl Maxim, who was young and in perfect health, and then I think of Doc. He's near seventy, Jim, and has this whole town on his shoulders!

JIM

He's a naturalized Vermonter by now; he'll live longer than Old Man Beecher, so stop worrying. Is that what Darryl Maxim died of, a coronary?

BEA

(*Nods.*)

Thirty-two years old.

JIM

Mmh. He must have had *something* wrong with him.

BEA

Nothing.

JIM

Really?

BEA

Look for yourself. So I *can't* stop worrying about a man twice as old who works twice as hard. Now listen, don't you get me in dutch with Doc.

(JIM *goes to a file drawer—not one that* DOC *looked into earlier—and opens it.*)

You make out as if I didn't say anything about anything, and taking an EKG is your own idea—because he doesn't look right to you.

JIM

(Flicking through the file cards.)

Okay.

BEA

I'd better check the ink and paper.

(goes UPSTAGE *and opens one of the sliding doors partway.)*

Do you think you can cope with our old antique?

(She slips into the examining room and turns the light on. JIM *draws a card from the file. An anatomy chart and the end of an examining table can be seen through the door.)*

JIM

The new ones aren't that different . . .

BEA

(Calling from within.)

I'm going to lay out the electrodes for you!

JIM

(Comes DOWNSTAGE, *studying the card, and after a moment calls to* BEA.*)*

What does R stand for?

BEA

(Off.)

What?

JIM

(Louder.)

What does R stand for?

BEA

(*Comes to the door.*)

R?

JIM

On Darryl Maxim's card. On the line before where the coronary is entered.

(BEA *comes* DOWNSTAGE; JIM *shows her the card.*)

BEA

I don't know. Doc has all his little symbols and abbreviations . . . the G's and the B are for Darryl's children, two girls and a boy. I don't know what the R is. You see how clean his card is?

JIM

You were right.

(*Going back to the open file.*)

I thought he might have had something in his childhood that affected his heart. It's funny he didn't.

BEA

(*Going back* UPSTAGE *to the door.*)

I laid out the electrodes but I didn't plug them in. So it wouldn't look too prepared in advance.

(*Reaching in, she turns the light off in the examining room.* JIM, *still holding* DARRYL MAXIM*'s card, is lifting out other cards, glancing at them, and tucking them back into the file.* BEA *closes the examining-room door.*)

I wish you'd think more about what I said, Jim; about coming in with Doc.

JIM

Here's another one with an R on it. Hannah Meserve.

BEA

Oh what a sour old woman that was. Sour and selfish. You wouldn't remember her, would you.

JIM

(*Studying the card, comparing it with* MAXIM*'s.*)

Mm-mmn.

BEA

The joke was that she should have been named "Hannah Serve-me" instead of "Hannah Me-*serve*." That was what everyone used to say. She was Essie Bullit's mother, and after her husband Howard died she moved in with Essie and Ben and made servants out of them; had them fetching and doing for her, Essie and Ben and all four kids.

(DORA *enters from the kitchen, carrying her coat and a paper bag.*)

She used to sit in the parlor all day long, playing bridge from a book against Ely Culbertson—this is Hannah Meserve—and all day long saying "Bring me this" and "Go and do that," slapping the children with this ivory back-scratcher she had.

DORA

(*Putting her coat and the bag on a chair.*)

Hannah Serve-me is what she *should* have been called, not Hannah Me-*serve*. It's five after.

BEA

Essie never *could* say boo to her, and Ben was too kind-hearted to send her packing. He got an ulcer, he was so upset.

DORA

Her funeral was remarkable in that it was so poorly attended.

(BEA *goes to the coat rack and gets her coat.* DORA, *sitting, directs a question to her.*)

Pneumonia it was, wasn't it?

BEA

That's right.

JIM

That's right. Preceded by R.

BEA

(*Coming back in, putting on her coat.*)

Ask Doc; he'll tell you what it means.

(JIM *puts the cards on the desk and helps* BEA *with her coat.*)

Thanks. I told Jim about Doc and he's going to check his heart.

DORA

And the other?

BEA

He's going to think about it. Aren't you? This is the finest little town in Vermont and you know it.

JIM

(*To* DORA.)

I like Chicago.

BEA

But his girl friend likes a small town. Show her the picture.

JIM

I think it's rubbed away by now.

(*Gets out the wallet and the snapshot.*)

BEA

You call me if you have any trouble with the cardiograph.

JIM

(*Giving the snapshot to* DORA.)

I will.

DORA

Oh, my!

BEA

Isn't she a beauty?

DORA

But sensible looking too. She'd fit in here perfectly.

BEA

(*To* JIM.)

Try to call me *after*, but don't let him hear you.

JIM

I'll try.

BEA

Good night, Dora.

DORA

(*Giving the snapshot back to* JIM.)

Good night. Tell May about the baby clothes.

BEA

Clean forgot! Good night, Jim.

JIM

Good night. See you in the morning.

BEA

You'd better give Ray and Jean a call.

JIM

I'm going to.

(BEA *exits* LEFT. JIM *puts the snapshot away.*)

DORA

Congratulations.

JIM

Don't rush me.

DORA

You can make your call if you want. Marshall picks me up at ten after—

(*Gesturing* LEFT.)

—in front of Elias's. He's working up at the asbestos mill now.

JIM

Is he?

DORA

They're running two shifts, because of the space race.

JIM

You mean asbestos from Greenfield is used in the rockets?

DORA

In the gantries; there was a big story in the *Courier*. And we're getting a little plant that's going to make transistors too, on the other side of Hart Mills on Route Fourteen.

JIM

The town is waxing wealthy.

DORA

Yes, Jim, that's right. I don't know what you'll find in Chicago that you won't find here.

JIM

Well, hospitals and other doctors, and theatres, restaurants, museums, libraries, department stores—

DORA

I'll tell you *one* thing you won't find there—happier people.

JIM

No, I won't; I know. I've never been anywhere else where life seemed so good and satisfying.

DORA

We're blessed. It's as simple as that. Even Davistown, Hardwick, Morrisville, they don't have the good fortune we do. Oh, I know, you were no choirboy to begin with and you're probably an all-out heathen by now, but God has smiled on this town and given it His special love and protection; I know that for a fact. The Legion picnic in 1962; three hundred and fifty of us could have perished that day—that's how many of the sandwiches there were—but we all came through with only upset stomachs, and the one who did die, the only one, was Lloyd Zachary. Now don't you think God had a hand in that someplace?

JIM

No, I don't.

DORA

We'd still have the three one-room schools if Lloyd hadn't died, and be fighting in the courts the way Davistown is. God watches this town, and when He takes, He takes for a reason. Like Hannah Meserve we were talking about, spreading un-happiness all around her.

JIM

What about Darryl Maxim?

DORA

I don't say the reason's always crystal-clear to human eyes. Darryl, your mother, Laura Scoville . . . who can say why? But more often than not you can say why; even with the little ones, where it's almost always the ones that have something wrong with them—humpbacked, like the McClure baby, or not all there, like Perry and Barbara Booth's.

(*She finds a loose button on her dress and winds the thread around it.* JIM *watches her, motionless, held by thought.*)

I had this same talk with Darryl, just a day or two before he died. He stopped by here. Right around this time of day it was.

JIM

What was wrong with him?

DORA

Nothing, he just wanted to talk to Doc. And Bea was gone and Doc was out and I was waiting for Marshall. And we talked about God's judgment on each of us—the Reverend had preached about it that Sunday in honor of Old Man Beecher's birthday.

(JIM *goes back to the file.*)

And Darryl said it was wonderful that nice people like Livvy Sawyer and Old Man Beecher lived to such ripe old ages . . .

(JIM *takes a card out,* DORA *watches him.*)

. . . and mean people, like George Suggs who had died a few weeks before . . . is that Darryl's card?

JIM

(*Studying it.*)

Lloyd Zachary's.

(*Picks up the other two cards from the desk, looks at* DORA.)

Go ahead, I'm listening.

DORA

Well . . . that's all. I talked with Darryl the way we're talking now.

JIM

Did *he* look at any of these cards?

DORA

No. Why should he? He wouldn't have understood them even if he had. He asked me if there'd always been—nobody seriously impaired in the town, and I said no, long ago there'd been Anne Arkham, who was blind, and Sax Rousseau and a few others, but they'd all died or been cured or moved away, like Anne did. That's all. And then Doc came back and I went out. And I'd better be going out now.

(*Rises and begins putting on her coat.*)

JIM

When I came to Chicago, I was—surprised to see blind people, and mute people finger-talking, people with an arm or a leg missing; I knew they existed, of course, but I was—surprised at the sight of them . . .

DORA

It's what I said; we're blessed. Vermont is the most favored state in the Union, and we're the most favored town in Vermont. The Lord takes good care of us.

(*Picks up her bag.*)

Now look, that table is all set in there, so don't you let Doc eat in here. The world won't come to an end if he's not right next to the telephone; you tell him I said so.

JIM

All right.

DORA

There's lamb stew and chocolate cream pie. I hope you enjoy it.

JIM

I will.

DORA

Good night.

JIM

Good night, Dora.

DORA

(*Takes a final loving look at him.*)

My, you've grown up nicely.

(*She exits* LEFT. JIM *stands looking after her for a moment, then moves to the desk. He turns the desk lamp on—it has grown quite dark outside—and sits down in* DOC*'s chair. He looks at the three cards in his hand, studies them intently, takes down one of* DOC*'s medical books.* ELIAS *enters* LEFT. *and comes softly through the waiting room, he looks in.*)

ELIAS

Doc?

JIM

(*Turning.*)

It's me.

ELIAS

Oh. I thought you were Doc, sitting there with the cards in your hand.

JIM

He's out on a call. He should be back—in a few minutes.

ELIAS

Will you give him a message for me?

JIM

Sure.

ELIAS

(*Coming into the room.*)

Tell him it got dark before I could take out the yew tree but I'll come by and do it tomorrow afternoon. All right?

JIM

I'll tell him.

ELIAS

Thank you.

JIM

How do you like being constable, Elias?

ELIAS

Fine. There's nothing to it, really. When the kids have a dance I make sure there's no alcohol, and when Iz Rausch and his wife start throwing dishes I go quiet them down. Any real trouble, I call the State Police. There never is any, though.

JIM

(*Rising.*)

No sin or crime in Greenfield Town.

ELIAS

Not with George Rousseau in the Army, there isn't.

JIM

And George Suggs dead.

ELIAS

Yes.

JIM

What do you do when somebody dies?

ELIAS

Do?

JIM

As constable.

ELIAS

(*Shrugs.*)

Nothing. Doc makes out a certificate and gives it to Evalyn. Evalyn Ruth. She's the clerk now.

JIM

What if it's a—suspicious death?

ELIAS

Well . . . Doc is the regional medical examiner, so he would report it to the state pathologist. In Montpelier. There's never been a suspicious death though; Doc always knows what people die of.

JIM

Yes. Of course.

ELIAS

The truth is I'm getting paid for doing next to nothing. Only don't say I said so.

JIM

I won't.

ELIAS

Don't forget to tell Doc about the yew tree, because otherwise he's going to see it there in the morning and think the sticker fell off and go all the way out to put on another one.

JIM

The sticker?

ELIAS

That's how he tells me what to do, now that I don't come in on regular days any more. He has these little orange stickers—they glow, sort of—and he takes them in his pocket whenever he goes out in the garden. Anything he wants me to do, he just puts a sticker on the plant or whatever and marks it; P for prune, T for transplant, and so on. We have a whole code he worked out. That way, I can find something to do any time I come by, even if he's out, or busy with someone and can't speak to me.

(*Backs* LEFT *to go.*)

When you're through eating why don't you come over and say hello to Helen? She's looking forward to seeing you.

JIM

Maybe I will . . .

ELIAS

Try to. We've got a color television.

(*He turns and goes.* JIM *glances at the cards in his hand and looks up again.*)

JIM

What does R stand for, Elias?

ELIAS

(*Stops and turns.*)

Remove. Did you see one of the stickers on your way in?

(JIM *stands motionless.*)

Jim?

(JIM *looks at him.*)
Did you see one of the stickers on your way in?

JIM

(*Nods.*)
Yes.

ELIAS

There's not a weed or a dead branch or a hurt plant that Doc doesn't notice it and see that it's put right, either by him or by me. That's what keeps the garden so perfect all the time. (*He exits* LEFT. JIM *sits and puts a hand over his eyes.)*

THE CURTAIN FALLS

ACT TWO

AT RISE: *Ten minutes later.* JIM *is standing at* RIGHT *watching intently as* DOC *lets himself in at the door* LEFT. JIM *has put back the cards* HE *took from the file and closed it. His suitcase is where it was.* HE *has been pacing and stewing.*

DOC

Hi.

JIM

(*Gathers himself.*)

Hello.

DOC

(*Going to the desk and putting down his bag.*)

I stopped in at the Hopwoods', right across from Frank Prugo. Their baby has God-awful eczema.

(*Taking off his coat.*)

You were right about Frank's flu, but it's good I went anyway. Sharon looks terrible; she's lost over ten pounds in the last two months and she was underweight to begin with. I made her promise to come in Monday or Tuesday.

(*On the way to the coat rack he sees the suitcase.*)

Haven't you unpacked yet?

JIM

No.

DOC

(Hanging up his coat and cap.)

Did you make your calls?

JIM

No.

*(*DOC *turns and looks questioningly at him.)*

I was talking with Bea and Dora. And Elias.

DOC

He's gone?

JIM

Yes. They're all gone.

*(*DOC *returns to the desk.)*

He said he'll come over tomorrow and—take out the yew tree. It got too dark.

DOC

(Sitting.)

Mm.

JIM

He didn't want you to go out and put another sticker on it.

DOC

(Looking at a slip of paper.)

Ann Zachary?

JIM

She called just a few minutes ago.

DOC

(*Picking up the phone.*)

Did she say what for?

JIM

No.

DOC

(*Jiggles the crossbar.*)

Zenia? Oh? What are *you* doing on the board at this hour? Oh. Ring Ann Zachary for me, will you? Thanks.

(*To* JIM.)

Would you turn that lamp on, please, Jim?

(JIM *goes silently* RIGHT.)

Hello, Ann? Yes.

(JIM *turns another lamp on, then stands watching* DOC, *who is searching the desktop for Frank Prugo's card while he listens.*)

Oh sure, that's perfectly all right. Anything she wants, at this point. No, no, whatever she wants. I only meant that for the first three days. You can give her anything she asks for. Good, that's fine. I'll stop in sometime during the weekend. Good-by, dear.

(*Hangs up, uncaps his pen, and begins writing on Prugo's card.*)

I'll be with you in a minute. I want to get my notes down while they're fresh in my mind.

JIM

Go ahead.

(DOC *writes,* JIM *watches him.*)

DOC

(*Exchanging cards.*)

Why don't you unpack now?

JIM

I will. In a minute.

(DOC *writes again.* JIM *moves* LEFT. *a wary, watchful crossing.*)

I was looking at—some of your records.

DOC

Mm?

JIM

(*Takes a deep breath.*)

Some of your—abbreviations and symbols are—hard to figure out.

(*An amused, self-satisfied grunt from* DOC.)

What does—R stand for?

(DOC *goes on writing. After a moment:*)

DOC

R?

JIM

That's right.

DOC

(*Writes more.*)

It's hard to say, right off. That's one I haven't used in quite a while. I have so many of them.

(*Turns farther away from Jim to file the card he was writing on.*)

JIM

You used it on Darryl Maxim's card. In July.

DOC

Did I?

JIM

And George Suggs's, not long before.

DOC

Rest. It means I told them to rest.

(*Rises, smiling at* JIM.)

I have so damn many of those little short cuts that I—

JIM

It's on Susanna Booth's card too. She was twenty-two months old and mentally retarded. Did you tell *her* to rest?

DOC

It means something else in relation to children. It means *repeat*—a treatment or prescription that I gave before.

(*Going to* JIM *with a laugh, clapping him on the shoulder.*)

Listen, forget about my damn records, will you? I ought to move half of 'em out to the garage and have some room in here! Listen, Jim. Listen, you go up and unpack your suitcase, okay? And I'll go in and see what Dora made for us, and we'll eat, and then—I'll share you with Ray and Jean, and Mary and the Reverend. Everyone is so anxious to see you, Jim. This town's been talking about nothing else for two whole weeks! Now you go on, okay? Go on up and unpack.

(*He starts* JIM LEFT. JIM *crosses from him slowly, unwillingly.*)

Say, do you know what I've got? A bottle of very fine wine that Earl Booth gave to Jack Brenner and Jack Brenner gave to me. Last Christmas. The only problem now is going to be finding it.

(JIM *stops near the doorway to the foyer and turns around and faces* DOC.)

Dora probably put it God-knows-where. I'll find it though. I can't think of a better occasion for opening it.

(JIM *stands looking at him in pained indecision.*)

What is it, Jim? What's wrong?

JIM

Doc . . .

DOC

Yes?

JIM

This may sound awfully crazy, but do you know what I think R stands for?

DOC

I *told* you what it stands for, Jim; rest or repeat. Now what are you going on about it for?

JIM

I think it stands for—remove.

(*A pause.*)

DOC

Well it does. In the garden. But—not in here. That *does* sound crazy, Jim. Remove? Why would I put "remove" on somebody's record? You remove—*plants*, you don't remove people! Not that I wouldn't like to once in a while, believe me!

(*With a laugh he moves away from* JIM. JIM *takes a step after him, pointing at the drug cabinet.*)

JIM

The poison on that bottom shelf; you've got more than Cokely Memorial has with six floors and an annex.

DOC

(*Turning sharply.*)

Were you in that cabinet?

JIM

I looked through the glass. I read the Latin now. Doc?

DOC

(*A pause, a nod.*)

Yes, I've got more poison than you'd expect. I don't get fresh supplies every day or two, the way your hospital does. I've got more bandages than you'd expect too, in the closet in there. I've got six gallons of Zephiran sitting out in the garage. This isn't the heart of Chicago; this is a little town that's snowbound more winters than not.

JIM

Kinds of poison, Doc. You've got things there's no reason to have.

DOC

(*A pause, then he laughs at* JIM *and points at him.*)

You've been working too hard, that's what's going on here! Studying for your tests after a year of interning. Rest is what *you* need. R, for rest. Shall I get your card out and mark it on it?

(*He laughs,* JIM *doesn't.*)

JIM

Doc . . . have you killed anybody?

DOC

It wouldn't surprise me; you've seen me on Saturday mornings, getting them in and out in ten seconds.

JIM

Intentionally! I mean intentionally.

DOC

No, Jim. No, I haven't. I haven't "removed" anybody.

(*A pause.*)

JIM

(*Gesturing at the cabinet.*)

What do you need with mercuric chloride?

DOC

I used to use it for a disinfectant. I still do sometimes. I'm set in my ways.

(JIM *turns and moves away, uncertain, then turns to* DOC *again.*)

JIM

Dora thinks the town is blessed, because the right people die. Lloyd Zachary, George Suggs . . .

DOC

The Reverend thinks that too. He's so complacent about God's love that it makes you wish for an earthquake.

JIM

But the right people *do* die.

DOC

So do the wrong people, like anywhere else.

JIM

There's nobody blind, nobody crippled.

DOC

It's a small town, with good Vermont stock.

(*Goes to* JIM *and claps him fondly on the shoulder, laughing.*)

Jimmy, Jimmy . . . I suppose I ought to be offended, being accused of killing off my patients, but I honestly can't bring myself to believe you mean what you're saying. How did you— get such an idea?

JIM

(*Not yet won over but wanting to be.*)

I saw the R on some of the cards, and talking with Dora I realized they were people who—*should* have died. Except Darryl Maxim. And then Elias mentioned what R stood for.

DOC

In the garden.

JIM

In the garden . . .

DOC

(*Nods, smiles.*)

Did Elias mention what T stands for?

JIM

Transplant?

DOC

That's right. And you'll find a lot of cards with T on them in the files, but none of my patients, to my knowledge, has ever been "transplanted." A lot of them, though, have been given tetanus shots.

(*Pushes* JIM *on his way, smiling.*)

Now take your things upstairs and get ready for dinner.

JIM

Why did you tell Darryl Maxim to rest when he was in perfect health?

(*A pause.*)

DOC

In a minute I *am* going to get offended, Jimmy. Go on upstairs.

JIM

I'm not Jimmy any more, I'm another doctor. Questions have been raised in my mind, and unless you can satisfy me that you're answering them truthfully, I'm—duty-bound to take them to—someone else.

DOC

"Duty-bound" . . .

JIM

Yes.

DOC

You really *are* twenty-seven years old, aren't you.

(*Another clap on the shoulder.*)

All right, Dr. Tennyson, just let me refresh my memory a bit.

(*Going to the file.*)

I can't remember everyone's history, as much as I'd like to. Maxim . . .

(JIM *watches as* DOC *finds the card, takes it out, and comes* DOWNSTAGE *studying it. After a moment:*)

Let's see now . . . yes, I remember how it was. He came in and said he'd had a couple of dizzy spells. He hadn't told his wife because he didn't want to worry her. He hadn't told anyone else either. I gave him a quick check-over, which was negative, and he was going to call the next day and make an appointment for a full examination. He had to see when his next free time would be. In the meantime I told him to take things as easy as he could.

(*Turns the card toward* JIM.)

To rest. July twelfth, that was.

JIM

You didn't enter anything about the dizzy spells or the negative check-over.

DOC

It would have all been in the notes on the full examination. He didn't make the appointment, though, and two days later, on the fourteenth, he died.

JIM

Why didn't you give him a full examination when you had him here?

DOC

I couldn't; the waiting room was jam-packed. It would have taken over an hour. Are you satisfied?

JIM

No. I'm not. Dora said he came after office hours. Just around this time.

(*The telephone rings.* DOC *backs to it, his eyes staying locked with* JIM*'s. The telephone rings again.* DOC *picks up the receiver.*)

DOC

Yes? Yes. Is he in pain? No, not if he can walk on it. Just pack some ice around it and if it doesn't look any better in the morning, bring him in and I'll take an X-ray. Twenty minutes, half an hour. No, no, you didn't. Good-by.

(*Hangs up. A pause.*)

That's right. I'd forgotten. He came after hours and I didn't give him the full examination because I wanted to have Bea here to help with the tests.

(*A pause.*)

JIM

Doc, please, level with me.

DOC

I *am* leveling with you.

JIM

(*Shakes his head.*)

It doesn't *feel* that way.

DOC

Look, you of all people ought to believe me when I tell you something! And not—quiz me this way, cross-examine me as if I were—you had no business going into my files in the first place! That's a god-damn unprofessional thing to do!

JIM

I know, I know it is; I wish I hadn't.

DOC

Well . . . let's let—bygones be bygones, and forget all this—crap. And have the nice visit we were planning to have; what do you say, Jimmy?

JIM

How can we?

DOC

What do you mean?

(JIM *looks at him wordlessly, then turns and goes* LEFT *to the foyer.*)

Where are you going?

JIM

(*Gets his coat from the rack and turns, putting it on.*)

Over to Elias's. I'm going to call—I don't know, the state police or the medical board or somebody; I don't know who.

DOC

You're going to make a fool of yourself.

JIM

I hope so.

DOC

You're going to get into trouble; I can promise you that! I'm not going to let anyone smear my name and get away with it, not even you!

(JIM *picks up his suitcase and starts to go.* DOC *tries to maintain his show of anger but it cracks and goes and leaves him defenseless.*)

Wait, wait. Wait a minute. All right. All right, come on back, Jim. Come on. Put it down. All right, I'll—level with you. Come on back.

(*He backs* RIGHT, *gesturing appeasingly for* JIM *to follow.* JIM, *having turned, stands watching him.*)

Come on. Put it down. I'll level with you.

(*Sits on a hassock or low stool* DOWNSTAGE RIGHT.)

Come on.

(*He rests his face in his hand for a moment,* JIM *slowly lowers his suitcase and stands feet-astride in the doorway, staring at* DOC *at a loss for understanding.* DOC *lowers his hand, looks at* JIM, *and looks away.*)

JIM

You've—killed people?

DOC

(*Nods.*)

It's—what I told you before, about getting involved, caring what happens. When a Lloyd Zachary or a George Suggs is doing harm to the town—

JIM

There are *lawful ways of dealing with him.*

DOC

Twenty years we tried to deal lawfully with Lloyd Zachary!—tried to break up his bunch of tightwads and know-nothings and get ourselves a decent school! Twenty years! And every year a different legal maneuver up that frayed sleeve of his. So five hundred kids, and you're one of them, got less education than they should have, and had to work harder for what little they got. I gave him every chance to square himself—pleaded publicly with him at meetings and privately here in this office; didn't make my mind up finally till 1961! And who misses him? Nobody. Not a damn soul.

JIM

What did you use?

DOC

I don't remember now. What difference does it make?

JIM

(*Moves a step closer to* DOC.)

Did you give Susanna Booth a chance to square herself?

DOC

Oh Jimmy, that was a vegetable, not a child! She ate what was put in her mouth and went to sleep when she was put down. She didn't react or respond or even lift a hand of her own volition. And poor Barbara dressed her up once a week and tied a ribbon in her vegetable hair and sat her in a stroller and wheeled her into Simms' and the Bluebell, just daring anyone to see something wrong. It was a cloud over the town for two years. Perry thanked God when she died, and so did the grandparents. Every one did, and Barbara's glad now too.

JIM

(*A pause.*)

Darryl Maxim caught on . . .

DOC

(*Nods gravely.*)

That was—hard. He was a fine person and my real friend. I'd have sooner cut off my arm if I'd had the choice. The Reverend preached a stupid sermon about God's account books—a few weeks after George Suggs died—and Darryl came here and questioned me . . .

(*He sits thinking, troubled,* JIM *moves another step closer to him.*)

JIM

How many, Doc? How many people have you—done it to?

DOC

(*Turns, looks at him.*)

How many people's lives have I saved; first ask me that.

JIM

It's not relevant.

DOC

Not relevant? Why isn't saving a life relevant if taking one is? Helen Hart smashed into Earl Booth's truck last winter and was almost torn in two. Any doctor with a brain in his head would have let her go, she was that close to the edge. Not me though, not on your tintype! Eight straight hours I worked on her, piecing her back together again; and now she's alive and doing things, giving Elias his dinner this very minute!

JIM

Saving one life doesn't—

DOC

Old Man Beecher had a CA of the intestine eight or nine years ago! Bea says, "Doc, what are you killing yourself for?" Well he's a hundred and eight years old now, and tall and strong, and it makes you feel majestic just to look at him. That's what I was killing myself for.

JIM

Saving one life doesn't give you the right to take another. God Almighty, Doc, you know that!

DOC

No. One thing I know, one thing only! This town is the *happiest* town, and the *healthiest* town, in the entire state of Vermont! Maybe in the entire country! Maybe in the entire *world!* Now you just stop and think about that for a minute; the happiest, healthiest town in the entire world! It very well may be!

JIM

Not for Lloyd Zachary and—

DOC

(On *his feet.*)

Lloyd Zachary gave up his right to be happy and healthy—

JIM

He *didn't!* He *didn't!*

DOC

—when he—he *did!*—when he deprived five hundred kids of a decent education!

JIM

That wasn't for you to decide!

DOC

Then who does decide if I don't? God and his account books?

(*He waits,* JIM *is momentarily checked.*)

Eh?

JIM

Nobody decides. You leave it to chance. Zachary was an ignorant bastard facing in the wrong direction but he was within his legal rights.

DOC

Tch!

(*He turns scornfully away and moves* UPSTAGE. JIM *takes a following step.*)

JIM

How many? How many altogether?

DOC

(*At his desk, muttering.*)

Go ahead, you keep quizzing me; this is really rich.

JIM

Zachary, Maxim, Susanna Booth, George Suggs, that Me-serve woman—how many others? Dora mentioned a baby with a hump-back.

DOC

Don't let anybody ever tell you that there's no such thing as poetic justice in the world.

JIM

What do you mean?

DOC

That's what this is, you poking away at me like this: poetic justice, only I don't know who's giving it and who's getting it.

JIM

I don't understand what you're talking about.

DOC

Don't ask me; I might tell you.

JIM

Are you going to tell me how many others?

DOC

No.

(*A pause.*)

JIM

Those poisons all leave traces. Everyone who died since you came here is going to be—disinterred and examined.

(*Turns and starts toward the foyer.*)

DOC

IT WAS YOU WHO STARTED IT!

(JIM *wheels.*)

You—righteous—twenty-seven-year-old—It was you who started it!

JIM

(*A baffled whisper.*)

What are you talking about?

DOC

Your arm! Your dripping mangled arm! And your mother, with the belt-buckle bruises on her stomach and her back! And your drunken hulk of a father!

(JIM *stares mutely.*)

What do you *think* he died of? *Your secret wishes?*

JIM

Cerebral hemorrhage . . .

DOC

He died of my bottom shelf! You—! And he was number one! The first! The beginning!

JIM

Oh Jesus no.

DOC

Oh Jesus yes!

(*He paces around, bringing down the pitch of his anger.* JIM *stands motionless, eyes closed.*)

Do you remember the other beatings he gave you?

(JIM *nods.*)

Every time she begged me not to tell; swore he was sorry, swore she'd keep him dry. She was afraid you'd be taken away from them, or he'd be *put* away and you'd have the shame to grow up with. But then the arm; I couldn't let that go by. I'd never cut down *any*one until then! Three, four, five times I'd seen situations where I could have, where I *should* have; where someone good was being hurt and mistreated. But I'd never had the nerve. Until then. Until I saw what he'd done to your arm.

JIM

I wanted him alive, so I could get bigger than he was.

DOC

You never would have made it; he'd have killed you before you were seven or eight. Or if you *had* made it, you'd be him all over again today: a millhand, drinking, giving a little boy what he gave you, and what his old man gave him. Beatings get handed down the same as land and money. So I killed him and you've grown up straight, and now you're a doctor, and you look at my records, and you quiz me, and you're going to go call the state police because it's wrong for me to kill. Do you see what I mean about poetic justice?

(JIM *is staring at him, stunned.* DOC *goes to him and takes his arm earnestly in both hands.*)

Never in anger, Jim. Never quickly. Never without months, sometimes *years*, of weighing, deciding. Always aware of the—awful responsibility, but accepting it; for the town, for Greenfield; to feed the good in it, to cut out the bad.

JIM

It's—a town, not a garden.

DOC

It's a perfect town. Why should a garden be perfect but not a town? People deserve more care than flowers do.

JIM

Than weeds do too.

DOC

No, no, Jim. Lives aren't all of them sacred. If you've got a gun and see a man stabbing a child, you shoot to stop him, don't you?

JIM

Yes.

DOC

If you've got cyanic acid and see a man beating a child and brutalizing him . . .

JIM

There are courts and judges.

DOC

But never enough justice! Look out there, no farther than Davistown and Hardwick; and look here, in Greenfield!

JIM

It's *wrong* . . .

DOC

Why? Because you've been *told* it's wrong since you were two years old? It's *right!* The proof is in the town; the happiness, the *love,* the way they all flock into church on Sundays and sing their thanks up to heaven. And let me tell you this, Jimmy: every doctor does it, more or less. When it's a Helen Hart who's almost dead, you break your back to save her; when it's a Lloyd Zachary, you don't.

JIM

No—

DOC

Just wait. Wait. Wait till you're on your own, just you and the patient, with no resident peeping over your shoulder.

JIM

You do your best for everyone.

DOC

I'd have said so too, at twenty-seven. Just wait. You'll make your choices. We all make choices.

(*Moving away from* JIM, UPSTAGE *toward his desk or the* Flower and Garden *cover.*)

I'm not so unique. A little more willing to shoulder responsibility than most men, but not so unique, no . . .

JIM

(*Watches him.*)

How many, Doc?

DOC

(*Turning.*)

How many what?

JIM

People.

DOC

Oh. Thirty.

JIM

(*A pause.*)

Thirteen?

DOC

No, thirty. In twenty-one years. Hurt people. People who'd been hurt so badly and for so long that all they could finally do was hurt other people. Your father and Bruce Hart and Hannah Meserve. Ned Ingles, P. T. Fletcher . . . and some who were in terrible pain and for whom there was no hope, and they were draining the life and the happiness of the people around them, Reba Sanford and Sax Rousseau. Fred Allbright. No, it was Leonard. Leonard Allbright.

JIM

Who else?

DOC

Children. Oh, those are the ones I hate to think about. Susanna Booth, and the McClure baby—that was the humpbacked one—and a monstrous baby that Ruth Scudder had when Bob was in Korea, and Reuben Wilcox.

JIM

Because of his legs?

DOC

That's right.

JIM

(*A pause.*)

Who else, Doc?

DOC

The troublemakers. Mack Bullit. Diana Rausch.

JIM

George Suggs.

DOC

No! He really had empyema!

(*Laughs, points upward.*)

God finally took a look at the account books! Isn't that a laugh? And that was the one that made Darryl suspicious!

(*The laugh ends and he grows sober again.*)

And before Darryl there was Ted Ruth senior.

JIM

He got suspicious too?

DOC

(*Nods.*)

I'd sooner have cut off my right arm if I'd had any choice about it. Ted was my good friend, you know. He's the one who made my greenhouse in there.

JIM

(*Pause.*)

Who else?

DOC

Let's see now . . .

JIM

My mother? So I'd have the insurance money?

DOC

What are you talking about? No! Are you crazy?

JIM

I don't know! I don't know, Doc! I don't know *who* died naturally!

DOC

You *saw* how I sweated over her, didn't you? Weren't you beside me, helping me? I was going to give you the money for school, you know that. I *cherished* your mother! Orrin Sanderson! He was taking eight-and nine-year-old girls into that shed behind his shop. *That's* what I pull out, not someone like your mother! I *cherished* her! Joe Schmidt! And the handyman at Grievers', I've got his name there, the Polish one.

(*Sits* RIGHT *tiredly.*)

And that couple who came here from Canada. Jefferson. Herb and Dorothy. They weren't husband and wife, they were brother and sister. She confessed it to me when she got pregnant. That isn't all thirty, is it?

JIM

No.

DOC

Did I mention Mack Bullit?

JIM

Yes.

DOC

Never in anger, Jimmy. And never quickly. This is the best town in the whole state, and you know it. And that's not just Chamber of Commerce talk either.

(*He sits silently brooding.* JIM *closes his eyes for a moment, then draws a breath, blows it out, and opens his eyes. He looks at* DOC.)

JIM

Doc . . .

(DOC *looks at him.*)

There's so much that I owe you—

DOC

That's the truth, Jim.

JIM

I don't mean—my father. I mean—the things you taught me, the—the image you gave me of what I might some day be . . . look, this has to stop, you think it's right but it's wrong. The law says it's wrong and I say it's wrong, and I'm not going to debate it with you, I'm just going to tell you that it has to stop. Completely. The *garden* is your garden, not the town. The garden. And it ends at the picket fences. Now nothing on earth is going to bring any one of those thirty people back to life again, so because of what I owe you, and because I love you, and because the town needs you *when you're being the doctor and not the judge and the jury*—because of those reasons I'm going to keep my mouth shut, but *only on one condition*. Do you understand? I'm going to become an accessory, after all your thirty facts, but only on one condition, no *two* conditions.

(*Goes closer to him, pointing.*)

One: you've got to give me your solemn vow right here and now that you're never going to poison anyone ever again, never going to *kill* anyone ever again in any way or by any means. And two: we've got to work out some kind of way for me to be sure that you're—fulfilling your vow. Not because I don't trust you, but because—well we've *got* to, that's all. Otherwise I can't keep quiet. All right?

DOC

What happens to the town?

JIM

What do you mean?

DOC

What happens to the town? What keeps it from going to seed?

JIM

Doc, *gardens* go to seed. Towns—muddle along. All right, somebody is going to be in pain. A kid is going to have a father who breaks his arm and kicks him. Somebody is going to—do terrible things to little girls. Doc, those are things that are *still* not as bad as *killing*. The town can take care of them legally. And the things the town *can't* take care of—it will simply have to live with and get used to. Boy oh boy, if you lived in Chicago!

(*Pantomiming it broadly.*)

Twenty-eight hours a day you'd be handing out the strychnine and the arsenic! Okay?

DOC

I don't have any choice, do I?

JIM

No, I guess you don't.

DOC

(*Rising.*)

All right, you've got my word.

JIM

I want to hear it.

DOC

I said you've got it.

JIM

I want to hear it, Doc!

DOC

(*A pause.*)

I swear I won't poison anyone—

JIM

Won't *kill* anyone!

DOC

—won't kill anyone ever again. In any way or by any means.

JIM

(*A pause.*)

All right.

(*He realizes that he has his coat on and takes it off.* DOC *watches him.*)

DOC

And what are you going to do, go on my rounds with me?

JIM

That's a good question; what am I going to do.

(*Thinks, dropping his coat over a chair.*)

Okay, I'll *tell* you what I'm going to do. I'm going to have the *Courier* sent to me every week and I'm going to read it very carefully, especially the obituaries. And I'm going to keep in *touch*, with the Reverend and Ray Higley. I'm going to know what's going on. And I'm going to visit, every couple of months or so. If the right people keep on dying, or if I even *suspect* that the right people are dying, then I'm going to tell. There'll still be plenty of proof up at the cemetery; at least in the last few arrivals, there will.

DOC

The thing for me to do now, I guess, is remove some of the *wrong* people.

JIM

You remove nobody ever again. Don't you forget it.

DOC

I was making a joke, that's all.

JIM

(*Looks at him for a moment.*)

Christ Almighty, Doc. If people ever found out . . . !

(*Shakes his head.*)

DOC

Make no mistake; plenty of them would thank me.

JIM

(*Nods.*)

Some would, I suppose.

DOC

A *lot* would. Plenty! The whole damn town!

(*A pause.*)

JIM

I want the key, Doc.

DOC

The key?

JIM

To the cabinet.

DOC

You've got my vow.

JIM

I want the key too. Tonight or tomorrow we'll go through that stuff down there and get rid of what you don't really need. And we'll measure out what you *do* really need and you're going to have to keep a record for me of what happens to every last grain and particle.

(*Puts his hand out for the key.*)

I'm sorry, Doc. It's the only way.

(*A pause, and then* DOC *takes a key-chain from his pocket and ruefully begins detaching one of the keys.*)

DOC

My young helper Jimmy is taking my key from me . . .

JIM

Life's little ironies.

(DOC *detaches the key and puts it on* JIM*'s palm.* JIM *holds and examines it, looks at the cabinet.*)

DOC

It's the right one.

(JIM *looks at* DOC *and pockets the key.*)

JIM

I'll give it back when we've—cleaned things out.

(DOC *turns and moves away, his hands in his pockets. He looks older, resentful.*)

What it all comes down to simply is—the good old end doesn't justify the good old means. You've got a whole town ecstatically happy, in neat rows with no bugs and no crabgrass; but thirty people are lying in the cemetery and they didn't get a chance to say one word in their own behalf. Who knows? Maybe I was one of the many small boys who *deserve* to be kicked and beaten.

(DOC *doesn't smile, he rocks on his heels, unforgiving.*)

Well, debate ended. You garden in the garden.

(JIM *picks up his coat and goes* LEFT. DOC *turns.*)

DOC

Are you going?

JIM

No. Do you want me to?

DOC

No.

JIM

I could stay with Ray and Jean.

DOC

(*Letting go his resentment.*)

No, no; don't be silly.

(JIM *goes to the coat rack and hangs up his coat. He turns toward* DOC *again in the foyer doorway.*)

JIM

I don't feel any differently toward you, Doc; damned if I know why, but I don't. Maybe I will in a week or so, I don't know. I hope not. And I hope you don't feel any differently toward me.

DOC

Of course I don't, Jimmy.

(*Smiles.*)

I'm just a little sorry I didn't chase you home all those times your mother said I should.

JIM

(*Smiling back.*)

You and Dr. Frankenstein, turned upon by your own creations.

DOC

I didn't create you, Jimmy; you know that. If I helped a little, then I'm still glad and still proud.

JIM

Thank you, Doc.

(*Picks up his suitcase.*)

I'll go unpack.

(*He goes quickly up the stairs and out of sight.* DOC*'s smile fades away, he comes* D. *and stands troubled and brooding, his fists in his pockets. He sniffs, thinks, rocks on his heels, frowns. After a moment the telephone rings.* DOC *doesn't seem to hear. He thinks more, sniffs again, worries. The telephone rings again.* DOC *goes back to the desk and without breaking out of his mood takes up the receiver.*)

DOC

Yes? Oh. Yes, he is. He—he just went upstairs, Ray. He was going to call you and Jean and then we got talking and—Ray. Hold on, will you? Just hold on a minute.

(*He lays the receiver on the desk, looks up at the stairs, and goes quietly across the office to the waiting room. He closes the connecting door partway, looks out, and then takes up the receiver of the reception-desk telephone. He is genuinely upset and perturbed.*)

Ray? I'm in the waiting room now. I don't want Jim to hear me. I—I don't know what to say, Ray. I don't know what to tell you. He's so dear to me. He's like a *son* to me, you know that. And I'm—I'm afraid there's something wrong with him! I know I shouldn't say anything, but he looks so fine, so apparently healthy, and while we were talking he got this—what looked like some kind of cerebrovascular disturbance. His speech got all jumbled and meaningless and he wasn't even aware of it. And his father died of a cerebral hemorrhage—you remember, Ray?—and before he did, *he* had the same kind of disturbances. When I think that Jimmy may end up the same way his father did, I'd sooner cut off my arm. I swear that's the truth, Ray; I'd sooner cut off my arm! Listen, Ray; I'm being foolish and a—a foolish man. I'm sure he's all right. Forget what I said, will you?

(*Another look out through the doorway.*)

He's just been pushing so hard, that's what it is, with the interning—you can't imagine what a grind that is—and then the examinations right after, and now he's got some kind of appeal pending with his draft board. I'm *sure* he is. Don't upset Jean, now. Don't say anything to *her*. He'll probably call you later on and—yes, yes. You too, Ray, you too. Good-by.

(*He hangs up and stands thinking unhappily for a moment, then looks into the office again and opens the door and goes on. Going to the desk, he quietly hangs up the telephone there, looks up toward the top of the stairs, listens. He thinks again, and reaches a reluctant decision. Going* DOWNSTAGE RIGHT, *he stands on tiptoes and, from atop a high book or door frame, takes an unseeable something with which he goes* DOWNSTAGE LEFT. *He crouches and—the something is a key—unlocks the drug cabinet. He takes a small bottle from the bottom shelf, inspects it thoughtfully, then takes out a second bottle, weighs them, and puts back the first. He closes the door, reopens it, rearranges the bottles so that no gap is visible among them, then closes the door again and locks it. Rising, he goes* DOWNSTAGE RIGHT *again and returns the key to its hiding place.* JIM *calls from upstairs.*)

JIM

Doc?

(DOC *goes near his desk and stands facing the stairs, holding the small bottle behind his back in one hand.*)

DOC

Yes? What is it?

(JIM *comes down the stairs far enough to see and be seen.*)

JIM

Do I have time to take a shower and put on a clean shirt?

DOC

Sure. Of course. Go ahead, Jim.

JIM

I'll be as quick as I can.

(*He goes up and out of sight again.*)

DOC

Don't rush. Whenever you're ready—that's when we'll eat.

(*He exits quickly, determinedly, into the kitchen, as*)

THE CURTAIN FALLS

ACT THREE

AT RISE: *Half an hour later.* JIM *is standing by the desk laughing into the telephone.* HE *is combed and clean looking in a fresh sport shirt, and has a napkin in his hand.* DOC *is sitting at the desk quietly eating a plate of stew. A second plate, half eaten, is on the hassock or low stool* DOWNSTAGE RIGHT, *which is serving as table to a nearby chair. Outside the house there is total darkness.*

JIM

(*Laughing.*)

You didn't! To all three cars?

(*Laughs more.*)

You're a nut, you're an absolute nut!

(*And a little more.*)

How does Fran feel about it? Well, good for her. She's a nut too. No, not tonight; there are—things Doc and I want to talk about. Look, why don't you come by in the morning, around nine or so, and you can run me out to South Green. I want to see Charley and Chris and—Perfect. I'll see you then. So long, nutto.

(*Hangs up and laughs.*)

Did you hear how he let Rudy know he was quitting?

DOC

(*Nodding, smiling.*)

Yes, I did. We all did.

JIM

He should have done it long ago.

DOC

He never should have started working there at all. He's capable of much more than fixing cars.

JIM

You've got to hand it to him; it takes nerve to change now, with a wife and a child and another on the way.

(*A pause, as he thinks about it.*)

DOC

You haven't finished your stew.

JIM

Oh. Yeh.

(DOC *watches as* JIM *goes* DOWNSTAGE RIGHT *and suddenly turns.*)

Listen, would you like me to stay around and give you a hand tomorrow morning?

DOC

No.

JIM

'Cause I can go to South Green in the afternoon just as well.

DOC

No, no, go in the morning, the way you planned.

JIM

(*Sitting.*)

Bob's free all day, so just say the word and—

DOC

No, really, there's no need for you to—stay around.

(JIM *takes a fork from the plate.*)

Things are quiet now anyway.

(JIM *forks up a piece of stew and puts it into his mouth.* DOC *watches, then follows suit. Both chew, and it might be noted at this moment that their plates are of different colors.* JIM *swallows.*)

JIM

What was I telling you? Oh, my nemesis, Dr. Kalebjian.

DOC

And the woman whose pressure dropped.

JIM

Mm. Well it was way down—ninety over forty or something—and she was just barely breathing. With an IV running, glucose and water.

(*He takes another bite,* DOC *watches.*)

According to the chart Kalebjian had given me, she had a couple of pints of blood on stand-by and she was slated for a bone marrow biopsy in the morning. Now what am I supposed to do?

DOC

If you give her the blood, the biopsy has to be postponed.

JIM

Exactly.

(*Another bite.*)

So I'm standing there trying to make up my mind when suddenly I notice that there's no IV ordered on the chart. There it is stuck in her arm but it's not on the chart. And according to the work-up she's forty-four years old, and this woman I'm looking at is—

(*The telephone rings.* DOC *picks up the receiver.*)

DOC

Yes? Hello. How are you? I'm sorry to hear that, Livvy. Is it as severe as last time?

(JIM *goes on eating.*)

No, that doesn't necessarily follow. Do you still have the drops? You take three of them in a glass of water and get into bed. Janet's there, isn't she? You do as I say and don't worry. I'll look in some time tomorrow afternoon. Only if you can't sleep, but you'll sleep fine, you'll see. Of course I won't. Good-by.

(*Hangs up, takes his pen and jots a note.*)

Livvy Sawyer.

JIM

How old is she now?

DOC

(*Swinging around toward* JIM.)

One hundred and two years.

JIM

That's great.

DOC

(*Meaningfully.*)

She had uremia three years ago, and hepatitis and cirrhosis before that.

(*A pause.*)

JIM

Doc, I know there are dozens of people who would be dead now if it weren't for you. That's true of every doctor. *I've* even saved one life that everyone had pretty much given up on.

(DOC *eats.*)

Does every doctor have the right to kill?

DOC

This is a *special situation here*, where I know the whole town inside and out!

JIM

Does every Vermont doctor who's the only doctor in his *town* have the—

DOC

There's no point in talking about it now.

JIM

There is. There is, though. I don't want you feeling resentful and angry at me.

DOC

There's no point in talking about it.

JIM

There *is*, Doc.

(*He sniffs at a fork of stew and eats it, fleetingly it doesn't taste as it should, but then it does.* DOC *watches with sharpened interest for a moment.*)

DOC

I'm not angry at you, Jim.

JIM

You just sounded angry.

DOC

No, I can see how someone your age would automatically take the conventional view . . .

JIM

For Pete's sake, Doc, it has nothing to do with my age and nothing to do with convention! It's a matter of logic and—

(*Someone has tried the door* LEFT, *found it locked, and now the doorbell rings—one of the old-fashioned turnscrew kind.* DOC *looks around and sits motionless.*)

Did you lock the door already?

DOC

Yes.

(*A pause.*)

JIM

Shall I—?

DOC

(*Rising quickly.*)

I'll get it, you stay.

(*He goes into the foyer and unlocks and unbolts the front door.* ELIAS *is outside.*)

ELIAS

You locked up early.

DOC

Jim and I are talking.

ELIAS

I've got something for him. For you too.

DOC

Thanks. I'll—

ELIAS

Let me bring it in. It's more for him than for you.

(DOC *stands aside and* ELIAS *comes in, carrying a napkin-covered pie plate.*)

JIM

Hi.

ELIAS

It looks like I timed this just right.

(DOC *closes the front door and comes to the foyer doorway.* ELIAS *stands before* JIM.)

Guess what it is.

JIM

A pie.

ELIAS

What kind?

JIM

(*Thinks.*)

Pumpkin?

ELIAS

No . . . Helen's own peach!

(*Uncovering it.*)

From out of the freezer and part of it eaten, and we both apologize to you.

JIM

Apologize? That's great! Boy, I haven't seen anything so beautiful in years!

ELIAS

(*Including* DOC *in his explanation.*)

She took it out yesterday and we had some last night, and all through supper just now she was fretting and upset that she hadn't thought to take out two. "I'll bring them what's left of this one," I says, but she says no, you can't bring someone half a pie. "Why not?" I says. "It's the same as with bread. Half a *pie* is better than none the same as half a loaf is!"

JIM

You were absolutely right! Thanks a million. And thank Helen too.

ELIAS

I'll put it over here; you go on eating. Doc, go on eating; don't let me interrupt you.

(*He puts the pie in an out-of-the-way place.* DOC *moves reluctantly toward the desk.*)

While I'm here I've got a question I want to ask you, Jimmy.

JIM

(*Eating.*)

What's that?

ELIAS

A little thing that's been annoying me. I'm getting to be like you, Doc, wanting to be sure everything is settled and orderly the way it's supposed to be.

JIM

What is it?

ELIAS

You said before that you saw one of the markers—one of the stickers I told you about—you said you saw one with an R on it and that was how you knew R was one of the letters in Doc's and my code that we use.

JIM

(*A pause.*)

That's right.

ELIAS

Well where is it? Because I couldn't find it when I went out of here. It was still light enough to see and I looked all over the front.

(*To* DOC.)

I thought I was finally caught up with things, except for the yew tree. Did Jim tell you about that?

DOC

Yes.

ELIAS

I'll come by around three or four.

DOC

That'll be fine.

ELIAS

Where was it, Jim? The sticker you saw.

JIM

On one of the bushes.

DOC

I took it off. I went out on a call after Jim came in and I stopped and took it off. It was on one of the dwarf lilacs but I changed my mind.

ELIAS

You think there's too many?

DOC

No. I did, but I changed my mind.

ELIAS

Well that explains it.

(*To* JIM.)

I was going to come back in right then and ask you, only Helen started waving to me from the porch. It bothered me though, not finding it, and that as much as the pie is why I came over.

DOC

(*Smiling.*)

And now you've taken care of both reasons.

ELIAS

That's right, so I'll get out of your way and let you go on with your supper.

DOC

No, no . . .

(JIM *breathes deeply and slaps his chest.* ELIAS *and* DOC *look at him.*)

JIM

I'm short of breath.

ELIAS

You mustn't eat too fast.

DOC

Thank Helen for the pie, will you, Elias?

ELIAS

Sure thing.

JIM

Tell her that—

(*Another deep breath.*)
—half of one of her peach pies is better than all of anyone else's.

ELIAS

(*Backing* RIGHT.)
Right. Come visit with us when you're done, why don't you? Have you seen any color TV yet, Jim?

JIM

A little.

DOC

(*Following along with* ELIAS.)
We'll try, but don't count on us.

ELIAS

If not, I'll see you tomorrow.

JIM

Good night. Thanks again!

DOC

(*Seeing* ELIAS *out the door.*)
Good night, Elias. Thank you.

ELIAS

(*Out of sight.*)
Don't even mention it, Doc.

(DOC *closes the door and locks it and bolts it.* JIM *considers another forkful of stew, decides against it, and puts the fork down on his plate. He sits without moving, puzzled by his shortness of breath.* DOC *comes to the foyer doorway and looks at him.*)

DOC

You didn't finish telling me about Dr.—I don't remember his name.

JIM

(*A pause.*)

Kalebjian . . . Wolf N. Kalebjian . . .

DOC

That's quite a monicker.

JIM

(*Another pause. Not looking at* DOC.)

The woman was—according to the chart she was supposed to be forty-four. But the woman on the bed looked—late fifties, almost sixty.

(DOC *moves* DOWNSTAGE RIGHT, *ostensibly listening to* JIM*'s slow, numbed narration. He draws a window shade, closes curtains.*)

And the chart said—five feet six, but the woman was shorter than that—about five-two.

(*A pause.* JIM *looks at* DOC, *who stands casually by the covered window.* JIM *squints uncomfortably at him.*)

Would you turn the lamp off, please? My eyes hurt.

DOC

Sure, Jim.

(DOC *turns the lamp off.*)

JIM

Thank you.

DOC

You're welcome.

JIM

(*A pause.*)

All of a sudden—it dawned on me—that he had given me—the wrong chart.

DOC

(*Crossing quietly* UPSTAGE *of* JIM.)

Do you think he did it on purpose?

JIM

Of course he did. He never made a mistake in his whole life, the—

DOC

(*Drawing the shade and curtains of a window* LEFT *more openly than before.*)

He probably did it to see if you would notice.

JIM

(*Nods.*)

That's what he said when I—went back to him on it. He was "testing" me.

(DOC *goes into the waiting room. He closes curtains and checks the lock and bolt of the rear door.*)

But that was no time for testing. I think he wanted me to give that woman the other woman's two pints of blood. It wouldn't have hurt her any, her pressure so low—they were the same type—but it would have got me into—

(DOC *comes back into the office and stands listening to* JIM.)

—six kinds of trouble with—Harris and Benjamin.

DOC

(*A pause.*)

Shall I turn this lamp off too?

JIM

(*Turns, grimaces.*)

Please.

(DOC *turns a second lamp off.* JIM *rubs his closed eyes.*)

I don't know what it is, that's made my eyes so sensitive . . .

(DOC *picks up* JIM*'s plate with the fork on it, and puts a hand on* JIM*'s shoulder.*)

DOC

I'm going to take the plates into the kitchen now and get the coffee. You sit right here and wait for me—

(*A glimmer of pained sympathy.*)

—all right, Jimmy?

JIM

Sure, Doc.

DOC

I'll just be a minute or two.

(*Goes to the desk, picks up his own plate and fork, and continues* UPSTAGE LEFT.)

You stay right there.

(*He goes out into the kitchen.* JIM *sits motionless for a moment.*)

JIM

She was Dr. Benjamin's patient . . .

(*A pause, and then he blinks, frowns, and feels his heart. He takes his pulse, and after a few seconds of soundless counting realizes that it's far slower than it ought to be. He looks about, rises, licks his lips. He looks toward the kitchen,* could it be? *He goes to the drug cabinet, tries it, finds it locked, stands uncertainly, then searches in his pockets and finds the key. He unlocks the cabinet, locks and unlocks the opened door, stands straight and calls out in frightened confusion.*)

Doc?

(*No answer. He gasps for breath, then turns, drops to his knees by the cabinet and pulls bottle after bottle from the bottom shelf, trying to find one missing or disturbed. He gives up, and gasping—nearly suffocating—rises and turns to the sliding doors of the examining room. He tries to pull one open, it sticks, he pulls harder, strains, it flies open and* DOC *stands before him.* JIM *falls back, startled.* DOC *comes out, tense, keyed up.*)

DOC

Sit down, Jimmy. Sit down over there. That's right.

(JIM *sits* UPSTAGE CENTER, *gasping.* DOC *glances at the opened cabinet.*)

Did you figure out what I gave you? Sodium cyanide.

(*Takes the bottle from his pocket, shows it.*)

See? It's slower than potassium cyanide but faster than anything else except cyanic acid.

(JIM *groans, gasps.* DOC *puts the poison back in the cabinet.*) You'll have some convulsions in a minute or two and then you'll go into a gradual paralysis and then you'll die. The antidote is inside there—don't move! It's all ready in a pan; a shot of sodium nitrite, and another of sodium thiosulfate, and amyl nitrite for inhalation.

JIM

Doc! Please, Doc! I beg you!

DOC

You forced me into this. I don't enjoy scaring you this way, maybe killing you. You're almost my son. But what am I supposed to do? Let you come in here and ruin the whole town? After all the love and the labor I've put into it? Over thirty years I've been working here!

(JIM *gives an agonized gasp and undergoes a violent racking convulsion.* DOC *leans forward and watches compassionately. When the final spasm ends,* JIM *is sprawled limp and sweating in the chair.*)

That's the worst, Jim. The first one's the strongest and then they get weaker.

JIM

I'll go away. I won't come back. I won't say a word to anyone. I swear to God!

DOC

Security! I've got to have some kind of security! I can't just take your word, don't you see that?

(*Moves his chair a bit closer to* JIM.)

What I'm hoping, praying, is that you've got something *you* don't want told, just the way I do!

JIM

Something I—

DOC

Something secret! Something people might not understand about, and then I can forgive you and trust you and give you the antidote. Tell me something, Jim. I don't take pleasure in killing.

(JIM *cries out and undergoes a second convulsion, shorter and less violent than the first.* DOC *watches, waits, moves a bit closer.*)

Tell me something. Did you try drugs at the hospital?

JIM

No.

DOC

Did you steal anything? Sell anything?

JIM

I—I did—

DOC

Did what?

JIM

Did an abortion, on Liz.

DOC

Your girl?

JIM

Yes.

DOC

When?

JIM

Last June.

DOC

Where?

JIM

In the hospital. Sneaked her in. Nurses helped me.

DOC

You performed the abortion in the hospital?

JIM

Yes.

DOC

It was your baby?

JIM

Yes.

DOC

(*A pause.*)

Is this the truth, Jim?

JIM

Have proof. Letters where she mentions it. She went home after. Wrote to me. Have them here.

(*A third convulsion, shorter and less racking than the*

second. After it, JIM *sprawls motionless, as a general paralysis begins setting in. His speech becomes slower and slurred, seemingly disinterested, his eyes close and his breathing becomes quick and shallow.*)

DOC

(*Warily.*)

You have the letters here?

JIM

My suitcase . . . lent my room to a friend . . . was afraid he might find them . . .

(DOC *backs toward the foyer.*)

DOC

Where in your suitcase?

JIM

Side pocket . . . blue envelopes . . . three blue envelopes . . .

(DOC *backs farther, onto the first step of the stairs. He watches* JIM, *who lies motionless, eyes closed, gasping weakly. After a moment* DOC *comes down off the step. He puts the bottle on the desk and goes into the examining room. He comes out with a white enamel pan and, not hurrying, goes to* JIM*'s side and puts the pan somewhere handy. He takes a capsule from it and breaks it at* JIM*'s nostrils. He lifts* JIM*'s head.* JIM *winces, moans.*)

DOC

Come on, breathe it in . . .

(*He waits a moment and then lowers* JIM*'s head and throws the capsule into the pan. He undoes* JIM*'s left cuff, pushes* *up the sleeve, and ties a length of rubber tubing around the arm. He takes a syringe from the pan, tries it, and injects it below the tubing. When the syringe is empty he draws it out, puts it in the pan, unties the tubing, and rubs and flexes* JIM*'s arms.* JIM *watches him.*)

Don't worry, you'll be all right. It would take more than a little sodium cyanide to knock off a bozo like you . . .

(*Undoes the other cuff, pushes up the sleeve and, taking a second syringe from the pan, goes around to* JIM*'s other side.*)

That was the nitrite, this is the thiosulfate.

(*Ties on the tubing.*)

In case you care . . .

(*Tests the syringe and injects it, then draws it out, unties the tubing, rubs the arm.*)

Abortion right in the hospital; you're a pretty nervy young fellow.

(*Reaching over* JIM, *he puts the second syringe and the tubing into the pan and then flexes both* JIM*'s arms simultaneously.*)

Not as smart as you should have been, though. You know how many keys I've got to that cabinet? Four. The one I carry, one on top of the books there, one up in my bedroom—

(*Tries* JIM*'s pulse.*)

—and one in a little magnet-thing stuck up inside the fender of the car, along with an extra set of car keys. It's getting to you, isn't it?

JIM

Mm.

DOC

(*Going back around him.*)

In half an hour you'll be yourself again. Do you know much about poisons and antidotes?

JIM

Mm-mmn.

(DOC *breaks another capsule at* JIM'*s nostrils,* JIM *raises his head a bit and breathes deeply of it.*)

Ooof!

DOC

(*Helping him sit erect, holding the capsule.*)

Oh, I'm glad you told me what you did so I could spare you, Jimmy! Seeing you die would have been terrible. I'd always rather be merciful than cruel, but most times there's just no room for choice. We're better friends now than we were before, aren't we? Because we know about each other, we don't have any secrets between us! That's rare, that's a rare condition, Jimmy. Listen, I want to tell you one more thing. I worry. I do. Because I'm human, you know, I'm not God. I have my emotions. And there's an element of *pleasure* that enters into killing someone—even when it's done for valid reasons—there's an element of pleasure in making the decision and carrying it out and being triumphant and still alive—and sometimes I worry, in the case of Herb and Dorothy Jefferson, for instance, I worry that the element of pleasure might be playing a part in my decisions. But incest is wrong biologically, not only morally, isn't it?

(JIM *nods.*)

Or Laura Scoville. Now a teen-age girl, especially a pretty one, she's *always* going to bring emotion into the picture and complicate things, isn't she?

JIM

(*A pause.*)

What did she do?

DOC

Laura?

JIM

Yes.

DOC

(*A pause. He puts aside the capsule.*)

Well, that's something I'd rather not go into, Jim. It's really not important. What *is* important is that pleasure didn't enter into my decision, because if it had, if pleasure were a factor of any importance at all, then I would have killed *you*, right?

JIM

Right.

DOC

I would have sat there and watched you gasping and sweating and I wouldn't have given you any chance at all to save yourself. But I did, I had mercy on you, and now you're looking much better, young Dr. Tennyson! How do you feel?

JIM

(*Watching* DOC.)

Dead.

DOC

You were an interesting shade of blue there for a few minutes. Can you move your legs?

(*Still watching* DOC, JIM *weakly lifts one foot and then the other.*)

That's fine. Do you know what we have to do now?

JIM

What?

DOC

Wash out your stomach. I'm sorry, but we do. I'll go get things ready. Don't try to walk yet. Here, sniff a little more.

(*Taking the pan, he gives* JIM *one of the capsules and goes* RIGHT; *gestures toward the cabinet and turns.*)

I had the potassium cyanide in my hand, you know that? And I thought, no, no, that's too quick. Even then I meant to be fair with you and give you a chance . . .

(*He turns again and goes into the examining room and out of sight.* JIM *sits listening, the capsule to his nose.*)

If I didn't show mercy to *you*, I'd be a pretty unspeakable creature, wouldn't I? Even *with* the whole town at stake.

(*He falls silent. There are sounds of a drawer being opened and closed, of water running. Quietly* JIM *rises from his chair. He leans unsteadily against it, takes a final sniff at the capsule and puts it down.* DOC *calls from the examining room.*)

How are you doing?

JIM

A little better!

(*Begins making his way to the waiting room, holding on to one piece of furniture and then another.*)

DOC

I want you to stay the weekend the way you planned, otherwise everyone's going to wonder. You can leave on Monday morning.

(JIM *makes his way through the waiting room to the door.*)

I'll be ready in a minute. Keep sniffing the amyl.

(JIM *tries the door, finds it locked. He unlocks it and tries it again but it still won't open.*)

I had to do this to a three-year-old boy yesterday. Jill Stormer's little fellow. Swallowed some furniture polish.

(JIM *is reaching up to open a bolt high on the door when* DOC *comes out of the examining room.* JIM *freezes in the near-darkness.*)

It took Jill and Bea *and* Dora to hold the poor kid down while I—

(*He sees the empty chair, glances* RIGHT *and moves to look up the stairwell. Then he turns and looks* LEFT *and grows chill and hostile.*)

What are you doing there?

JIM

Going. Isn't that what you want?

DOC

I want you to stay the weekend. Otherwise everyone's going to wonder.

JIM

(*A pause.*)

I'm going.

DOC

To—tell . . .

JIM

Doc . . . you need help.

DOC

(*Pointing upstairs.*)

I'll show those letters!

JIM

There are no letters. No abortion.

(*He turns and unbolts the door. Erupting into fury,* DOC *races across the office, through the waiting room, and catches* JIM *with both hands by the back of his shirt. He swings him around and hurls him forward—into the office, where he falls on hands and knees.* DOC *is right after him, kicking at him.*)

DOC

Liar! You liar! THOU SHALT NOT LIE!

(*He locks his fists and raises them to club* JIM*'s head, but* JIM *catches him around the waist and tries to bear him downward. They grapple. After a few moments* DOC *succeeds in working free and landing a blow that sends* JIM *sprawling on his back.* DOC *throws himself on him, grabs a cushion from the davenport, and clamps it over* JIM*'s face, holding it with all his strength against the weak flailing of* JIM*'s arms. At first it seems as if* JIM *will be suffocated, but after several futile tries he manages to get his arms between* DOC*'s and throws him off.* DOC *climbs to his feet and looks about for a weapon, breathing curses.* JIM *rolls over and drags himself to the desk.* DOC *gets a metal ashstand from the waiting room, as* JIM*, by the desk, reaches up.* DOC *swings,* JIM *ducks away, and the ashstand strikes the* *desktop.* JIM *grabs the shank of the stand and pulls himself up to his feet. The two men struggle for the ashstand, and finally* JIM *wrests it from* DOC *and falls back a few steps, holding it before him in readiness.* DOC *snatches up a letter opener from the desk but drops it, suddenly open-mouthed. He puts both hands to his chest and turns wide-eyed to* JIM.)

Heart!

(JIM *stands motionless, caught up short.*)

Real. Real.

(*Collapses into the desk chair, pale, sweating.*)

Tablets. Cabinet. Nitroglycerin.

(JIM *puts down the ashstand.*)

Top shelf. Quick. Bad one.

(*Activated,* JIM *steps to the cabinet and finds the right bottle on the top shelf.* DOC *winces with pain.*)

Quick. Two of them.

JIM

(*Trying to uncap the bottle.*)

I can't get it—

(*Stops. Looks at* DOC. *A pause.*)

—open . . .

(*Their eyes lock, and then* JIM *drops back a step.*)

DOC

Jim. Please. Be merciful. I was merciful to you, wasn't I? Now *you* be merciful to me.

(*He gasps at the worsening pain. There are tears in his eyes.* JIM *takes another step away from him.*)

JIM

Oh God, Doc, I think that's what I'm doing!

DOC

(*Almost laughs.*)

Jimmy, little Jimmy . . . you see? You see—how it—begins?

(*He slips forward to his knees, then tumbles sideward and lies still.* JIM *looks at him, looks at the bottle in his hand. He is stunned, in a turmoil. He puts the bottle back on the shelf, goes hesitantly to* DOC *and stands looking down at him. He crouches, feels* DOC*'s chest, tries his pulse. Rising, he thinks and then goes unsteadily into the foyer. He unlocks and unbolts the front door. Opening it, he cups his hands and shouts at the top of his lungs.*)

JIM

E-LI-AS!

(*Listens for a moment and then goes back into the office and to the desk, picks up the phone and jiggles the crossbar.*)

Zenia? Ring Elias Hart, will you please? Yes, it is. Please, get Elias. It's urgent.

(*Listens, tries to compose himself.*)

Elias? Yes, I did. Listen, something's happened here. Doc has—had a heart attack. Yes. Yes, very. He's dead. We were—

(*Stops, looks about, thinks.*)

—we were—*talking* about how it was when *he* was an intern, and he started laughing at this story he told me, he started laughing very, very hard . . . all right, please do.

(*He hangs up. A pause, and then he sets hastily to work. He closes and locks the cabinet, weighs the key, and goes to* DOC *and crouches by him. He tucks the key into* DOC*'s pocket and minimizes the disarray of* DOC*'s hair and* *clothes. Rising, he picks up the ashstand and brings it back to its place in the waiting room. He puts the cushion back on the davenport and sets the furniture as it was before the fight. Hearing* ELIAS *approaching, he hurriedly puts right the last sign of the fight, takes a position near* DOC*'s body, and tucks in his shirt and smooths down his hair.* ELIAS *comes to the part-way-open front door and enters. He comes into the office, looks at* DOC *and wordlessly, painfully, at* JIM.)

He had an attack before. Bea knows about it.

ELIAS

I do too. She told me.

(*Looks down at* DOC *again.*)

God help us now.

(*And up at Jim.*)

Was it Zenia on the board when you called me?

JIM

Yes.

ELIAS

We'd better put something over him. The whole town's going to be here in a minute.

(JIM *weaves unsteadily.*)

Are you all right, Jim?

JIM

No, not completely.

ELIAS

Is there a blanket around?

JIM

In there . . .

(ELIAS *gets a blanket from the examining room. Headlights flash across the* LEFT *window.*)

ELIAS

What did I tell you? Here comes a car now.

(*As* JIM *and* ELIAS *cover* DOC, *the headlights come to rest on the open front door, and are turned off. Simultaneously there is the sound of a car motor approaching and stopping, and then a car door slamming.*)

JIM

I have to go inside. Excuse me.

(*He goes hurriedly out of sight* RIGHT, *leaving* ELIAS *looking after him.* BEA *enters* LEFT, *distraught, her coat pulled on over a housecoat.*)

BEA

Zenia called me . . .

(*She looks, then turns away with a hand to her eyes.*)

oh God . . .

(ELIAS *goes to her side and pats her shoulder, sighing and shaking his head.*)

Where's Jim?

ELIAS

Inside. I think he's—being sick. Poor Helen near passed out when *she* heard.

BEA

Jim was going to check him over this very evening! That's why I wrote him, got him to come here . . .

(*She cries.* ELIAS *gives her a handkerchief, she rubs at her eyes.*)

thank you . . .

ELIAS

Listen, Bea; we've got to get Jim to *stay*. For a few weeks, at least.

(*Blinking away tears,* BEA *looks at him.*)

Shoreham lost their doctor last summer and they *still* haven't found a new one.

BEA

I asked him before, to come in with Doc, and he didn't want to. But now maybe he—

(*She stops and they draw apart as* JIM *comes back into the examining room and out to join them. He has washed and freshened himself, and the effects of the poison are completely gone. He comes to* BEA *and puts a consoling hand on her shoulder. She looks up at him sadly.*)

it was—too late, wasn't it?

JIM

(*Nods.*)

It happened quickly, though. I don't think he even had time to realize.

ELIAS

Will you write a certificate for me to give to Evalyn Ruth?

JIM

(*A pause.*)

Of course I will.

ELIAS

Otherwise I'd have to call in the doctor from Davistown.

BEA

We were just saying that we hoped you'd stay on a while and look out for us here.

ELIAS

He hasn't got time for Greenfield, the doctor in Davistown.

JIM

I—I can't. I have to be in Chicago Tuesday morning. To see my draft board.

ELIAS

You stay put here, you'll be back under our draft board.

BEA

You said that your girl likes small-town living.

JIM

No. No, I—I don't want to be the only doctor, with nobody else to—share the load.

(*The telephone rings.*)

I'd like to help out, but I'm sorry, I can't.

BEA

(*Picking up the receiver.*)

Yes?

ELIAS

You're not going to let us all down, are you, Jim?

JIM	BEA
Ah, don't put it that way, Elias. I know it's—	Oh, no! What was she doing there?

(JIM *and* ELIAS *turn to listen.*)

BEA

Oh my goodness! Of all nights . . . hold on a minute, Zenia.

(*Covers the mouthpiece, looks at* JIM.)

Peggy Scudder fell off of Patman's Rock.

(JIM *and* ELIAS *wince and draw breath.*)

They're afraid to move her; she's unconscious and bleeding from the mouth.

(*A pause.*)

JIM

All right. I'll go.

(*Goes* LEFT *into the foyer.*)

BEA

He's on his way, Zenia. Tell them he'll be there in ten minutes.

(*Hangs up.*)

JIM

(*Getting his coat from the rack.*)

Why the hell isn't there a higher fence up there?

ELIAS

Because Tom Lick won't have one. Doc warned him someone would fall but Tom is getting stubborner and stingier the older he gets!

(*Getting into his coat in the foyer doorway,* JIM *freezes for a moment.*)

BEA

Take my car; it's blocking the driveway anyway.

JIM

(*Buttons his coat.*)

I can probably postpone my meeting with the draft board for a day or two, long enough so that I can stay here for Doc's funeral. But that's as long as I'm *going* to stay. I don't want you to think I'm going to change my mind or stay on temporarily or anything. You'd better start right in looking for somebody else.

ELIAS

All right, Jim, we will. The first thing tomorrow morning.

(BEA *takes* DOC*'s bag from the desk and holds it out to* JIM. *He hesitates, then steps forward and takes it. He hefts the unfamiliar-familiar weight for a moment, and then, adjusted to it, goes determinedly from the house.*)

THE CURTAIN FALLS

THE END

VERONICA'S ROOM

(1973)

INTRODUCTION

(*VERONICA'S ROOM*)

The poster design for the 1982 film adaptation of Ira Levin's *Deathtrap* featured a stylized Rubik's Cube, intended to convey the myriad complexities of its interweaving plot. *Veronica's Room* takes that Rubik's cube and thrusts it inside a kaleidoscope. Few works of the theater offer such a thicket of overlapping identities and realities. Almost every "scene" (there are no conventional scene divisions) is playing out on multiple concurrent levels (as you'll eventually see), and its four roles are, accordingly, some of the meatiest in the theater canon—each a true actors' workout.

While *Interlock* featured its share of gaslighting, *Veronica's Room* points stadium floodlights into our retinas. Nothing here is as it appears, nor is anyone either. Is Susan actually *Susan*? Are we in 1973, or *1935*? Whatever our feelings were about our previous hosts, Mrs. Price and Dr. Cook, we could at least rely on their being whom they *claimed* to be—here, *everything* is up for grabs.

Levin accomplishes all of this without any special effects or trickery—just iron-clad stagecraft. The further brilliance of his approach is that we the audience are kept in the same position as Susan and Larry—knowing only as much as they do, and sharing each increasingly tortured step, as the proverbial noose incrementally tightens around Susan's neck . . . or *does* it?

After you've read through *Veronica's Room*, you may wish

to go back and reread some or all of it when you're clued in to the multiple layers on which its events are occurring. (It's also intriguing to speculate as to what events might have preceded, or followed, its own.)

Like *Interlock*, *Veronica's Room* features another of Levin's forceful female leads (to put it mildly). There's a passing detail in *Interlock* that appears to have been enlarged here, regarding Mrs. Price's sister, who died prematurely of rheumatic fever at age sixteen. You might also choose to flip back to *Dr. Cook's Garden* (after finishing *Veronica's Room* of course), where passing reference was made to a certain Northern couple who might've lingered in Levin's authorial imagination.

Levin was an intrepid writer, unafraid to turn the story of Mary and Jesus on its head in *Rosemary's Baby*, resurrect *Hitler* in *The Boys from Brazil*, and rig an entire apartment building with hidden cameras in *Sliver*. But one wonders what odds *Veronica's Room* stood on Broadway in 1973, given its dark-as-night contours—even today, it still rattles and unnerves. Its Broadway contemporary that year, *Equus*, was also formidably dark—but its violence played out *offstage*. Interestingly, both plays also incorporated prominent nudity. Though organic to the plot, Levin later removed this, leaving it as an option for companies who wished to retain it—having found that the nudity "*not only offended the audience but also brought the play to a halt while that same offended audience tried to see what it could see, ignoring the other actors onstage.*"

Two main factors led Levin to write *Veronica's Room*. There was, at the time, a string of unsolved disappearances of college-aged women in the greater Boston area, leading him to ponder what might have actually befallen the missing parties. Beyond that was an experience Levin described in a 1973 Associated Press interview: "*One day I sat down at the typewriter, and I really saw an image and couldn't get rid of it. As clear as I've ever seen anything in a theater. A man and woman were entering a room in which all the furniture was covered with sheets. A girl was waiting in the doorway and a young man was standing behind her. That took a year and a half to figure out.*"

How do you write an *intermission*? Unlike the previous two plays in this volume, the later *Veronica's Room* is structured in just two (vs. three) acts. Although it was not the first two-acter of Levin's stage works, its elegant *Susan/Veronica* partitioning almost demands it. The show's two acts result in a single intermission, which Levin was (quoting) "*persuaded*" by the original Broadway production to relocate from its original "*organic and more elegant placement . . . on the grounds of 'theatricality'.*" For this edition, we've restored the intermission's original placement. Over the years, Levin found that presenting the play without any intermission at *all* further intensified the proceedings—there being nothing to break the ratcheting tension; this appears to have been his preferred mode of presentation.

As promised—"the domestics" of our earlier two offerings have returned: here, as *Maureen* and *John Mackey*—the *Lucille* and *Everett* of *House Brabissant.*

Veronica's Room has been captivating audiences globally with years-long runs ongoing in locales from Argentina to China, and in 2020 the black metal band *Secrets of the Moon* released an eponymous song inspired by it. While its film rights have been routinely under option over the decades, no adaptation has yet been realized.

Don't look now—but that older couple at the next table keeps looking over at us . . .

Nicholas Levin
January 2025
New York City

VERONICA'S ROOM

Veronica's Room was first presented on October 25, 1973, by Morton Gottlieb at The Music Box Theatre in New York City with the following cast:

(*In Order of Appearance*)

THE WOMAN . . . . *Eileen Heckart*
THE MAN. . . . .*Arthur Kennedy*
THE YOUNG WOMAN . . . .*Regina Baff*
THE YOUNG MAN. . . . . *Kipp Osborne*

Directed by Ellis Rabb
Scenery by Douglas W. Schmidt
Costumes by Nancy Potts
Lighting by John Gleason

THE SCENE

The play is set in a room in a house about half an hour's drive from Boston. The time is an evening in spring.

ACT ONE: SUSAN
ACT TWO: VERONICA

ACT ONE: SUSAN

A WOMAN *and a* MAN *come into a dim, sheet-shrouded room. In its lighted doorway, a* YOUNG WOMAN *stands waiting. A* YOUNG MAN *stands behind her. The* WOMAN *and the* MAN *move familiarly among the sheeted shapes, the* WOMAN *lighting a wall bracket and a lamp, the* MAN *partly raising a window without drawing its pale breeze-stirred curtain. The* YOUNG WOMAN *comes into the room, looking about with interest as the* WOMAN *uncovers and lights another lamp. The* YOUNG MAN *follows the* YOUNG WOMAN; *he too looks about, but with an air of misgiving. The* MAN *lights a wall bracket. The* WOMAN *lights a hanging glass-shaded lamp over a round table. The room is a bed-sitting room in a turn-of-the-century Victorian house, ornate and somewhat ominous. The door is large and solid. The bed, a single one, is in an angled alcove. A window in the wall beyond it is lightly curtained like the other window. There are doors to a closet and a bathroom. Later the room will be seen to be feminine and attractive within the framework of its heavy architecture. Its decor is of the 1930's, though most of the furniture is a generation older. A chaise longue, the round game table, a desk before the window, a Victrola next to the desk, an artist's easel, a dresser, chairs, bookcases, etc.—all sheeted now.*

The WOMAN *and the* MAN *are pleasant looking, in their early or middle sixties. The* WOMAN *is neatly and plainly dressed, the*

MAN *a bit rumpled in a worn blue suit. The* YOUNG WOMAN *is twenty, slim and engaging, with long straight hair. She wears flared pants, a heavy turtleneck sweater, several necklaces. The* YOUNG MAN, *stocky and in his late twenties, has a bushy mustache and wears old sports clothes. The* WOMAN *lifts the cover carefully from the game table, on which lies a partly completed wooden jigsaw puzzle.*

WOMAN

(*She has a slight brogue.*)

Here's the puzzle she was workin' on, *exactly as she left it.* "Hunters in the Black Forest" is the name of it. Eight hundred pieces. And no picture on the box for assistance!

(*The* YOUNG WOMAN *comes closer to the table. The* MAN *is uncovering the desk. The* YOUNG MAN *wanders over to look briefly at a painting on the wall.*)

She did two or three of these a month, and just before Christmas, Mr. Brabissant would take all the ones she'd done the year before—they were kept in that chest on the landin'; did y' notice the oak chest there?

YOUNG WOMAN

Yes, I did.

MAN

That's a val'able antique, that chest is.

(*He too has a slight brogue.*)

WOMAN

And he would give them—give all of them puzzles costin' *ten and twelve dollars each*—to the Walpole firemen, to give to the children. She didn't like to do one she'd done before. A new one was like a new world to move into, she used to say. And of course . . .

(*A tender smile.*)

. . . they *did* indulge her in that.

YOUNG WOMAN

They knew she was going to die?

WOMAN

Oh yes, oh yes. There was no hope at all in those days. Not for bad cases like hers. *They* knew it, and *she* knew it too, from when she was fifteen years old.

YOUNG WOMAN

Oh wow.

(*Looking at the* YOUNG MAN.)

It must be awful, knowing it, at that age. Ooh!

(*She winces and shudders; the* YOUNG MAN *nods. The* YOUNG WOMAN *looks again at the* WOMAN, *who is gathering the dust cover together.*)

WOMAN

She never let it get her down though. Used to sit here hummin' a melody, happy as could be.

MAN

(*Lighting a lamp on the desk.*)

Susan dear, if you'd look over here . . . This is where she made the pins and bracelets we told y' about.

(*The* YOUNG WOMAN *goes toward the desk. The* YOUNG MAN *moves toward the game table, hands in pockets, looking about. The* WOMAN *puts the dust cover aside.*)

All her tools, her silver wire, bits of colored glass . . . Here's a pin she made just a day or two before.

(*Giving it to the* YOUNG WOMAN.)

Just look at that work, will y'?

YOUNG WOMAN

Wow, this is *beautiful!* Larry, come look!

(*She holds the pin in the lamplight. The* YOUNG MAN *goes toward her. The* WOMAN *begins uncovering a bookcase.*)

MAN. She made bracelets, earrin's, all kinds of things.

YOUNG WOMAN

(*Shows the pin to the* YOUNG MAN.)

Isn't it beautiful?

YOUNG MAN

(*Looks, nods.*)

Yeh, it is. It really is.

YOUNG WOMAN

(*Taking an arm's-length look.*)

She could sell these on the street today and make a *fortune!*

(*Gives the pin back to the* MAN.)

WOMAN

Here's some of her books and magazines . . . There are more by the bed, her favorite ones. And these are her paintin' things. She did that castle there. From her imagination, believe it or not; not copyin' anythin'.

(*The* YOUNG WOMAN *goes toward the painting on the wall.*)

YOUNG MAN

Did she do anything else, like make ships in bottles?

(*He has a Massachusetts accent. The* WOMAN *looks sharply at him.*)

MAN

Ah well, she had a lot of time to fill, y' know, stuck in the room here seven whole years.

YOUNG WOMAN

(*Looking at the painting.*)

What sign was she born under?

(*Turning, looking at the* WOMAN.)

Do you know?

WOMAN

Sign?

YOUNG WOMAN

You know, of the zodiac. Gemini, Capricorn . . .

WOMAN

(*Thinks for a moment.*)

June eighth was her birthday . . .

YOUNG WOMAN

That's Gemini. That's *my* sign. I'm June thirteenth.

(*A pause, the* WOMAN, *the* MAN, *and the* YOUNG MAN *looking at the* YOUNG WOMAN.)

MAN

Well now. Isn't *that* a coincidence . . .

(*Another pause, the* YOUNG WOMAN *uncomfortable, having been reminded of something.*)

WOMAN

Everythin' is how it was. Her clothes are in the closet, her comb and brush and all are in the bathroom. There's a half-done paintin' on that easel there . . . The Brabissants wouldn't change a *thing*, rest their souls. After she died they used to come in here almost every evenin' and just sit for a while, her over there and him over here, not sayin' *anythin'*. I had to keep the room as clean as any of the others.

MAN

I had to keep the trees by the window cut back, like as if she still needed the light to paint by!

WOMAN

Oh, they adored that girl . . . And John and I did too.

MAN

She used to wave to me when I was workin' this side of the house, as cheerful as if—as if she'd never even *heard* of TB, as if it was someone's *initials* or somethin'!

YOUNG WOMAN

(*Looking about approvingly.*)

It was lovely of them to keep everything . . . Like making a *shrine.*

YOUNG MAN

I don't think it was lovely. I think it was—unhealthy.

(*The* YOUNG WOMAN *looks at him with curiosity, the* WOMAN *and the* MAN *resentfully.*)

I'll bet this is why—

(*A movement of his head toward the door.*)

—Cissie wound up the way she is.

MAN

Oh no, no, no, no, no. Cissie was *always* the—

(*A waggle of fingers near his temple.*)

—peculiar one of the three.

YOUNG WOMAN

But maybe Larry's right. If the room had been changed, had been *used*, if—Veronica's things had been put away, maybe it would have been easier for Cissie to, you know, *understand*. This must have just *reinforced* everything.

WOMAN

You've got it all *wrong*, dear. She *did* understand, in the beginnin'. It's only these past few years, when she's near dyin' herself, that she's come to think Veronica's alive.

MAN

She's *gone back in time*, that's what Cissie's done. She's in 1935 now; Veronica's alive, *she's* goin' to the Boston Secretarial School—she does her shorthand every night, mind y'!—and Conrad's in his room at the end of the hall.

WOMAN

The three of them was close as fingers.

YOUNG WOMAN

Where's Conrad really?

WOMAN

He died in World War Two. In Japan.

MAN

Lieutenant in the Air Force. That was what finished the Brabissants, him getting' killed. First their oldest was taken, and then their youngest . . .

(*A pause, the* WOMAN, *the* MAN *and the* YOUNG MAN *watching the* YOUNG WOMAN, *who remembers again that she has a decision to make.*)

WOMAN

Will y' do it, Susan? Please? It'll make Cissie so happy.

MAN

It'll only take half an hour or so, and then I'll drive y' right back to town! You'll still have plenty of time for your walk by the river, and the—

(*Winks at the* YOUNG MAN.)

—moon'll be nice and high to shine on y'!

(*To the* YOUNG WOMAN *again.*)

What d'y' say, dear? Will y'?

WOMAN

Y' see the way the room is; we only have to take off the rest of the covers.

YOUNG WOMAN

(*Looks indecisively at the* YOUNG MAN, *and at the* WOMAN *again.*)

I—don't know . . .

(*The* WOMAN *and the* MAN *look anxiously at each other.*)

YOUNG MAN

Does she *really look* that much like Veronica?

WOMAN

Oh Lord, yes!

MAN

She could be her *twin* practically! I never *seen* anythin' like it!

WOMAN

When the two of y' came into that restaurant I thought I was seein' a *ghost*, so help me!

(*To the* YOUNG WOMAN.)

And the more so, the closer y' got.

MAN

I thought Maureen was havin' a stroke or somethin'! I had me back to y', remember, and didn't see till y' sat down.

(*To the* WOMAN.)

Remember, dear. I grabbed your hand and asked if y' was all right?

(*To the* YOUNG MAN.)

I really thought the old girl was dyin' on me!

(*Looking at the* YOUNG WOMAN.)

And then *I* saw . . . Oh yes, she really looks that much like Veronica. Enough to fool *anyone*, not just poor Cissie.

YOUNG WOMAN

You said you'd show us a picture.

WOMAN

That's right, of course; go get it, John. Sneak in there without wakin' her. The big one the photographer took. *You* know.

(*The* MAN *goes out.*)

She's got 'em all lined up, on the mantel and the tables; pictures of all of 'em.

(*Moves closer to the* YOUNG WOMAN.)

You'll see. It's yourself, standin' right here, with your hair brought back and gathered behind—

(*Taking the* YOUNG WOMAN'S *hair in both hands, arranging it.*)

—and a nice bright smile on your face. There . . .

(*Bites her lip, awed.*)

Oh Lord, seein' y' in this room of hers, it scares the daylights out of me!

(*She lets go of the* YOUNG WOMAN'S *hair and moves away, rubbing her hands distressfully. The* YOUNG WOMAN, *combing down her hair with her fingers, looks helplessly at the* YOUNG MAN, *and at the* WOMAN *again.*)

YOUNG WOMAN

I guess I have a common face. There was a girl back home who looked like me.

(*To the* YOUNG MAN.)

She was a year ahead of me, in school I mean, and kids were always stopping me and asking me about assignments I never heard of!

(*To the* WOMAN'S *back.*)

And the same thing used to happen to her.

YOUNG MAN

Did you ever purposely trick anyone?

YOUNG WOMAN

No. But we could've, if we'd wanted to. We weren't friends though. She was kind of a creep.

(*Smiles at him.*)

Gorgeous, but kind of a creep.

WOMAN

(*Turning to the* YOUNG WOMAN.)

Are you *sure* no part of your family's from here?

YOUNG WOMAN

Positive. My parents were born in Ohio, and my grandparents are from Poland and Germany.

WOMAN

(*Throwing off her discomfort.*)

Well, maybe over there then; who knows? Mr. Brabissant's folks were from Belgium originally. All them places are in there together, aren't they?

(*The* YOUNG WOMAN *nods, smiling.*)

YOUNG MAN

It's a continent, Mrs. Mackey. It's pretty big.

(*The* MAN *comes in, a small framed picture in his hand.*)

MAN

She's up, workin' on her *shorthand.*

(*Closes the door most of the way. To the* WOMAN.)

Didn't even know we was back.

(*To the* YOUNG WOMAN.)

I couldn't think of an excuse for the big one, but I sneaked this one out.

(*Gives the picture to her.*)

WOMAN

Oh that's no good! She's twelve or thirteen in that one!

MAN

I couldn't pick and choose, Maureen; it was nearest me hand.

(*The* YOUNG MAN *joins the* YOUNG WOMAN *looking at the picture. The* WOMAN *goes to them.*)

WOMAN

There. And that's Cissie and Conrad and *Mrs.* Brabissant. On the swing on the porch. It's gone now.

YOUNG WOMAN

She does look like me at that age . . . Except for the braces. On me I mean, not her.

YOUNG MAN

Braces?

YOUNG WOMAN

On my teeth.

YOUNG MAN

Oh.

WOMAN

She had lovely teeth. Nice and straight.

YOUNG WOMAN

So did I, but my father's a dentist.

(*Looks for another moment, then makes sure the* YOUNG MAN *is through and gives the picture to the* WOMAN.)

WOMAN

Later on, while Cissie's in *here*, John'll go in and get the *good* picture. We'll show it to y' after.

YOUNG MAN

Now just a second; Susan hasn't said she's going to do it.

WOMAN

Oh y' must, Susan! Please! All she keeps sayin', morning' and night, is "Why is Veronica angry with me? Why won't she let me come visit no more?"

MAN

The doctor says she felt *guilty when Veronica died.* Sometimes a child'll *do* that, he says, even when it's natural causes. And now she's a child again, eighteen in her head, not—fifty-six or whatever.

WOMAN

We're askin' so little of y'. Y' put on a dress, y' pin back your hair. Y' say "Hello, Cissie, I'm glad you're lookin' so well. No, I'm not angry with y', Cissie, it's just I don't want y' to catch the TB." It's so little, and it'd be such a blessin' for her.

YOUNG WOMAN

I'm—not sure it's a good thing to do.

MAN	WOMAN
What are y' talkin' about?	How could it *not* be, when it's the one thing she's longin' for?

YOUNG WOMAN

(*Gathers her thoughts.*)

Look, I—I know you *mean* well, and you think we'd be doing her a favor . . . But—I've studied some psychology. I'm a *sociology major*. It's not good to—play along with somebody's delusions. It just makes them *more* dependent on—

WOMAN

(*Interrupting her.*)

She's *dyin'*, Susan! She is *dyin'!* Didn't we make that clear in the car? She's dyin' of cancer! It's too *late* to get rid of her delusions! All we can do now is—make her a little *happy* when we've got the chance!

(*Upset, she turns from the* YOUNG WOMAN, *moves to the game table and puts the picture down on it. The* MAN *touches the* YOUNG WOMAN'S *shoulder gently.*)

MAN

A few weeks is all she's got. A month or two at the most. That's quotin' the doctor now.

(*The* YOUNG WOMAN *looks at the* YOUNG MAN; *he shakes his head doubtfully, rubbing the back of it. The* MAN *looks angrily at him.*)

What are your objections, Larry? Perhaps you'll tell us.

WOMAN

(*Having steadied herself, she turns to the* YOUNG WOMAN.)

Susan . . . We've never gone to that restaurant before. We go to a place on State Street, where John has a cousin who's waiter. Tonight, walkin' from the parkin' lot. I suddenly felt we should go someplace different this week. Don't ask me why' cause I don't know. "Let's go in *there,*" I says to John, "it'll be a change." "We'll have to tip," says John. "What the hell," says I . . . So in we go. And five minutes later *you and Larry come in.* And sit down next to us. Now don't you think—that someone, somewhere, was guidin' our steps tonight? *Your* steps, *our* steps? *Puttin'* us together so we could do this kind thing for Cissie?

YOUNG MAN

Making us not have any plans for the evening?

WOMAN

Yes! Even that! Maybe even that. Yes!

(*Pins him with an angry stare, then looks at the* YOUNG WOMAN *for her answer.*)

YOUNG WOMAN

Could Larry and I talk together please? Just for a minute or two?

(*The* WOMAN *stays looking at her.*)

MAN

Sure y' can. Of course.

(*Taking the* WOMAN'S *arm.*)

Come on, Maureen, let's let 'em talk it over.

(*The* WOMAN *lets the* MAN *take her toward the door.*)

We'll look in on Cissie. Y' can't blame 'em for hesitatin', dear. It's not everyone that wants to involve themselves in—oops!

(*About to draw the door closed, he leaves the* WOMAN *outside it and goes quickly to the game table and takes the picture. He smiles apologetically on his way back to the* WOMAN.)

Better slip this back before she misses it; eyes like a hawk! Come on, dear.

(*He draws the door closed. The* YOUNG WOMAN *looks at it for a moment, and turns to the* YOUNG MAN.)

YOUNG WOMAN

She *is* dying, and it *would* make her feel better . . .

YOUNG MAN

Oh, I *guess* so . . . But maybe they've got other reasons. Did you think of that?

YOUNG WOMAN

What do you mean? *What* other reasons?

YOUNG MAN

(*Crossing the room.*)

Well . . . it's not hard to imagine some . . .

YOUNG WOMAN

It's hard for *me* to. Like what?

YOUNG MAN

(*Turns to face her.*)

All right, the parents are dead, right? Mr. and Mrs. Brabissant?

YOUNG WOMAN

Yes.

YOUNG MAN

And Veronica's dead, and Conrad is dead . . .

(*The* YOUNG WOMAN *nods.*)

Only Cissie is alive, and she's dying.

(*The* YOUNG WOMAN *looks at him.*)

Maybe she knows something, where some money is hidden, or—some papers or something, and *she'll tell Veronica*, but she won't tell—

(*A thick brogue.*)

—the kindly old family servants, bless their darling' shamrock hearts!

(*The* YOUNG WOMAN *stares at him.*)

It's possible, isn't it? Or maybe they want her to sign something.

YOUNG WOMAN

Man, you really *are* a lawyer, aren't you!

YOUNG MAN

Did you think I wasn't?

YOUNG WOMAN

Well, guys bullshit.

(*Moves toward him.*)

You don't *look* like one, with that mustache.

YOUNG MAN

It's fake. I take it off before I go into the courtroom.

YOUNG WOMAN

All they want me to *say* is that I'm not *angry* with her.

YOUNG MAN

That's all they've told you *so far*. Maybe they'll have some other suggestions later on.

(*The brogue again.*)

"An' by the way, dear, would y' ask her t' tell y' where she's hidin' the old lady's *joolery?*"

YOUNG WOMAN

Shhh! Not so *loud* . . .

YOUNG MAN

You're right; they're probably listening.

YOUNG WOMAN

Oh man. Look, if you're so suspicious *now*, how come you were so unsuspicious in the restaurant? I don't remember you kicking me under the table or anything.

YOUNG MAN

We were just going to go look at a picture; they weren't saying anything then about—you putting on an act.

(*The* YOUNG WOMAN *moves away from him.*)

And I was afraid if I said no, you'd think I was in too much of a hurry to get down to the river.

YOUNG WOMAN

Oh great.

(*Turns to him.*)

I was afraid you'd think I was in too much of a hurry!

(*They look at each other. He smiles.*)

YOUNG MAN

I guess we should have been more open.

YOUNG WOMAN

(*Looking around dispiritedly.*)

You can say *that* again . . .

(*Decides, and looks at him.*)

I'm going to do it. I am. It'll be fun. I was Cordelia in *King Lear.*

YOUNG MAN

High school?

YOUNG WOMAN

(*Nods.*)

It'll be a good deed too. If they tell me to ask her anything, I just *won't,* that's all.

YOUNG MAN

I . . . *guess* they're on the level. They could twist her arm and *make* her tell, if there was something she was—keeping from them.

YOUNG WOMAN

Do you *always* mistrust people? I hope not. Oh wow, they forgot about my voice; what if I don't *sound* right?

YOUNG MAN

You must or they wouldn't think you could do it.

YOUNG WOMAN

I can do a Baaston aaccent. For a few minutes, at least.

YOUNG MAN

Can you keep from saying "oh wow"?

YOUNG WOMAN

Oh wow. Oh—something. What did they *say* in 1935?

YOUNG MAN

(*Shrugs.*)

I don't know. Boop-boop-a-doop.

YOUNG WOMAN

Oh wow. *Ooh!*

(*She slaps her forehead, and winces and smiles at him. He smiles at her.*)

YOUNG MAN

Should I call the leprechauns?

YOUNG WOMAN

(*Raises her hand.*)

No, wait a minute.

(*Moves closer to him, and stands before him.*)

Touch me.

(*He looks at her, not moving.*)

You haven't touched me yet, do you know that? I mean not even my elbow crossing the street. Let alone my more interesting features.

YOUNG MAN

It's—only our second date.

YOUNG WOMAN

Our first. Sunday doesn't count.

YOUNG MAN

So?

YOUNG WOMAN

Touch me; I'm promiscuous.

(*He touches her shoulder, and withdraws his hand. She looks feelingly at him.*)

She really bugged you, didn't she. That *mother* of yours, I mean. You're very uptight.

YOUNG MAN

(*Uncomfortably.*)

No I'm not . . . Jesus Christ, we're in a house out past Walpole, in a room covered with sheets, where a dead girl did jigsaw puzzles—all right, yes, I'm uptight! . . . I'll touch you later. Everywhere.

YOUNG WOMAN

(*Smiles at him.*)

Okay.

(*Goes toward the door, and turns and looks back at him.*)

If not, we'll just talk!

(*She opens the door and calls into the hallway.*)

You can come in now!

(*She smiles at the* YOUNG MAN. *The* MAN *and the* WOMAN *come in. The* YOUNG WOMAN *nods happily to them.*)

I'll *do* it!

WOMAN

(*Claps her hands.*)

Oh thank y', darlin'!

(*Hugging the* YOUNG WOMAN.)

Bless y'! You're an angel!

MAN

I knew y' would! I knew it all along! I just now made a dollar bet with her; "She'll *do* it," I said. "She has a *warm heart!*"

(*Snaps his fingers at the* WOMAN.)

Come on, Maureen, pay up! Come on, come on, where's me dollar? Hand it over.

WOMAN

(*Waving her hand at him.*)

Oh shut up, you and your bets.

(*Moves to the door.*)

MAN

You're welshin' on me?

(*To the* YOUNG WOMAN.)

Y' see what she is? She's a welsher!

(*To the* WOMAN.)

Come on now, Maureen! Y' made a bet, y' gotta—

WOMAN

(*Her back to the door, closing it; interrupting him.*)

Shut up, John.

(*The* MAN *falters to silence. The* WOMAN *looks steadily at him.*)

We've got to get the covers off, and Susan fixed up.

(*A pause. The* MAN *nods.*)

MAN

Of course, of course . . .

YOUNG WOMAN

Can I help? With the covers, I mean.

(*The* MAN *goes toward the bed.*)

WOMAN

Of *course* y' can, dear! The more *hands* there is, the less *work* there is! Get that one there.

(*She begins gathering the cover from a chair. The* YOUNG WOMAN *moves to the desk chair.*)

YOUNG WOMAN

Oh listen, is my *voice* all right? Do I *sound* like Veronica?

WOMAN

Y' do near enough! The sight of y' 'll be so perfect, I'm sure Cissie won't pay much mind to the sound!

MAN

(*Gathering the bed's dust cover.*)

Her hearin' ain't that good anyway; it's her eyes that're sharp, not her ears.

(*The* YOUNG WOMAN *begins gathering the desk chair's cover. The* YOUNG MAN, *having been looking on with an air of lingering disapproval, turns and begins gathering the cover from the dresser. The* WOMAN *puts her cover on the chaise.*)

WOMAN

Put 'em all on the chays here; then we'll bundle 'em up in the one.

YOUNG WOMAN

I can do a Boston accent a little; should I? Veronica must have had one.

WOMAN

Yes, that'd help y' sound right . . .

(*Takes the cover from a side table.*)

YOUNG WOMAN

(*Putting her cover on the chaise.*)

I'll paak my caa in Haavaad Yaad.

(*She starts toward the Victrola as the* YOUNG MAN *brings his cover to the chaise.*)

WOMAN

We're grateful to y', Larry, for lettin' Susan *do* the favor for us.

YOUNG WOMAN

(*Turning.*)

Letting me? He didn't *let* me; I make my *own* decisions.

(*The* YOUNG MAN *goes around the game table.*)

MAN

Oho, so you're a liberated woman, are y'!

YOUNG WOMAN

Bet your—*life* I am.

YOUNG MAN

(*Taking the cover from the chair before the puzzle.*)

How come I paid for dinner?

YOUNG WOMAN

(*Taking the cover from the Victrola.*)

Because *you asked*. When *I* ask, *I'll* pay.

MAN

(*To the* YOUNG MAN; *bringing the bed's cover to the chaise.*)

I'da paid if y'da let me.

YOUNG WOMAN

Hey, what *is* this?

WOMAN

(*Picking up the desk's dust cover from the floor.*)

The Victrola.

MAN

Record player, phonograph.

YOUNG WOMAN

Oh wow.

(*Turning to the* WOMAN.)

Hey, that's something else: what did Veronica say instead of "oh wow" and "oh man" and things like that?

WOMAN

(*Takes the cover from the* YOUNG WOMAN'S *hands and brings it with her own to the chaise; considers as she puts them down.*)

I believe she kept silent . . .

(*The* YOUNG WOMAN *is given pause. The* YOUNG MAN *smiles, gathering another cover. The* MAN *is uncovering a bookcase on the far side of the bed. The* YOUNG WOMAN *opens the Victrola's top, looks inside, twists her head.*)

YOUNG WOMAN

"Shuffle Off to Buffalo" . . .

WOMAN

(*Gathering a cover.*)

Oh, that was real popular then. It must have been the last record she played . . . Tsk-tsk.

(*Shakes her head and sighs.*)

YOUNG WOMAN

Does this work? Can we hear it?

WOMAN

I guess it does; try it and see.

MAN

(*On his way to the chaise.*)

Y' wind it on the side there, the handle.

YOUNG MAN

We want to get this over with, don't we?

YOUNG WOMAN

(*Winding the Victrola.*)

I want to hear it; it'll help me get in the mood.

(*The* YOUNG MAN *gives an Oh-God look. The* MAN, *having put his cover on the pile, reaches for the ones the* YOUNG MAN *holds. The* YOUNG WOMAN *fiddles in the Victrola's top.*)

WOMAN

John, get the one off the mirror there.

YOUNG WOMAN

It's turning, but the arm doesn't move.

WOMAN	MAN
Y've got to do it yourself.	Just pick it up and set it down there.

YOUNG WOMAN

Oh.

(*Doing it.*)

That's not very handy . . .

(*We hear a 1933 or '34 recording of "Shuffle Off to Buffalo," with vocal. While the record plays, the restoring of the room is completed. The* MAN *and the* YOUNG MAN *gather the last of the dust covers, while the* WOMAN *sets out various decorative objects that she takes from drawers in tables and the dresser. The* YOUNG WOMAN *helps some, but her interest is mainly in the song. "Oh, I've heard* this!" *she says after a few bars, and she hums along and sings, "Off we're gonna shuffle, shuffle off to Buffa-lo," sharing her enjoyment with the others in looks and smiles. The* MAN, *enlisting the* YOUNG MAN'S *help—"Gimme a hand here, will y'?"—encloses the heap of dust covers in the covers of the chaise; he carries the bundle from the room—the* YOUNG MAN *opens the door for him and closes it after him—and he returns a few moments later with a towel which he brings into the bathroom. The* WOMAN *gives various instructions throughout: "This goes on the night table. John, get a towel from the closet! Will y' put these on the bookcase there?" etc. As the record nears its end, the room looks warm, attractive and thoroughly lived-in. Another lamp may have been lighted, or secondary bulbs in the lamps already lit. The only jarring note is the unfinished painting on the easel, an agony of twisted tree branches, bare and black. The* YOUNG WOMAN *becomes aware of it, and moves from the Victrola to stand before it. The* MAN, *watching her from the side of the chaise where he sits resting, sings along with the final "Off we're gonna shuffle, shuffle off to Buffa-lo!" The* YOUNG MAN, *leaning against the dresser with his arms folded, watches him. The* WOMAN, *at the side of the Victrola, lifts its arm, switches it off, and closes its cover.*)

YOUNG MAN

They don't write them like that any more.

MAN

(*Turning to him.*)

Ain't it the truth! The *junk* they call *songs* now! Honest to God!

(*The* YOUNG WOMAN *doesn't turn. The* WOMAN *watches her, and looks uncomfortably at the painting.*)

WOMAN

She was—kind of downhearted at the end, I guess.

YOUNG WOMAN

That's not *downhearted*, ooh, that's—*anguished. Ooh!*

(*Turns from the painting wincing and hugging her arms.*)

MAN

Well, y' can't blame her, poor thing, knowin' what was ahead.

WOMAN

(*With a hand movement.*)

Turn it around, John; Cissie may not like it.

(*An inviting gesture to the* YOUNG WOMAN.)

Come on, dear. Now that the *room* is fixed up, it's *your* turn!

(*She goes to the closet. The* MAN *rises and starts toward the easel, watching as the* WOMAN *opens the closet. It's filled with colorful garments, most of them light and silken, and a rack of shoes hangs on the door. The* YOUNG WOMAN *approaches slowly. The* WOMAN *takes out an attractive 1930's-style dress on its hanger, and another one.*)

This here is one she liked a lot, and this here one too.

(*Displaying them both.*)

What d'y 'like, dear? Choose. Whichever y' want.

YOUNG WOMAN

(*Looks, and turns coolly to the* YOUNG MAN.)

I did not, you will notice, say "oh wow."

(*He smiles. The* YOUNG WOMAN *turns to the closet.*)

I sure *felt* like it though . . .

(*The* MAN *carefully turns the easel and painting around to face the wall, while the* YOUNG WOMAN *separates and looks at the garments in the closet.*)

It's like the Walpole branch of Paraphernalia!

WOMAN

Of what?

YOUNG WOMAN

This boutique in Cambridge that has all kinds of marvelous far-out things.

(*Takes a dress out and inspects it at arm's length.*)

You know my poncho? That's where I got it.

WOMAN

Oh.

(*The* YOUNG WOMAN *goes before the mirror over the dresser and holds the dress against herself.*)

I was wonderin' . . .

YOUNG WOMAN

It's Peruvian. Shepherds wear them.

(*Takes one of the dresses from the* WOMAN *and compares it with the other she's holding.*)

WOMAN

Well, these are what Veronica wore. Which'll it be?

YOUNG WOMAN

(*Shows them to the* YOUNG MAN; *moves toward him.*)

Which do *you* like?

YOUNG MAN

The one that goes on and off the quickest.

YOUNG WOMAN

(*Makes a face at him and goes back to the* WOMAN.)

This one.

WOMAN

I'da chose it too! It's a good color for y'.

(*She takes the other dress from the* YOUNG WOMAN.)

MAN

Well. I guess it's time for Larry and me to be getting' out.

YOUNG WOMAN

(*To the* YOUNG MAN.)

Sorry about that.

(*The* WOMAN *is hanging away the unchosen dresses. The* YOUNG MAN *stands straight.*)

YOUNG MAN

Can I come back and watch from somewhere, while Cissie is here?

(*The* WOMAN *turns from the closet; she and the* MAN *look at the* YOUNG MAN.)

MAN	WOMAN
Oh no.	No, y' can't do *that.*

MAN

There's no place to watch from.

(*The* YOUNG MAN *starts to gesture toward the bathroom.*)

WOMAN

She's liable to want to *use* the bathroom.

MAN

She goes a hell of a lot.

(*A pause.*)

WOMAN

And she might even want to—see something' in the closet. No, I really don't see how y' can—

MAN

(*Interrupting her, beckoning to the* YOUNG MAN.)

Susan'll tell y' the whole story! Come on, I'll make y' comfortable downstairs. I'll even give y' a sip of Irish whiskey, what d'y' say to that?

YOUNG MAN

(*Going to him.*)

Oh faith an' begorrah, that'll be a treat.

(*The* MAN *laughs. The* YOUNG MAN *looks across the room at the* YOUNG WOMAN. *She waves her fingers at him; he smiles.*)

Have fun.

YOUNG WOMAN

I expect to. It's a bigger part than Cordelia.

WOMAN

Have y' acted in plays?

YOUNG WOMAN

In high school.

WOMAN

Oh, *that'll* help us . . .

(*The* YOUNG MAN *goes to the* YOUNG WOMAN, *looks at her, and puts his hand to her cheek. She smiles at him, and puts her hand to his cheek. The* WOMAN *watches, surprised. The* YOUNG MAN *turns and goes back to the* MAN, *who, opening the door, throws a fatherly arm about the* YOUNG MAN'S *shoulders.*)

MAN

Come along, son, and I'll show y' where there's a nice comfortable chair in front of a TV set!

(*They go out, the* MAN *drawing the door almost closed after them. The* YOUNG WOMAN'S *smile lingers, as does the* WOMAN'S *puzzlement.*)

WOMAN

Y' belong to a *lodge* or somethin'?

YOUNG WOMAN

(*Turns to her with a broader smile.*)

No. He's—shy about touching me.

WOMAN

Oh.

(*A glance toward the door.*)

He seems to be getting' over it.

YOUNG WOMAN

(*Nods.*)

I think he will.

(*Taking the hanger from the dress she holds.*)

He had this awful rejecting mother. She told him right to his face that she never wanted him.

(*Gives the hanger to the* WOMAN.)

WOMAN

Oh dear.

YOUNG WOMAN

She probably never touched *him*, so now *he* can't touch. At least not easily.

WOMAN

(*Hanging the hanger in the closet.*)

Can that be?

YOUNG WOMAN

Oh yes. Yes . . .

(*Undoing the back of the dress.*)

Kids should be touched like crazy. All the time.

WOMAN

(*A pair of shoes in her hands.*)

Can y' wear size—

(*Looks in them, squints.*)

—seven B?

(*Goes to the* YOUNG WOMAN.)

YOUNG WOMAN

(*Takes them, looks.*)

—I guess so. I may *moan* a little.

WOMAN

(*Smiling.*)

It won't be for long.

(*Fixes the* YOUNG WOMAN *with a frank, steady, moment-of-truth gaze.*)

Y're not wearin' a brassiere, are y'.

YOUNG WOMAN

God no! Nobody does.

WOMAN

Speak for yourself.

(*Turns to the dresser, opens a drawer.*)

Y' better have one with that; it's kind of clingy. Are y' wearin' stockin's?

YOUNG WOMAN

No.

WOMAN

(*Finding them in the drawer.*)

Stockin's . . . Garters . . .

YOUNG WOMAN

Garters?

WOMAN

(*Turns and looks at her.*)

Y' ain't goin' to keep 'em up by prayin'.

(*Turns back to the drawer.*)

A slip . . . Here's a nice slip for y' . . .

(*Looking at the* YOUNG WOMAN *again.*)

Y' *are* wearin' *pants . . .*

(*The* YOUNG WOMAN *nods.*)

Saints be praised.

(*Turning, she tucks the handful of lingerie into the crook of the* YOUNG WOMAN'S *arm.*)

Now go on in there and put 'em on. I'm goin' to dust around a little.

(*The* YOUNG WOMAN *goes into the bathroom.*)

Oh, wait a minute, there's a belt that goes with that dress. Go ahead. I'll get it for y'.

(*Turns to the dresser, closes the open drawer, opens another, lifts out a skein of belts.*)

Narrow satin belt . . . Here it is.

(*Puts the others in the drawer, closes it, and brings the belt to the bathroom doorway.*)

Here y' are.

YOUNG WOMAN

(*Taking it.*)

Thanks.

(*The* WOMAN *closes the door partway, and standing in the lee of it, draws a neckchain from her dress. Taking in her hand something attached to the chain, she lifts it off over her head.*)

WOMAN

Have y' known Larry long?

YOUNG WOMAN

(*Off.*)

No, we just met Sunday.

WOMAN

(*Trying to open the chain, and having difficulty.*)

Y' seem to know a lot about him.

YOUNG WOMAN

(*Off.*)

I'm good at drawing people out. And picking up clues.

WOMAN

Clues? What d'y' mean?

(*Uses her teeth on the clasp.*)

YOUNG WOMAN

(*Off.*)

Oh, like the fact that he's got a big mustache and short hair. That means that he's *trying* to be open and self-accepting, but part of him is still kind of closed and defensive.

WOMAN

(*She has the chain open now and is drawing it up from the object in her hand.*)

Oh, that's *interestin'*. . . Can y' do that with everybody?

YOUNG WOMAN

(*Off.*)

More or less, when I'm not all wrapped up in *myself.*

WOMAN

(*Tucking the chain in a pocket and going toward the door to the hall.*)

My oh my, you're a very smart girl!

(*Standing before the almost-closed door, she draws it to her and puts the object, a key, into the outside of it. She tries it; the bolt, a large one, slides smoothly out and in.*)

YOUNG WOMAN

(*Off.*)

Mrs. Mackey?

WOMAN

It's Maureen, dear! Call me Maureen!

(*Puts the door as it was, leaving the key in it, and moves away.*)

YOUNG WOMAN

(*Off.*)

I ought to know more about people and things that Cissie is liable to mention. Who was Veronica's doctor, for instance?

WOMAN

(*Looking critically at the chaise.*)

Dr. Simpson, that was. He was everybody's doctor, the whole family's.

(*Moves the chaise a little farther away from the lamp table by it.*)

YOUNG WOMAN

(*Off.*)

Simpson?

WOMAN

That's right. And there was a cook then named Henrietta, with a little boy Morgan who used to hang around and make a pest of himself.

(*Adjusts the position of a decorative pillow on the chaise.*)

YOUNG WOMAN

(*Off.*)

Were there any friends or relations?

WOMAN

(Taking a handkerchief from a pocket, moving about flicking it at various surfaces, blowing dust from things.)

None that Cissie's likely to mention. The Brabissants was above most of the folks around here, and they weren't that close with their families neither.

He hated hers and *she* hated his. From what I seen at the funerals they were *both* of them right.

(She flicks and blows. The YOUNG WOMAN *comes out of the bathroom, fastening the belt of the mid-calf-length dress; it's quite becoming to her.)*

Oh isn't that nice now!

YOUNG WOMAN

It fits perfectly.

WOMAN

(A small pause.)

I knew it would; you're just the right size.

YOUNG WOMAN

Even the shoes are all right. Either my *feet shrank* or they made sizes bigger in those days.

(Takes a heavy bracelet from her wrist and smiles at the WOMAN, *who stands looking at her.)*

What do we do with my hair?

WOMAN

(Looks for another moment.)

I don't suppose y'd—let me cut a little, would y'?

YOUNG WOMAN

Oh no. No. No way.

WOMAN

Well, we'll just have to make it *look* shorter, then.

(*Pocketing her handkerchief, going toward the bathroom.*)

Sit down, I'll get pins.

(*The* YOUNG WOMAN *moves toward the desk. The* WOMAN, *passing her with a touch on the arm, goes into the bathroom. The* YOUNG WOMAN *puts her bracelet on the corner of the desk and sits in a chair.*)

YOUNG WOMAN

If she notices I'll just say I'm letting it grow. She hasn't *seen* Veronica in a long time. I mean even by *her* standards.

WOMAN

(*Off.*)

That's right; it'll be fine, don't worry. I pay too much mind to little details; John's always tellin' me that.

(*Comes out of the bathroom shaking dry a comb. She gives the* YOUNG WOMAN *a handful of hairpins.*)

Hold these and give' em to me, all right?

YOUNG WOMAN

Sure.

(*During the following, the* WOMAN *combs the* YOUNG WOMAN'S *hair back loosely over her ears and pins it up at the back of her neck in as close an approximation of a 1930's hairdo as she can manage. The* YOUNG WOMAN *hands back pins when the* WOMAN *reaches or asks for them.*)

WOMAN

I rinsed the comb . . .

YOUNG WOMAN

It was clean; I saw it. The whole bathroom is.

WOMAN

Oh, I come in and clean around once in a while . . .

(*A moment of silence, the* WOMAN *working with great concentration. The* YOUNG WOMAN *puts her hand to her mouth and coughs. Another moment goes by.*)

YOUNG WOMAN

Was that all right?

WOMAN

Was *what* all right?

YOUNG WOMAN

My cough.

WOMAN

Oh! Oh *yes*, that was very good, very good. Just like hers. That was very good . . . Real little actress . . .

(*Another pause, the* WOMAN *working, the* YOUNG WOMAN *thinking.*)

YOUNG WOMAN

How come Veronica wasn't in a sanitorium? The Brabissants could have afforded it, couldn't they? This *house*, and all the *land* . . .

WOMAN

Oh yes, they were *loaded.* He had a big mill over in East Walpole. Textile mill. Even in the Depression they were sittin' pretty.

YOUNG WOMAN

Then why didn't they send her—

WOMAN

(*Interrupting her.*)

Well y' see, it was that they *loved her so much;* they couldn't bear to have her away from them.

YOUNG WOMAN

But wouldn't she have lived longer, in a place like in *The Magic Mountain?* A sanitorium in the Alps . . .

WOMAN

Ma*ybe;* I don't know. All I know is they kept her here . . .

(*Another pause, the* YOUNG WOMAN *thinking, and looking down at herself uneasily.*)

Another . . .

(*The* YOUNG WOMAN *puts a pin in the* WOMAN'S *hand.*)

YOUNG WOMAN

Maureen?

WOMAN

Mm?

YOUNG WOMAN

These clothes, and the room and all; it's—safe, isn't it?

(*The* WOMAN *looks at her suddenly wary. The* YOUNG WOMAN *turns.*)

There's no danger of—

WOMAN

(*Understanding, relieved.*)

Oh of *course* it's safe, darlin'! The whole room was fumigated and all the clothes was taken out and cleaned! No, no, no, no, don't worry about *that!* Of *course* it's safe! I wouldn't be in here meself if there was any danger, would I? Oh no, no, no. Everythin' was cleaned and made all right again.

(*She comes around in front of the* YOUNG WOMAN, *lifts the* YOUNG WOMAN'S *chin, and looks judiciously at one side of her head and the other.*)

And germs don't live thirty-five, forty years anyway, do they?

YOUNG WOMAN

I don't know; I don't *think* so . . .

WOMAN

(*Fixing a strand of the* YOUNG WOMAN'S *hair.*)

No, I'm *sure* they don't. Everythin's clean; don't you worry. Tell me, d'y' have any brothers and sisters?

(*Going around in back again.*)

YOUNG WOMAN

One brother.

WOMAN

Older or younger?

YOUNG WOMAN

Older. He's in Portugal. Wait till I write him about—oh wow! Wait till I tell my *roommates!* They're going to think I made the whole thing up!

WOMAN

Are they? Oh, they wouldn't doubt your—

YOUNG WOMAN

(*Interrupting her.*)

Fact, absolute *fact!* This *one*, Diane, is the complete skeptic! I tell her I found a *penny on the sidewalk*, she doesn't believe me!

WOMAN

Oh my goodness . . .

YOUNG WOMAN

You're going to have to give me a *note* or something, some kind of *proof* that this whole thing *happened*.

WOMAN

(*Smiling at her, leaning close to share a secret.*)

It's *fun* dressin' up and playin' a part, isn't it?

YOUNG WOMAN

(*Nods, smiling.*)

Yes, it is. At least when there's a good reason for doing it.

WOMAN

Mmm, yes!

YOUNG WOMAN

You can rationalize it then; otherwise it's just—kid stuff. But kid stuff's *okay* once in a while; I don't think people ought to *not* allow themselves to—

(*A knock at the door stops her.*)

MAN

(*Off.*)

It's me. Can I come in?

WOMAN

Yes, come on in, John!

(*The* MAN *comes in and closes the door at his back. He looks at the* WOMAN, *and at the* YOUNG WOMAN, *admiringly.*)

We're just finishin'.

MAN

You're Veronica. As God is me judge!

(*The* YOUNG WOMAN *smiles, pleased.*)

WOMAN

Doesn't she look grand?

MAN

Marvelous, marvelous!

YOUNG WOMAN

What's Larry doing?

MAN

Watchin' TV. A basketball game.

YOUNG WOMAN

Oh? Who's playing?

MAN

Didn't notice.

WOMAN

Go and get her things out of the bathroom.

(*The* MAN *goes to do so. The* WOMAN *tells the* YOUNG WOMAN.)

In case Cissie goes in there. I'll put 'em in the linen closet.

YOUNG WOMAN

Is Cissie her real name?

WOMAN

Cecilia.

YOUNG WOMAN

Oh.

WOMAN

There. That looks right enough.

(*The* YOUNG WOMAN *rises, touching her hair tentatively. The* WOMAN *smiles and mock-curtsies.*)

Please don't bother to tip me, miss.

YOUNG WOMAN

(*Smiling.*)

Okay, I won't.

(*She goes and looks at herself in the dresser mirror. The* WOMAN *watches her happily. The* MAN *comes out of the bathroom with the* YOUNG WOMAN'S *clothes over his arm, her shoes and necklaces in his hand; he too watches her.*)

It's nice. I like it!

(*Turning to them.*)

Can I go show Larry?

WOMAN

Oh no, what if she sees y' out of the room?

MAN

I'll bring him up after the *performance;* y' can give him an *encore.*

YOUNG WOMAN

(*Smiling.*)

Okay.

(*Hugs her arms, rubs them.*)

"Performance" is right; I've got goosebumps!

MAN

Ah, it'll be a breeze! Don't worry about it!

WOMAN

(*Putting a chair in its proper position.*)

Just say you're not angry with her. I won't let her stay more' n two minutes.

YOUNG WOMAN

You'll stay here *with* us, won't you? In case she—

WOMAN

(*Over her.*)

Oh sure I will.

YOUNG WOMAN

—says anything I don't understand? Asks a question I can't answer?

WOMAN

I'll be *right here*. I'll tell her the doctor says y' mustn't talk too much. And let's turn off a light or two, to make it even *more* convincin'.

(*Turns off the lamp by the chaise.*)

MAN

(*Turning off the desk lamp.*)

Eyes like a hawk, she's got.

YOUNG WOMAN

(*Standing by the game table; to the* WOMAN.)

How old is *Conrad?*

WOMAN

(*Turning off the wall bracket.*)

You're twenty, she's eighteen, Conrad is seventeen.

(*The* MAN *turns off the other bracket. The* WOMAN *moves near the door and takes a final satisfied look at the* YOUNG WOMAN *and the room. The man joins* her.)

Well, I guess we're about ready now, don't y' think?

MAN

(*Looks, considers.*)

Yes . . . I'd say we was all set.

YOUNG WOMAN

(*With a relieved smile.*)

Larry thought you would tell me to *ask* Cissie something.

WOMAN — What d'y' mean?

MAN — Ask her somethin?

YOUNG WOMAN

Where *money* is hidden or something like that.

WOMAN

Oh for goodness' sake.

MAN

Is that why he was against your doin' it?

(*The* YOUNG WOMAN *nods; they shake their heads.*)

WOMAN — Tsk!

MAN — Oh my . . .

YOUNG WOMAN

I guess lawyers become suspicious of people.

WOMAN

Sure they do, from bein' amongst *lawyers* so much!

YOUNG WOMAN

(*Smiling.*)

He changed his mind, so don't tell him I told you.

MAN

(*Raises his right hand.*)

He'll never know.

(*Opens the door partway.*)

WOMAN

It's goin' to take us a couple of minutes to get her ready; she'll want to fix herself up and all.

MAN

We'll hurry her along as much as we can.

WOMAN

You make yourself at home.

(*Going to the desk.*)

Do some work on the puzzle there.

(*Picking up the* YOUNG WOMAN'S *bracelet.*)

Or look at a book, or play some records.

YOUNG WOMAN

Are you kidding? I'm going to *rehearse!*

(*The* MAN *opens the door wide; the* WOMAN *waves a hand at the* YOUNG WOMAN *and goes toward it.*)

WOMAN

Ah, y' don't need to! You're perfect, y' couldn't be better!

(*She goes out past the* MAN. *He stands looking amiably at the* YOUNG WOMAN, *her clothes over his arm.*)

MAN

No, you're right, Susan. You rehearse a little.

(*Conspiratorially, with a wink.*)

Practice bein' Veronica!

(*He goes out and draws the door closed. After a moment the bolt is heard striking home. The* YOUNG WOMAN'S *smile gives way to an uncertain frown. She crosses the room, tries the door, and sure enough it's locked.*)

YOUNG WOMAN

Mr. Mackey? Maureen?

(*Listens, hears nothing, and calls louder.*)

Mr. *Mackey?* John?

(*She's puzzled. She stands for a moment, thinking, and then—what can she do?—shrugs her puzzlement off and moves into the room. She wanders thoughtfully, touching the back of the chaise, the edge of the Victrola, picking up one of Veronica's mementos, examining it, putting it down. She turns, faces the door, and smiles warmly.*)

Hello, Cissie! Oh, it's so good to see you! You're looking—

(*It's awful; she throws it away with both hands and girds herself for another try.*)

Hello, Cissie! You look maavelous! Angry? *Me?* With *you?* Oh Cissie, how could you think—*Hello,* Cissie! Oh, I'm *so* glad to see you!

(*Coughs.*)

Angry? With *you?* Oh *no,* dear, it's all Dr. *Simpson's* fault! He's such—

(*Coughs.*)

He's such an old *fusspot* about keeping me *isolated!* Conrad hasn't been allowed in either, not for months!

(*Not bad; with a tentative nod of approval, she moves toward the door and sings to it, throwing her arms open.*)

Hello, Cissie!
Well, hello, Cissie!

(*Moves about, and sings slowly.*)

It's so nice—

(*Touches something.*)

—to have you back—

(*Turns, taking in the whole room.*)

—where you belong . . .

(*She continues a slow humming of "Hello, Dolly!" moving about, looking, touching. The end of the first part of the song finds her next to the game table. She stops and looks down at the puzzle. She picks up a piece, looks at it, looks at the puzzle, and sees where the piece goes. She pops it in, surprised and pleased with herself.*)

Ha!

(*She picks around at some of the other pieces, and sits down and studies the puzzle. The curtain of the partly raised window wafts and falls back. Moonlight has printed a black silhouette on the curtain: the window sashes and, overlying them, a barred grillwork that covers the whole of the window. The same shadow pattern is on the curtain of the window beyond the bed. The* YOUNG WOMAN *picks up the open box of the puzzle and rummages through the pieces. She finds a likely one and tries it in various places in the puzzle. She begins humming again—"Shuffle Off to Buffalo" in a quick perky tempo. She sings.*)

Ooooh, ooh, ooh.
Off we're gonna shuffle,
Shuffle off to Buffa-lo.

(*She hums the next few bars and sings again.*)

Oooh, ooh, ooh.
Off we're gonna shuffle,
Shuffle off to Buffa-lo.

(*She begins humming the bridge, as*)

THE CURTAIN FALLS

ACT TWO: VERONICA

(The YOUNG WOMAN is still working on the puzzle. *She stops short as the doorbolt clicks. She rises and readies herself, watching the door. It opens and the* WOMAN *comes in holding a glass of milk on a plate. She seems taller than before. Without looking at the* YOUNG WOMAN, *she brings the milk to the table by the chaise. The* YOUNG WOMAN *peers into the dimness, and glances at the open door.*)

YOUNG WOMAN

Is she coming?

(*The* woman, *having put the milk down, lights the lamp on the table and stands looking at the* YOUNG WOMAN. *She has changed her clothes and her hair style and looks now like a woman of the 1930's—and considerably younger than she looked before. The* YOUNG WOMAN *stares at her.*)

Hey, you look *terrific!* I didn't know *you* were going to change too.

WOMAN

What are you talking about?

(*Her brogue is gone.*)

YOUNG WOMAN

(*An uncertain pause.*)

What do you mean, what am I talking about? You—changed your dress, your hair . . . You look twenty years younger!

(*The* WOMAN, *with an annoyed headshake, turns and goes toward the door.*)

Is she coming?

WOMAN

(*Turns and looks at the* YOUNG WOMAN.)

Is *who* coming?

YOUNG WOMAN

Cissie.

(*The* WOMAN *stares angrily at her. The* YOUNG WOMAN *is unsure whether to laugh or not.*)

Are you—all right? Don't you remember?

(*The* WOMAN *keeps staring at her.*)

You and *Mr.* Mackey are bringing *Cissie* in. To *see* me. That's why I'm dressed up.

WOMAN

(*Looks down at her hands and rubs them, trying to decide how best to cope with this; looks at the* YOUNG WOMAN *with controlled hostility.*)

Now look, Veronica . . .

(*The* YOUNG WOMAN *stands motionless, looking at the* WOMAN, *who goes on—with a Massachusetts accent.*)

This is *not* the night to give us any trouble, do you understand? Conrad's in bed with a fever of one hundred and one degrees. It's Maureen's night off. And the men at the mill started a sit-down strike today and your father's *not happy* about it. So just drink your milk, and get undressed, and go to bed. Good night.

(She goes out and closes the door. The bolt clicks. The YOUNG WOMAN, *staring, moves a few steps toward the door. She turns, and looks at one of the windows with its grillwork-shadowed curtain. She turns farther, and looks at the other window. She turns all the way around, looking at the room and the closed door—fearfully, incredulously. She runs to the door, and finding it locked again, begins hitting it with her fists.)*

YOUNG WOMAN

Unlock this door! Let me out of here! Unlock this goddamn door, God damn it!

(She takes one of her shoes off, and holding it by the instep, hammers at the door with its high heel.)

Larry? Come up here! Larry!

(She stops and listens, then hammers again.)

LARRY! LARRY!

(She stops and listens, then crouches and puts her eye to the keyhole. She straightens, drops the shoe, and stamps on the floor with her shod foot several times. She listen, and hears nothing. She looks at the door, thinking, and at the desk, and at the bookcase. Taking her other shoe off, she drops it and goes quickly to the bookcase. She searches among art supplies and finds a large sketch pad. Opening it, she tears a sheet from it, drops the pad, and returns to the door. Crouching, she slides the paper under it. She puts it partway through and moves it against the jamb, below the keyhole. Rising, she goes to the desk and looks among the tools there. She comes back to the door holding a small pair of thin long-nosed pliers. Crouching again, she looks into the keyhole, then puts the pliers into it and

tries to work the key out on the other side. She stops and withdraws the pliers, looks down, and watches the end of the paper vanish under the door. She rises, and stands facing the door.)

Put the key back in and unlock this door.

MAN

(*Off.*)

Move away, Veronica.

YOUNG WOMAN

I'm not Veronica; I'm Susan.

MAN

(*Off.*)

Move away and we'll come in.

YOUNG WOMAN

Get Larry up here.

MAN

(*Off.*)

Move *away.*

(*The* YOUNG WOMAN *stays there, but after a moment she withdraws a few steps.*)

Further.

(*She withdraws farther, and stands watching the door. The key and the bolt are heard, and the door opens. The* MAN *and the* WOMAN *come in. The* MAN *moves a step or two toward the* YOUNG WOMAN; *the* WOMAN *stays by the open door. The* MAN *wears the vest and trousers of a 1930's business suit, with a white shirt and a loosened necktie. Like the* WOMAN, *he looks younger and more authoritative than he did before. Toying with the key in his hand, he looks disapprovingly at the* YOUNG WOMAN, *and down at the shoes on the floor before him. He moves one with the toe of his own shoe, and looks at the* YOUNG WOMAN *again.*)

Now what's all this banging and screaming about? Hm?

(*And he too speaks with a Massachusetts accent, not a brogue. The* YOUNG WOMAN *looks warily at him.*)

Well, young lady? What do you think you're doing?

WOMAN

Being her miserable *self*, that's what she's doing.

(*The* YOUNG WOMAN *looks at the* WOMAN, *and at the* MAN *again. He puts the key into a vest pocket.*)

MAN

Well? I'm waiting for an answer.

YOUNG WOMAN

I want to go now. Bring me my clothes.

WOMAN

Speak in your regular voice!

YOUNG WOMAN

(*Looks at her for a moment.*)

I'm speaking in it. It's—shaking a little, but this is it.

(*To the* MAN.)

Bring me my clothes, please.

MAN

(*Tries to make sense of that, but can't.*)

You're *wearing* them.

(*She looks at him. He points.*)

Well, *look*. That's not—*nothing!* It's a *dress*, stockings . . .

YOUNG WOMAN

(*As loud as she can, moving towards the open door.*)

LARRY!

(*The* WOMAN *slams the door and stands against it. The* MAN *blocks the* YOUNG WOMAN, *thrusting her back a step with a push at her shoulder. She drops the pliers.*)

MAN

Don't you raise your voice again! You hear me? You shout like that again I'll—I'll really give it to you! You hear me?

(*The* YOUNG WOMAN *withdraws another few steps, watching him and rubbing her shoulder.*)

You can talk any which way you like, but you're not going to *shout* any more!

(*He picks up the pliers. The* WOMAN, *with a sigh, moves from the door.*)

WOMAN

Anything to torment us, anything to make trouble . . .

(*She picks up the shoes; the* MAN *tosses the pliers to the desk.*)

MAN

(*To the* WOMAN.)

Go downstairs; I'll see that she goes to bed.

YOUNG WOMAN

Get Larry up here . . .

MAN

(*Turning angrily to her.*)

Who are you *talking* about? *What* Larry? Larry *Porcelli*, at the *mill?*

YOUNG WOMAN

The Larry who's downstairs! Larry Eastwood! The man I came here with!

(*The* MAN, *nonplussed, looks at the* WOMAN; *she's seething. The* YOUNG WOMAN *cries at her.*)

You just closed the door so he wouldn't hear me!

WOMAN

I closed the door because *Conrad* is *sleeping!*

YOUNG WOMAN

Conrad is DEAD! . . . Now *stop* it! This is *now*, this is 1973. You *know* it is.

WOMAN

Oh Lord!

(*The* MAN *stands staring at the* YOUNG WOMAN.)

YOUNG WOMAN

Get my clothes and let me out of here.

(*A pause, the* MAN *and the* WOMAN *staring at the* YOUNG WOMAN.)

MAN

You stop it, Veronica. We've had all we're going to stand for.

WOMAN

(*Going toward the closet, shoes in hand.*)

Hit her and *make* her stop; will you do that, please? Because if *you* won't—

(*The* YOUNG WOMAN *runs toward the door, evading the* MAN *as he grabs at her arm. He catches her from behind as she touches the knob.*)

YOUNG WOMAN

LARRY! LARRY! LARRY!

(*The* WOMAN, *having dropped the shoes, hurries over and helps the* MAN *drag the* YOUNG WOMAN *back to the room's center. She struggles and hits at them.*)

Let go of me! Let me—*out* of here!

WOMAN

Bitch! Little *bitch!*

(*They struggle further—for several moments, upsetting some bric-a-brac and a chair that the* YOUNG WOMAN *grabs onto—and finally the* YOUNG WOMAN *is thrown to the bed. She brings herself to a sitting position, winded, trembling, her hair half undone. The* MAN *goes to the door and locks it. The* WOMAN *sucks at her wrist.*)

MAN

(*Returning, pocketing the key, his hands shaking.*)

You stay there. You don't move from that bed till I say so. Or else I get the belt. Is that what you want? The belt?

WOMAN

That's what she *needs*, God damn her. Look at that!

(*She shows the* MAN *her wrist, and sucks at it again, glaring at the* YOUNG WOMAN. *The* MAN *tucks his shirt down into his trousers*)

MAN

Oh, you really take the cake! And it had to be tonight, didn't it!

(*Looks at the* YOUNG WOMAN *as he goes on fixing himself.*)

Do you *know* what kind of trouble I've had all day? We've *all* had all day? Do you *care?* No, *that* wouldn't interest you; *yourself* is all *you* care about. God knows you've proved *that* conclusively.

YOUNG WOMAN

I'm not Veronica. You *know* I'm not.

(*The* MAN *sighs. The* WOMAN *is fixing her hair and her dress.*)

I'm Susan Kerner. I'm a junior at B.U. My ID card is in my bag downstairs.

WOMAN

With *Larry.*

(*The* YOUNG WOMAN *looks at her, and at the* MAN, *who's righting the upset chair.*)

YOUNG WOMAN

It's on the—coatrack or whatever it is. The thing in the hall, with the antlers. That's where it *was,* anyway.

WOMAN

(*To the* MAN, *helping him pick up bric-a-brac.*)

I told you to let them have her, didn't I! But oh no, scandal must never touch the holy name of Brabissant!

MAN

All right, all right.

WOMAN

After *all*, there were Brabissants in Europe who were actually *street cleaners!* I'm talking about the *successful* ones, now.

MAN

Shut up, Nedra.

(*They straighten things; the* YOUNG WOMAN *watches them.*)

WOMAN

We could have spared ourselves *all* this *misery* . . . I won't even *talk* about the *expense.*

YOUNG WOMAN

Who are you?

WOMAN

Tch! "Who are we"!

MAN

(*Looks coldly at the* YOUNG WOMAN.)

I'm Amos. She's Andy . . . Now cut it out. Talk like yourself.

(*He goes back to straightening up. The* YOUNG WOMAN *watches.*)

YOUNG WOMAN

Do you *really believe* I'm—Veronica? Or are you—playing some kind of game?

WOMAN

You'll find out what kind of "game" we're playing if you don't start talking in your normal voice.

(*The* YOUNG WOMAN *looks about confusedly, and at herself, and her left arm. She shows the inside of it.*)

YOUNG WOMAN

Did Veronica have a scar like this? I was hit by an arrow, in camp, when I was eleven! Camp Allegheny, in Shanksville, Pennsylvania!

WOMAN

You did that yourself, with a pair of scissors. When you were fourteen.

MAN

You've never been to camp.

(*He and the* WOMAN *do the last of the straightening up. The* YOUNG WOMAN *sings at them, to the tune of "Buffalo Girls."*)

YOUNG WOMAN

Allegheny girls gonna stand up and fight!
  Gonna stand up and fight!
  Gonna stand up and fight!
Allegheny girls gonna stand up and fight!
  Gonna fight both night and noon!

(*The* MAN *and the* WOMAN, *having exchanged commiserating looks and headshakes, are near the door now.*)

MAN

You quiet down and get to bed. And in the morning you'd better be talking like yourself.

YOUNG WOMAN

(*Standing up.*)

Are you out of your *heads?* How long do you think Larry is going to *wait* down there? I'm surprised he hasn't come up *already;* it's been—I-don't-know-*how*-long since he went down—

(*Faltering, looking uncertainly at the* MAN *and the* WOMAN.)

—and he was anxious to—get it over with . . .

(*Stares at them.*)

MAN

Nobody is downstairs.

YOUNG WOMAN

Did you—do something to him?

WOMAN

(*To the* MAN.)

Will you make her stop this please?

YOUNG WOMAN

You were going to give him Irish whiskey . . . Did you—put something in it?

WOMAN

Why are you *standing there,* Lloyd? Give me the key; *I'll* get the belt!

YOUNG WOMAN

(*Withdraws a step.*)

My *God*, you're—you're *maniacs . . . !*

WOMAN

(*Turning on her.*)

We're maniacs? Oh that's a *hot* one, coming from *you*, Veronica!

MAN

(*Looking at the* YOUNG WOMAN.)

Call Dr. Simpson.

(*Gets the key from his pocket and holds it toward the* WOMAN.)

WOMAN

(*Looks at the key, and at him.*)

Are you *serious?* This is an *act* she's putting on! She doesn't *believe* this Larry business!

MAN

(*Turning to her, holding out the key.*)

Call Simpson.

WOMAN

For God's sake, he was here *twice* already today for Conrad! I'm not going to—

MAN

Will you for once in your life do what I tell you without giving me arguments, God damn it?

(*Takes her hand and claps the key into it.*)

Call him! Now!

WOMAN

All right . . . !

(*Turns to the door and unlocks it.*)

MAN

Tell him to hurry.

WOMAN

(*Turns, gives him the key, and glares at him.*)

Two dollars, right down the drain!

(*She turns, opens the door, and goes out. The* MAN *closes the door and locks it. He turns and looks at* YOUNG WOMAN; *she's staring at him fearfully.*)

MAN

Get back on the bed.

(*The* YOUNG WOMAN *withdraws a step. The* MAN *moves toward the table by the chaise, pocketing the key. He draws a deep breath and massages his forehead. The* YOUNG WOMAN, *watching him intently, sits on the edge of the bed. The* MAN *takes the glass of milk from the table and drinks some of it. He puts it down again, and takes a handkerchief from his pocket and wipes his mouth, and his forehead, and the palms of both his hands.*)

YOUNG WOMAN

I thought you . . . loved Veronica . . .

MAN

(*Scrubs a palm thoughtfully.*)

We did, long ago, and maybe we still could, a little—

(*Looks sadly at her.*)
—if you—didn't do things . . .

YOUNG WOMAN

I'm not Veronica.

(*The* MAN *sighs.*)

I'm Susan Kerner. I'm a junior at B.U.

(*The* MAN *sits on the foot of the chaise. He rubs his face with both hands.*)

And *you're not*—Veronica's father either. If she was twenty in 1935, he must have been—forty, at least. So now he'd be—

(*Puts a hand to her forehead and closes her eyes. To herself.*)

Oh God, thirty-five from seventy-three . . .

(*Works it out, lowers her hand.*)

He'd be almost eighty now. Maybe more. You weren't even that old *before!*

MAN

(*Patiently, not looking at her.*)

It's 1935. I'm forty-eight. Your mother is forty-six.

YOUNG WOMAN

(*A pause, watching him.*)

I know she is. But she's in Youngstown, Ohio . . . What do you want from me? Do you want me to—pretend I'm Veronica and stay here? Did you—*kill Larry?* Did you? Oh *God*, he'd be *up*, knocking at the door!

MAN

(*Sighs, shakes his head and looks at her.*)

Don't talk any more, all right? *That's* what I want from you. Don't talk. Let's just wait for Dr. Simpson.

(He looks away again, deeply troubled. The YOUNG WOMAN, *watching him, begins pulling the pins from her hair.)*

YOUNG WOMAN

There *is* no Dr. Simpson! *He'd* probably be *a hundred* by now!

(Glances at the door.)

What is she really doing?

(The MAN *doesn't answer.)*

Is she changing again? Who's she going to be *now*, Henrietta the cook?

MAN

(Looks at her, holding out a palm-up hand.)

You see?

YOUNG WOMAN

She *told* me about Henrietta!

MAN

(Looks away.)

Don't talk.

(The YOUNG WOMAN, *having removed all the pins, combs her hair down with her fingers. The* MAN *looks at her.)*

You've let your hair grow . . .

(The YOUNG WOMAN *glares at him. He looks away again.)*

It looks nice, hanging loose that way. Girls *ought* to let their hair grow long.

(A knock at the door brings the YOUNG WOMAN *instantly to her feet.)*

YOUNG WOMAN

Larry?

MAN

Sit down.

(*He rises and goes toward the door, taking the key from his pocket. The* YOUNG WOMAN *stays standing. The* MAN *unlocks the door and opens it, and the* WOMAN *comes in—as she was before except for a white Band-Aid on her wrist.*)

WOMAN

He's coming.

(*The* MAN *closes the door and locks it. The* WOMAN *looks at the* YOUNG WOMAN.)

How's Luise Rainer?

MAN

(*Turning, pocketing the key.*)

She's not acting. She really thinks it's 1973.

WOMAN

Sure. Tell me another.

YOUNG WOMAN

Turn on the radio.

(*The* WOMAN *and the* MAN *look at her.*)

You have a *radio*, don't you? They were invented by 1935!

(*To the* MAN.)

You said "Amos and Andy" before; they were *radio* stars!

MAN

(*Nods.*)

We have a radio . . .

YOUNG WOMAN

(*A step toward them.*)

Then turn it on!

(*The* MAN *looks at the* WOMAN.)

WOMAN

And how—do you expect us—to get it *up* here?

YOUNG WOMAN

(*Snaps her fingers and points at the* WOMAN.)

Ooooh, you're really quick there, Maureen! Nedra, Henrietta; you improvise *fantastically!*

(*Another step toward them, holding out her thumb and forefinger inches apart.*)

They're going to have radios no bigger than a pack of cigarettes, would you believe that?

MAN

I suppose it's—conceivable . . .

YOUNG WOMAN

You bet your *ass* it's conceivable!

(*She turns and strides across the room and swats at the dresser.*)

MAN

No filthy language.

YOUNG WOMAN

(*Turning.*)

That's *clean* language now!

MAN

Get back on the bed.

YOUNG WOMAN

All right, I will.

(*She turns toward the bed and whips into the bathroom, pulling the door closed. The* MAN *and the* WOMAN *glance at each other, undismayed.*)

WOMAN

There's no lock on the door, dear!

(*She sits in a chair and makes herself comfortable. The* MAN *sits on the foot of the chaise. After a moment the bathroom door opens and the* YOUNG WOMAN *comes out, looking balefully at them.*)

We took it out after the *first* time you did that.

YOUNG WOMAN

Now *look* . . . People don't go from sane to crazy just like that. You're pretending. Beautifully, I'll admit, but you're *pretending.*

WOMAN

(*To the* MAN.)

You know, I'm beginning to think you may be right.

MAN

I *am.* Look at her, for God's sake.

(*They look at the* YOUNG WOMAN; *she looks at them.*)

YOUNG WOMAN

We went to a restaurant, Larry and I!

(*To the* WOMAN.)

The Larry you were probably downstairs burying! . . . It was the Golden *something*, I forget the name, but *you* were at the next table, the *two* of you, about sixty years old—it was make-up, I guess—and you were talking with brogues that Saint *Patrick* would have been proud of! . . . You said you were Mr. and Mrs. Mackey, John and Maureen, and you—

WOMAN

(*Interrupting her.*)

John and Maureen?

YOUNG WOMAN

Yes! The gardener and the maid!

MAN

(*A pause.*)

We know who they are.

YOUNG WOMAN

You said that *I* looked like *Veronica*. We came back here to look at a picture of her. Does any of this ring a bell? Does any of this penetrate the miasma?

(*The* MAN *and the* WOMAN *shake their heads, utterly at sea.*)

You're lying, you've *got* to be . . . On the way here you told us about Cissie, and you asked—

WOMAN

(*On her feet.*)

Don't—you—mention—her—name!

(*Going toward the* YOUNG WOMAN, *pointing.*)

Not from your lips, her name! *Ever!*

(*She stands before the* YOUNG WOMAN, *who retreats a step, frightened. The* MAN *rises.*)

MAN

What did we tell you about her?

YOUNG WOMAN

You *know* what you told me, God damn it!

(*A pause.*)

MAN

What did we tell you?

YOUNG WOMAN

(*Retreats farther from the* WOMAN. *To the* MAN.)

That she's dying of cancer . . . That she thinks Veronica's alive . . .

(*The* WOMAN'S *anger is growing. The* YOUNG WOMAN *eyes her uneasily and speaks to the* MAN *again.*)

You asked me to pretend to *be* Veronica, to—tell her I'm not angry with her. She feels guilty about Veronica having died.

WOMAN

(*Claps her hands to her face and cries out.*)

Jesus and Mary!

(*A shivering whisper.*)

Hold me, Lloyd, hold me; stop me from—hurting her!

(*The* MAN *moves quickly behind the* WOMAN *and takes her by the shoulders. The* YOUNG WOMAN, *frightened and confused, looks at her and at the* MAN.)

MAN

Cissie alive? *Cissie* feeling *guilty?*

YOUNG WOMAN

And Veronica dead! That's what you told me! Tonight! In 1973!

WOMAN

(*In an agonized moan.*)

How can she *say* it . . .?

MAN

(*His lips by her ear, soothingly.*)

She *believes* it, Nedra, she *believes* it. Something has—switched over in her mind; I've heard of that happening, when people can't face reality.

YOUNG WOMAN

(*Shaking her head.*)

Oh no, no. That *is* reality. That's what you *told* me; in the *restaurant*, in the *car*, in this *room* here. It was—covered with sheets. We had to—fix it all up . . .

(*The* WOMAN *lowers her hands and looks at the* YOUNG WOMAN; *the* MAN *looks at her too.*)

I'm *Susan Kerner* . . .

WOMAN

Oh don't you *wish* you were . . . !

(*Peeling the* MAN's *hands from her shoulders.*)

Don't you wish you were *someone*, anyone, *years* from now, going to school, as free as a bluebird!

(*She moves toward the* YOUNG WOMAN; *the* YOUNG WOMAN *retreats.*)

With a boyfriend Larry to take you to restaurants! And a family somewhere that *loves* you; instead of *this* one, your *own*, that wishes you were *dead!*

(*The* YOUNG WOMAN *is retreating around the game table, keeping her distance from the* WOMAN, *who follows.*)

You think that's reality? That restaurant story? You're really not doing this to torment us?

YOUNG WOMAN

It *is* reality. It *happened tonight.*

WOMAN

(*Shaking her head.*)

I'm not going to let you *escape* that easily. I'm going to give you the *real* reality. You're *never* going to switch things around in your mind, not while *I'm* alive! . . . Why do you think you're kept in this room?

YOUNG WOMAN

I don't *know* why you're keeping me here!

MAN

(*Raising his hand.*)

You didn't put it right, Nedra.

(*Looks at the* YOUNG WOMAN.)

Why do you think—*Veronica* is kept in this room? *Was* kept in this room, in 1935.

YOUNG WOMAN

(*Looks at him for a moment.*)

You said—she had TB.

WOMAN

TB?

YOUNG WOMAN

Tuberculosis . . .

WOMAN

If you had TB . . . you would be in a sanitorium . . . If you had TB, your door wouldn't be locked, and your windows wouldn't be barred. *With wrought iron costing six hundred and fifty dollars* . . . If you had TB, it would be an enormous improvement.

YOUNG WOMAN

Then—why was she kept here?

WOMAN

You're kept here—because you *killed Cissie* . . . Does that "ring a bell"? Does that "penetrate the miasma"?

(*The* YOUNG WOMAN *shakes her head, staring at the* WOMAN.)

One afternoon when you were fifteen years old—Friday, November twenty-first, 1930, to be precise—you hit her on the head with a shovel, more than once, down in the cellar, and you hauled her into the coal bin, and put her beneath the chute. It was the day and time when a delivery was coming. It came. Five tons. I found her only a little while later; I had seen her go down there after you, and one of her legs was sticking out. I found *you* up *here*, scrub-a-dub-dubbing. You hadn't quite finished yet, unfortunately for you . . . Unfortunately for *me,* your father decided—

(*A nod to the* MAN.)

—for his own pea-brained reasons—

(*And back to the* YOUNG WOMAN.)

—not to hand you over to the police. And he has since spent more than twenty thousand dollars *keeping* our little secret. Five thousand dollars to Dr. Harvey, for overlooking the shovel marks—do you remember Dr. Harvey, before Dr. Simpson?

(*The* YOUNG WOMAN *shakes her head.*)

Another five thousand to the coroner; ditto, ditto, ditto. *Two* thousand dollars to someone at Devereaux, for keeping you on the records through graduation, though we took you out and put you here. You *do* remember Devereaux, don't you?

(*The* YOUNG WOMAN *shakes her head.*)

No? I could have sworn you *did.*

(*Sings, to the tune of "Buffalo Girls."*)

Devereaux girls gonna stand up and fight,
Gonna stand up and fight,
Gonna stand up and fight . . .

A thousand dollars every Christmas to John and Maureen—which, I suppose, is why in 1973 they'll be dining in restaurants; five hundred every Christmas to Henrietta; the same to Dr. Simpson, who wondered, of course, why we have a daughter in *stir;* and sundry miscellaneous expenditures—the grillwork, the jigsaw puzzles, the occasional broken mirrors and windows.

(*Lifts her wrist, points.*)

The Band-Aids . . . *That* is reality, Veronica. You killed Cissie. That's why you're kept here in *1935,* and that's why you'll be kept here in *1936,* and in *1937,* and in *1938,* and in *1973,* and in every year until you die. I swore that to Cissie, when I kissed her in her coffin.

(*She moves away. The* YOUNG WOMAN *stands shaking her head weakly. The* MAN *sits down again on the foot of the chaise. The* WOMAN *turns to the* YOUNG WOMAN.)

And you can stop dropping those notes out the window; Conrad won't help you. *He* feels the same way *we* do. When *we* die, *he'll* keep you locked here. *He* swore that to *me*, on the Bible . . . Now what were you saying about meeting us in a restaurant?

YOUNG WOMAN

(*Shakes her head weakly, her eyes closed.*)

I am not Veronica . . .

(*Opens her eyes, looks down at herself.*)

This is not my *dress* . . .

(*She catches the left sleeve of it and tears it from the shoulder. The* MAN *springs to his feet; he and the* WOMAN *hurry to her.*)

That is not my *puzzle!* . . .

(*They grab her and try to restrain her, but she manages to knock part of the puzzle to the floor.*)

MAN

Calm down, now! Calm down!

WOMAN

Get her arm!

YOUNG WOMAN

(*Screaming as they hold her.*)

This is—not—my—ROOM!

(*A loud knock at the door.*)

YOUNG MAN

(*Off.*)

Say, what's going *on* in there?

YOUNG WOMAN

(*A cataract of relief.*)

LAAAAREEEEE!

(*The* MAN *and the* WOMAN *stare at each other.*)

YOUNG MAN

(*Off.*)

Can I come in?

(*The door is tried.*)

YOUNG WOMAN

CALL THE POLICE! GO FIND—

(*The* MAN *claps his hand over her mouth but she forces it away.*)

GO FIND THE PHONE AND CALL THE POLICE! THEY'RE CRAZY! BOTH OF THEM! QUICKLY! CALL THE POLICE! THEY'RE INSANE! THEY'VE BEEN—*Let go of me!*

(*She breaks free of the* MAN *and the* WOMAN *and runs to the door.*)

CALL THE POLICE, LARRY! CALL THE POLICE!

(*She listens for a moment, then turns and faces the* MAN *and the* WOMAN, *her hands to her chest.*)

My *God!* My *God!* . . . Did you *hear* him? Or was *that* not reality?

(*The* WOMAN *sinks into a chair next to the game table, her face in her hand. The* MAN *touches her head soothingly.*)

He's calling them now. And if your *phone's* out of order he's getting them *somehow;* he'll run to the road and flag a car . . . My *God*, you are—very sick people! I don't even know the *name* for you! You—need *help*, very badly!

(*Holding her hand out, she goes to the* MAN, *who's looking mournfully at her.*)

Now give me that key *this instant* and *maybe*, just *maybe*, I will not press charges against you!

(*The* MAN *digs the key from his pocket.*)

Larry's a lawyer, don't you forget!

(*The* MAN *holds out the key; the* YOUNG WOMAN *snatches it triumphantly.*)

Good *grief*, you almost had me *believing* that *CRAP!* What kind of kicks did you *get* out of that? I thought maybe I imagined *everything;* myself, my family, school; *the whole rotten world, God bless it!*

(*She backs toward the door.*)

Camp Allegheny . . . I was even wondering if I made up little radios!

(*Turning, she puts the key in the door and unlocks it.*)

Hoo! What a *night* this has been! *Never again will I talk to strangers!*

(*With her hand on the knob, she turns for a final look at the* WOMAN, *who has raised her face from her hand and is looking at the* YOUNG WOMAN *dispassionately.*)

Oh lady, you are *very, very sick!*

(*She turns and opens the door. The* YOUNG MAN *stands there, holding a medical bag and wearing a fedora and an open topcoat over a 1930s vested suit. He has no mustache. The* YOUNG WOMAN *falls back several steps, staring at him. He smiles at her and comes into the room, taking off his fedora.*)

YOUNG MAN

Veronica . . .

(*Nods at the* MAN *and the* WOMAN.)

Mr. and Mrs. Brabissant . . .

(*The* YOUNG WOMAN *falls back farther. The* YOUNG MAN *moves to the desk and puts his hat and bag there. He starts taking off his coat.*)

I rang three or four times, and finally Conrad came down and let me in; I chased him back to bed.

YOUNG WOMAN

(*Staring at him.*)

You son of a bitch . . . it *was* a fake mustache!

(*He looks at her, startled, and looks at the* MAN, *who is on his way to the door.*)

MAN

She's been going on that way for half an hour now.

(*Closes the door and locks it.*)

YOUNG WOMAN

And a fake meeting in the restaurant! "Let's go in *here*, Susan, they've got great seafood. Let's sit over there. Hey, don't look now but you're being stared at"!

(*To the* WOMAN, *with a brogue.*)

"Oh don't y' think someone was guidin' our steps tonight, *your* steps 'n *our steps*, bringin' us together"!

(*Looking at the* YOUNG MAN *again.*)

Someone was guiding our steps, all right . . .

YOUNG MAN

(*Puts his coat over the back of the desk chair; to the* WOMAN.)

This doesn't *sound* like an act, Mrs. Brabissant.

MAN	WOMAN
(*Pocketing the key.*) Oh no, this is no act, Doctor; she's absolutely—	It did before, but I guess she's really—

YOUNG WOMAN

(*Over them, cutting them off.*)

And our meeting on Sunday! *That* was for this too, wasn't it! You *bastard* . . . And *I* thought *I* picked *you* up, you and your goddamn *dragon kite!*

(*Pointing overhead.*)

YOUNG MAN

(*Starting toward her cautiously, smiling, touching his chest.*)

Veronica, it's *me*, Dr. Simpson . . .

YOUNG WOMAN

Fuck you, you bastard!

(*The* YOUNG MAN *is taken aback; the* MAN *winces painfully; the* WOMAN *smiles.*)

WOMAN

That's the way they talk in 1973 . . . Sort of makes you want to die in '72, doesn't it?

YOUNG MAN

(*His eyes on the* YOUNG WOMAN *as he approaches her.*)

Be quiet please, Mrs. Brabissant.

(*The* WOMAN *makes an excuse-me face.*)

YOUNG WOMAN

All right, what kind of *scene* is this? What are you creeps up to?

YOUNG MAN

Your parents are worried about you. They asked me to come help you.

(*The* YOUNG WOMAN *looks narrowly at him as he comes nearer.*)

YOUNG WOMAN

Is Eric involved in this? Is this some kind of *gag*, to make me sorry? Are you a friend of his?

YOUNG MAN

"Eric"?

YOUNG WOMAN

Eric Sonneman!

WOMAN

He's downstairs with Larry.

(*The* YOUNG MAN *turns and looks reproachfully at her.*)

YOUNG MAN

I think you'd better leave the room, Mrs. Brabissant.

WOMAN

I'll be quiet.

YOUNG MAN

No, why don't you go take a look at Conrad?

WOMAN

(*Looks at him for a moment.*)

I *said*—I'll be quiet.

MAN

Let her stay, Doctor.

YOUNG MAN

(*Looks around at the* MAN, *and at the* WOMAN *again, and nods.*)

Okay . . .

(*Moves closer to the* YOUNG WOMAN.)

Who's Eric Sonneman?

YOUNG WOMAN

Forget it.

YOUNG MAN

No, come on, tell me; who is he?

YOUNG WOMAN

A better man than you are, Gunga Din.

(*The* YOUNG MAN *looks closely at her, studying her face and her eyes; she turns away.*)

YOUNG MAN

It's—1973?

YOUNG WOMAN

From coast to coast.

YOUNG MAN

(*Smiling, putting his hand into his jacket pocket.*)

Well, at least we're both in America, right?

(*Spreads coins on his palm and picks one up, a shiny penny; looks at it.*)

Nineteen-thirty-four . . .

(*He holds it out for the* YOUNG WOMAN *to look at; she turns, glances, and turns away.*)

Look at it.

YOUNG WOMAN

Collectors—have old coins that are new and shiny.

MAN

(*A despondent plea.*)

Oh Veronica . . .

(*The* WOMAN *shakes her head and sighs. The* YOUNG MAN *puts the penny back on his palm and examines his other coins.*)

YOUNG MAN

Nineteen-twenty-eight, 1933, 1931, nineteen—

(*The* YOUNG WOMAN *turns and slams his hand up, knocking the coins in his face and over his shoulders. He retreats a step and looks at her.*)

WOMAN

We've got Band-Aids if you want one.

(*The* MAN *picks up some of the coins. The* YOUNG MAN *still looks at the* YOUNG WOMAN.)

YOUNG MAN

It looks as if you're beginning to get violent . . .

MAN

(*Straightening up.*)

She began before you got here. *She* tore her dress, we didn't.

(*A pause, the* YOUNG MAN *and the* MAN *and the* WOMAN *looking at the* YOUNG WOMAN. *She points at the* YOUNG MAN, *and manages not to sound too frightened.*)

YOUNG WOMAN

Now you just watch your step, friend. My roommates know I'm out with you.

YOUNG MAN

Roommates?

YOUNG WOMAN

Roommates! Roommates!

YOUNG MAN

(*Touching his chest.*)

Know you're out with *me?*

YOUNG WOMAN

(*Her assurance leaks away; she eyes him deflatedly.*)

Who are you? What's your *real* name?

(*And now her fright shows.*)

Jack the Ripper?

YOUNG MAN

(*Smiling.*)

Samuel Simpson, M.D.

(*Reaching into his jacket.*)

Which stands not only for Medical Doctor but also for Massachusetts Driver; I'll show you my license.

YOUNG WOMAN

(*Backing a step from him.*)

Shove it wherever they *used* to shove things.

(*The* YOUNG MAN *makes a gesture of tolerant assent, puts back his wallet, and crouches and gathers a few coins. The* MAN *gives him the coins he picked up.*)

YOUNG MAN

Oh. Thanks.

YOUNG WOMAN

(*Looks at all of them.*)

So what happens? Do I get raped?

(*Looks at the* WOMAN.)

By all *three* of you?

(*The* WOMAN *glares; the* YOUNG MAN *smiles.*)

YOUNG MAN

Nobody's going to hurt you, Veronica; we all want—

YOUNG WOMAN

(*Interrupting him, going past him.*)

Oh stop that *Veronica shit!* It's a lie, all of it! You got this house, and you fixed up this room, and you *made up* that whole story!

(*To the* MAN *as she passes him.*)

You're some kind of *freaks,* with a *thing* for 1935!

WOMAN

Everything we told you is the truth.

YOUNG WOMAN

Bullshit! Why would she have done it? Girls don't kill their kid sisters. Their *parents* sometimes, like Lizzie Borden, but not their *kid sisters;* I've *never* heard of anything like that!

WOMAN

Let's not go into why you did it, please.

YOUNG WOMAN

Sure not! You forgot to make *up* that part of it!

(*Going to her, snapping her fingers.*)

Come on, Maureen, you're supposed to be the quick one! What's the matter, the old creative power beginning to *wane?*

WOMAN

(*Eyes closed; through her teeth.*)

Get away from me . . .

YOUNG WOMAN

No, no, come on, you can think of *something;* a lady who comes up like *that* with "How can we get the radio *up* here?"! Come on, why would a fifteen-year-old girl kill her two-years-younger sister? Huh? An argument over a game of Go Fish?

(*The* WOMAN *turns away and puts her face to her hand.*)

Well? Hmm? No ideas? No inspiration?

MAN

She knew what you were doing with Conrad!

(*The* YOUNG WOMAN *turns and looks at him.*)

She was *watching* you! Not letting you!

YOUNG WOMAN

Not—letting me?

MAN

(*Embarrassed.*)

Have—sex with him . . .

(*The* YOUNG WOMAN *stares at him.*)

You taught him how, and you made him do it with you, often.

YOUNG WOMAN

He was *twelve* then!

MAN

(*Nodding bitterly at her.*)

Twelve, yes, twelve. Your brother.

YOUNG WOMAN

Veronica's brother . . .

WOMAN

Your brother . . .

(*She has raised her face from her hand and is looking hatefully at the* YOUNG WOMAN'S *back.*)

MAN

Cissie caught you with him, in the garage, a few days before. You begged her not to tell us, you swore you would stop. She agreed to keep quiet, to spare *us*, but she—kept watch on you. That's why she followed you into the cellar. That's why you *meant* her to follow you . . . Conrad told us that night. He was glad to get free of you. You had—terrorized him.

(*He and the* YOUNG WOMAN *look at each other. The* YOUNG MAN *looks at the floor, shaking his head. The* WOMAN *watches the* YOUNG WOMAN, *who moves toward the* MAN.)

YOUNG WOMAN

I take back what I said . . . *You* are the quick one! That's *beautiful!* It fits in—like a piece of that puzzle! Forget about your mill; you can start writing soap operas! And by the way, don't worry: the Depression's going to get better; Roosevelt is going to fix the whole thing!

YOUNG MAN

(*Smiling.*)

That's what they say. Let's keep our fingers crossed.

YOUNG WOMAN

All *right*, we'll go through it *again*.

(*Going to the* YOUNG MAN, *chanting in a patient singsong.*)

It's 1973, it is not 1935. I'm Susan Kerner, I'm not Veronica. I go to B.U. I come—

(*Turning, going toward the* MAN.)

—from Youngstown, Ohio. My father's a dentist, room two hundred in the Hoover Building. My mother studied singing with *Rosa Ponselle;* she sings at—

(*Turning, going toward the* WOMAN.)

—parties, it's hard to stop her. I have a brother Sandy who's traveling in Portugal. Come home, Sandy!

(*The* MAN *and the* YOUNG MAN *look at each other; the* MAN *nods.*)

We live at Eight Winthrop Circle and our phone number's new but I'll think of it in a second. I live here on—

(*Turning, going toward the* YOUNG MAN *again; speaking faster now as if she might wind into a madness.*)

—Exeter with *two roommates!* Diane who's a dum-dum and Leslie who's heaven!

(*The* YOUNG MAN, *with the* YOUNG WOMAN *coming toward him, looks at the* WOMAN; *she head-signs toward the desk.*)

I have a paper on ethnicity that's due on Monday and all I've done is gather material!

(*Turning, going toward the* MAN.)

Nixon's in the White House—

(*Arms wide, triumphantly.*)

—*Richard M. NIXON!*

(*Pointing back at the* YOUNG MAN, *who was about to move.*)

George McGovern!

(*She goes on toward the* MAN. *The* YOUNG MAN *goes toward the desk.*)

Teddy Kennedy! *Ethel* Kennedy! *Jackie* Kennedy! Ari Onassis!

(*Turning, going toward the* WOMAN.)

The Rolling Stones! The Mothers of Invention! Mama Cass! Johnny Cash! Henry Kissinger!

(*The* YOUNG MAN *is at the desk, his back turned.*)

Dan Rather! Margaret Mead! R. D. Laing! Robert Redford! Robert Goulet! Robert *Stack!* Robert *anyone!* Gloria Steinem! Jane Fonda! Paul Newman!

(*Turning.*)

Joanne Woodward! Woody Allen!

(*She looks around. The* WOMAN *rises.*)

Woody Guthrie! Woody—*WOODPECKER!*

(*She sees the* YOUNG MAN *as he turns from the desk, his right hand behind his back.*)

What have you got there?

YOUNG MAN

(*Moving toward her harmlessly.*)

Nothing to hurt you. Just to calm you down.

MAN

(*Moving toward her too.*)

What were all those names you were saying?

(*She stares at them, then turns and runs to the dresser, grabs a piece of bric-a-brac and throws it at the* YOUNG MAN; *it smashes on the wall. She grabs another but the* MAN *catches her by her left arm and pulls her around, and the thrown object flies toward the bookcase. The* YOUNG MAN *runs over and locks the* YOUNG WOMAN'S *right arm under his left.*)

YOUNG WOMAN

Let go! Let go of me!

(*To the* YOUNG MAN.)

No needle! No needle!!

(*A hypodermic syringe is in the* YOUNG MAN'S *right hand. He and the* MAN *drag the* YOUNG WOMAN *toward the chaise.*)

No! No! No! No! All right! All right! All right! All right, all right. All right. I'm Veronica. I'm Veronica.

(*The* WOMAN *has gone quickly to the chaise, and as the* YOUNG MAN *and the* MAN *bring the* YOUNG WOMAN *to it, she snatches away the decorative pillow.*)

I'm Veronica. I'm Veronica. I'm Veronica. I'm Veronica.

(*The* YOUNG MAN *and the* MAN *get her onto the chaise and stand half-crouching on either side of it, holding her by her arms. The* WOMAN *comes around to the* YOUNG MAN'S *side, the pillow in her hand.*)

I'm Veronica. I'm Veronica. I'll calm down. I don't need any—needle. Really. I'm Veronica. I'm all right. I'll—stop pretending. You were right—Mother—I was only pretending. I'll stop though. I won't do it any more.

(*The* WOMAN *and the* MAN *watch her intently; the* YOUNG MAN, *syringe poised, watches them and her.*)

I'll—try to talk in my normal voice—

(*With a Massachusetts accent, trembling with fright.*)

—but I'm a little hoarse now and I probably won't sound like myself anyway. But I'm all right. I'll calm down. I'll go to bed quietly the way you said I should—Father. I'm—sorry I made so much trouble. I was—jealous because Conrad is getting all the attention. With his fever I mean. I'm sorry.

(*Tries to make a smile.*)

I'm all right. You can let me go now. I'll get undressed and go to bed.

WOMAN

(*Looks at her for a long cold moment.*)

Do you remember now why we keep you here?

YOUNG WOMAN

Yes. Yes, I do! I never forgot, I was only pretending.

WOMAN

Why do we keep you here?

YOUNG WOMAN

Because I—killed—(*Stops warily, looking at the* woman.)

WOMAN

Say it, say her name . . .

YOUNG WOMAN

(*A hesitant pause.*)

Cissie . . . I killed Cissie. I'm sorry, Mother. I swear I am!

MAN

And you know *why* you killed her?

YOUNG WOMAN

Because she knew what I was doing with Conrad. And she—wasn't letting me do it—any more.

(*Looks pleadingly at the* MAN, *and at the* WOMAN, *and at the* YOUNG MAN, *who has lowered the syringe. To all of them.*)

You see? I've stopped pretending. I'm Veronica. It's 1935. I—made up all those names, and those things about Susan. There *is* no Susan. I made it all up. Everything . . . Will you let go of me now? Please? I'll go to bed and I won't make any trouble. Tomorrow I'll—paint, and work on my puzzle. My voice will be back to normal. I'll stop dropping notes out the window. I'll be—good from now on.

WOMAN

That's what you said the last time. When you pretended you were French, and wouldn't speak English.

YOUNG WOMAN

(*A small pause.*)

This time I *mean* it, Mother. I swear I do.

(*The* MAN *releases the* YOUNG WOMAN's *arm and stands straight. The* YOUNG MAN *releases her other arm and puts the syringe on the lamp table. The* YOUNG WOMAN *rubs her arms, watching the* WOMAN, *who turns away, looks at the pillow in her hands, and looks to heaven.*)

WOMAN

Oh *God*, Lloyd, what are we going to *do* with her?

MAN

(*Shaking his head, looking at the* YOUNG WOMAN.)

I don't know, Nedra, I honestly don't know . . .

WOMAN

(*Turning to the* YOUNG WOMAN.)

You *say* you won't do this again, but there's so much—*evil* in you, how can you *not* try to—lie it away?

YOUNG WOMAN

I won't. I promise. Never again.

MAN

Cissie was an *angel*, and you murdered her . . .

YOUNG WOMAN

(*Nodding.*)

Yes . . . yes . . .

WOMAN

Conrad was an angel too, until you—did what you did with him.

YOUNG WOMAN

Yes . . .

MAN

We were a good family, a *fine* one, no matter *what* your mother says—and now we can't even have guests in the house, because of you!

WOMAN

You've locked *us* in, damn you! *We're* the prisoners, not you!

YOUNG WOMAN

(*A pause, and a hesitant suggestion.*)

Then—why not—let me go away? I'll go far away, and I—won't bother you. I'll—change my name . . .

(*A pause.*)

YOUNG MAN

There's an idea, Mrs. Brabissant . . .

WOMAN

(*Turns away, shaking her head, her eyes closed.*)

No, no, we can't let you go . . . I swore to Cissie . . .

YOUNG WOMAN

Angels forgive . . .

WOMAN

Not you, they don't . . . Not a girl who takes her twelve-year-old brother into the garage, and plays with him—(*Turning toward the* YOUNG WOMAN.)—and shows herself, and makes him touch, and kiss . . . ! Not a girl who leads her sister into the cellar, and hits with a shovel, and hits, and hits, and *hits!* And hauls her into the coal bin, and *waits*, and *watches! Nobody* forgives *you*, Veronica! Not even *angels!* Not even *Jesus!*

(*She goes toward the* YOUNG WOMAN, *who would flee the chaise, but the men catch her arms again and keep her there.*)

We *kill* you, we don't *forgive* you! *We kill you!*

(*The* YOUNG WOMAN *screams, a half-scream stopped by the pillow that the* WOMAN *presses to her face. The* WOMAN *sits on the side of the chaise and holds the pillow across the* YOUNG WOMAN'S *face with both hands. The men hold the* YOUNG WOMAN'S *straining arms. Her head moves from side to side, but the* WOMAN *holds the pillow tightly across it. The* YOUNG WOMAN *moans muffledly; her legs kick. The* MAN *catches them around the knees, holds them, and struggles one-handed with her left arm. The* YOUNG MAN, *restraining the* YOUNG WOMAN'S *right arm easily with both hands, watches the* WOMAN'S *face with interest. The* YOUNG WOMAN'S *moaning and straining grow more desperate. A while passes and they begin to weaken. Nothing else changes. Another while passes, a long one, and the* YOUNG MAN *puts the* YOUNG WOMAN'S *arm down to the floor. He stands straight and rubs the small of his back, still watching the* WOMAN'S *face. The* MAN *lets go of the* YOUNG WOMAN'S *legs and arm, watches the pillow and the* WOMAN'S *hands for another moment, and touches the* WOMAN'S *shoulder. He stands straight and massages his upper arms. The* YOUNG MAN *loosens the knot of his tie and unbuttons his collar. The* WOMAN *takes the pillow slowly from the* YOUNG WOMAN'S *face; its eyes and mouth are open, unmoving. The* WOMAN *rises, looks at the* YOUNG WOMAN *for a moment, and moves away. She flings the pillow away and lifts her arms in a gesture of relief and liberation. The* YOUNG MAN *crouches, slides his arms in under the* YOUNG WOMAN'S *back and knees, and lifts her from the chaise. He carries her around the foot of it and toward the bed. The* MAN *watches the* WOMAN *hopefully. The* YOUNG MAN *spills the* YOUNG WOMAN *onto the bed, rolling her off his arms so that she falls face down. He turns and looks at the* MAN *and the* WOMAN, *contemptuously, then draws back his sleeve and looks at his watch. He goes to the* WOMAN *and tries to put the watch before her face but she turns away. He taps at the watch with an insistent finger.*)

YOUNG MAN

Six minutes of eleven . . .

(*He brings the watch, still tapping at it, to the* MAN, *who looks angrily at him.*)

Ten-fifty-four.

(*Histrionically.*)

A new record! But *fated*—to be *broken!*

(*To the* WOMAN.)

When is the next one going to end? *Twelve, twenty, nine?*

(*To the* MAN.)

Three, oh, seven?

MAN

There isn't going to be a next one. This is the last. We all agreed. Didn't we?

(*The* YOUNG MAN *turns away scornfully and, with a fingerstroke, rips his vest unbuttoned. The* WOMAN *stands silently, her eyes closed.*)

It's the last. We agreed.

(*He stands uncertainly for a moment, then goes and takes the decorative objects from the bookcase. The* YOUNG MAN *stands rubbing the back of his neck angrily. The* MAN *brings the objects toward the desk.*)

Well don't just stand there, boy, get the dress off her.

YOUNG MAN

(*Starts toward the bed, stops, turns back.*)

I am too TIRED to get the dress off her!

(*The* MAN, *with a sigh, opens a desk drawer and puts the objects into it. The* YOUNG MAN *moves nearer the* WOMAN, *mimicking broadly with a thick brogue.*)

"Oh we usually go t' a restaurant on State Street, where John has a cousin who's a waiter, an' we don't have t' tip, praise the Lord, an' it's such a big *savin'* for us!"

WOMAN

(*Turns and looks acidly at him for a moment.*)

I wouldn't have had to go through all that if *you* hadn't been working *against* us! *That's* what gets worse every time, *you*, not *us!* The way you *needle* and *tease* and ask *questions* you're not *supposed* to ask!

YOUNG MAN

(*Looks at her.*)

Oh . . .

(*Gently, still with a brogue.*)

Well y' see dear, the reason I do that is it gives me an excuse to look at y' as if I don't like y' too much. 'Cause I'm not a good enough actor to pretend that I think you're charmin' and lovable.

MAN

All right, boy, shut your mouth and get the dress off her!

(*The* YOUNG MAN, *still angry, goes toward the bed. The* MAN, *gathering objects from the table near the chaise, watches the* WOMAN *as she moves toward the foot of it. She sits, and he turns and goes toward the desk. In the next minutes he returns all the room's decorative objects to the drawers from which they were taken in Act One.*)

YOUNG MAN

(*Holding the* YOUNG WOMAN *toward her side, unfastening her belt.*)

That whole first part has gotten too goddamned elaborate!

(*The brogue again.*)

"Here's where she made her pins an' bracelets. Here's her wire, here's her colored glass." How come you don't give a goddamn *PIN-making demonstration* while you're at it!

(*He undoes the back of the dress. The* MAN *pays him no heed. The* WOMAN *pulls her hair off; a wig. Beneath it is the hair she had in Act One; she fluffs it out. The* YOUNG MAN *starts taking the dress off the* YOUNG WOMAN.)

WOMAN

I didn't notice you rushing your doctor business any . . .

(*The* YOUNG MAN *turns and comes angrily toward her.*)

YOUNG MAN

What do you *want* me to do? Come in and say "Hello, Veronica, I'm Dr. Simpson; look at this needle I'm going to stick in your arm"? Is *that* what you want? Just say the word; it's fine with *me! I* don't need all this—

(*A gesture around him as he seeks words.*)

—this *Walpole Drama Society!*

(*Moves closer to her.*)

All I need—*darlin'*—is what's there on the bed, and I'd like to get to it *early* enough so that I can *stay awake* when I've *got* it!

(*The* WOMAN *turns the wig on her hand and picks at it as the* YOUNG MAN *lets that sink in.*)

MAN

(*Busy at the bookcase.*)

Will you *get on with it*, boy?

(*The* YOUNG MAN *goes back to the bed and resumes taking off the* YOUNG WOMAN'S *dress. The* WOMAN *toys with the wig.*)

YOUNG MAN

All right, fine! Next time the doctor part is going to take two seconds; you just *see* if she says what you want her to say!

MAN

There's not going to be any next time.

(*Goes toward the bathroom, his hands full of bric-a-brac fragments.*)

WOMAN

Save those pieces. Maybe I can glue it back together.

MAN

(*Stops, turns toward her.*)

I don't *think* so.

(*The* YOUNG MAN *slaps the dress around a bedpost.*)

WOMAN

Well, I want to *try*. Put them there.

(The MAN *puts the fragments doubtfully on the game table, clear of the puzzle. He brushes his hands off and looks around. All the decorative objects have been put away.)*

YOUNG MAN

(Taking off the YOUNG WOMAN'S *slip; grudgingly.)*

There's a new *silicone cement* that's supposed to be good.

WOMAN

There is?

(He doesn't respond. The MAN *takes the dress from the bedpost and finds its tear.)*

Do you know where to get it?

YOUNG MAN

No. These *her* panties?

WOMAN

Yes.

MAN

(Showing the WOMAN *the dress.)*

You want to sew this, don't you?

WOMAN

(Taking it.)

Mm-hmm.

(He reaches for the wig; she gives it to him. He goes toward the door, getting the key from his pocket. The YOUNG MAN *rolls the* YOUNG WOMAN'S *stockings down her legs. The* MAN *unlocks the door and opens it. The* WOMAN *fingers the dress in her lap. The*

MAN, *pocketing the key, goes to the desk and picks up the coat, the hat, and the medical bag. The* YOUNG MAN *unhooks the* YOUNG WOMAN'S *bra and bends one of her arms from its strap. The* MAN *goes out. The* YOUNG MAN *moves from the bed and calls after him.)*

YOUNG MAN

Hey, open my door while you're out there, will you?

(*He watches for a moment, then goes back to the bed and finishes taking off the* young woman's *bra, raising her middle to pull it from under her. He gathers the slip and stockings and tosses them with the bra into the bathroom. Moving to the side of the bed, he rolls the* young woman *toward him onto her back, crouches, and picks her up. He turns, holding her in his arms, and moves toward the* woman. *She fingers the dress, not turning. He stands looking at her for a moment.*)

Sure an' it's a good night I'm wishin' y', Mrs. Mackey. May the god Lord bless an' keep y'.

(*He carries the* YOUNG WOMAN *to the doorway, angles her through, and carries her out. The* WOMAN *fingers the dress, frowning. She looks in her mid-fifties now. She lifts the dress from her lap—and puts it behind her. She rubs her cheek, looks at her fingertips, rubs them with her thumb. The* MAN *comes in with the bundle of dust covers. He too now seems in his mid-fifties. He puts the bundle on the floor and spreads it apart, glancing uncertainly at the* WOMAN.)

MAN

It—spoiled things a little, didn't it, her saying all those names.

WOMAN

(*Nods.*)

A little . . .

MAN

(*Drawing loose a cover.*)

It was nice, her being able to do the accent though. I thought that was a big help.

(*The* WOMAN *nods. The* MAN *begins covering a chair nearby.*)

She *looked* good too.

WOMAN

(*Turning, surprised.*)

Did you think so?

MAN

Yes, definitely. She had the right eyes, the line of the jaw . . .

WOMAN

(*Waving a hand, turning away again.*)

No . . .

MAN

(*Returning to the bundle.*)

Yes! Not like the *first* one, of course. My *God*, we'll *never* find another one like *her!* That was *uncanny!* I mean—we *wouldn't* find another one like her. If we were going to *do* another.

(*He draws another cover from the bundle. The* WOMAN *looks at him.*)

WOMAN

Did I really terrorize you?

MAN

What do you mean?

WOMAN

That's what you said. "Conrad was glad to get free of you. You had terrorized him." And you said it with such feeling . . .

MAN

I was speaking like Father then, saying what *he* would have said.

WOMAN

Did you tell *them* I terrorized you?

MAN

(*Dropping the cover and going to her.*)

I never used the word in my whole life, until tonight. I don't even know what put it into my head.

(*Crouching beside her.*)

If you had "terrorized" me, I wouldn't have let you out of here, would I? I would have kept you locked in here after they died, the way I swore I would.

WOMAN

(*Smoothing his hair.*)

We *both* wanted it, didn't we? From the very beginning? It wasn't only *my* doing . . .

MAN

No, no, of course it wasn't! You didn't "terrorize" me, Veronica, honest to God you didn't!

(*They kiss each other lovingly. The* MAN *smiles at the* WOMAN.)

I got carried away being Father, that's all!

WOMAN

You were so like him tonight! I expected you to take out one of his *cigars* any minute!

MAN

You were Mother to a T! It was *fantastic!*

WOMAN

(*With her "Maureen" brogue.*)

And how about John and Maureen? Didn't we do them just wonderfully, darlin'?

MAN

(*With his "John" brogue.*)

Sure an' it's regular actors we are! Or could have been, if—if we'd *had* to be somethin'.

(*Rises from his crouching position and drops the brogue, suddenly grave.*)

Come on. Let's get out of here.

(*Backs from the* WOMAN.)

WOMAN

Conrad.

MAN

What?

WOMAN

(*Rising.*)

It really happened tonight. The way I always hoped it would. When she admitted everything, when you and Boy were holding her, she was *me* all of a sudden, and I was—me and yet *not me.* And after she was punished, I felt so *free* and so *clean!* As if I'd never done a single thing wrong in my entire life!

MAN

Good! Good!

WOMAN

And then *Boy* had to ruin it all shouting at me, bringing everything back . . .

MAN

(*Moving to her again.*)

God damn him!

WOMAN

We should have got rid of him the day he was born. I wanted to, remember? But you wouldn't let me.

MAN

A *baby*, Veronica!

WOMAN

Do you know what he told this girl? What *she* told *me?* That I didn't *touch* him enough! As if *touching* him would have made any difference!

MAN

But it *worked* tonight and we're done! We can close up this room forever!

WOMAN

It *didn't* work! He ruined it! I want to do *one more,* with him not having anything to do with it! We'll get the girl ourselves. We can do it. John and Maureen can . . .

(*Looking past him toward an imaginary young woman, speaking with her brogue again.*)

Oh darlin', excuse us for starin' at y', but you're the spittin' image of this girl we used to know a long, long time ago!

MAN

We're not going to do another! You said this would be the last!

WOMAN

The *next* one will be the last! I swear it will!

MAN

You *always* swear that!

WOMAN

But we know it can *work* now, if *he* doesn't ruin it! And I've *got* to make it work, Conrad!

MAN

She won't *admit* anything unless Boy is here holding the needle over her!

WOMAN

Oh yes she will . . .

(*With the brogue again, and focused again on the imaginary young woman.*)

She'll admit *everything*. What she done to poor Cissie, what she done with Conrad . . . The Mister and Missus'll get her to admit, sooner or later, and when *that* one's gone, she'll be gone forever.

MAN

We're not going to do another one, Veronica. We agreed. Come on, it's late.

(*Kisses her cheek.*)

Let's get to bed now.

(*He moves away from her and begins quickly turning out lamps. She stays focused on the young woman.*)

WOMAN

Veronica was her name. Y' could be her *twin* practically! Oh, how her father and mother loved her! Was all the time touchin' her! Kids—should be touched a *lot*, y' know.

(*The* MAN *is near the door, watching her with anguish.*)

MAN

Come out. Come out now . . .

WOMAN

(*Looks at herself, at the room.*)

I can't. I'm still locked in here.

MAN

(*Hurrying to her.*)

No, no, no, no, you're not! She's gone! She's dead! The door is open! Look! I unlocked it for you!

(*He takes her in his arms and kisses her. She stiffens in the embrace and pushes free.*)

WOMAN

Let—go of me!

(*Retreats, confused.*)

How can you *kiss* me that way? I—I don't even know who you are!

(*She retreats farther; they stare at each other.*)

Do you—*really* think I'm Veronica? Or is this some kind of *game* you're playing? We were—in the Golden *something*, Larry and I. *You* were at the next table, talking with a brogue . . . You said you were John Mackey . . .

MAN

Veronica . . . !

WOMAN

My ID card is in my bag downstairs! Get Larry up here!

MAN

(*Stares at her.*)

What Larry . . .?

WOMAN

Larry Eastwood! The man I came here with! Get him up here! And bring me my clothes! I want to go now!

MAN

(*Going to her.*)

What are you *doing*, Veronica?

WOMAN

I'm not Veronica! This is not my dress! This is not my puzzle!

(*Sweeps the bric-a-brac fragments from the game table to the floor.*)

This is not my ROOM!

MAN

All right! All right!

(*Backs hastily, fearfully, toward the door.*)

I'll get your clothes! I'll get everything! Be quiet!

WOMAN

What kind of scene is this? What are you creeps up to?

(*The* MAN *hurries out and closes the door. The sound of the bolt is heard. The* WOMAN *stares at the closed door.*)

It's—1973. It's not—1935.

(*She looks around the room, and at the barred window where the curtain lifts in a breeze.*)

Oh my *God . . . !*

(*She runs to the door and beats at it.*)

Mother? Father? Let me out! Please unlock the door, Mother! Please! Let me out of here!

THE CURTAIN QUICKLY FALLS

THE END